Functional Behavioral Assessment and Function-Based Intervention

An Effective, Practical Approach

John Umbreit
University of Arizona

Jolenea Ferro
University of Arizona

Carl J. Liaupsin
University of Arizona

Kathleen Lynne Lane
Vanderbilt University

PEARSON

Merrill
Prentice Hall

Upper Saddle River, New Jersey
Columbus, Ohio

Library of Congress Cataloging-in-Publication Data

Umbreit, John.
  Functional behavioral assessment and function-based intervention:
an effective, practical approach/John Umbreit, Jolenea Ferro, Carl Liaupsin.
    p. cm.
  Includes bibliographical references and index.
  ISBN 0-13-114989-X
    1. Behavior modification. 2. Behavioral assessment. 3. Operant behavior.
4. Educational psychology. 5. Problem children—Education. I. Ferro,
Jolenea. II. Liaupsin, Carl. III. Title.
  LB1060.2.U42 2007
  370.15'28—dc22

2006003616

**Vice President and Executive
  Publisher:** Jeffery W. Johnston
Senior Editor: Allyson P. Sharp
Editorial Assistant: Kathleen S. Burk
Production Editor: Sheryl Glicker
Langner
Production Coordination:
Jodi Dowling, *TechBooks GTS* York, PA

Design Coordinator: Diane C. Lorenzo
Cover Design: Thomas Borah
Cover Image: Super Stock
Production Manager: Laura Messerly
Director of Marketing: David Gesell
Marketing Manager: Autumn Purdy
Marketing Coordinator: Brian Mounts

This book was set in Garamond Book by *TechBooks GTS* York, PA. It was printed
and bound by R. R. Donnelley & Sons Company. The cover was printed by
R. R. Donnelley & Sons Company.

Pearson Education Ltd.
Pearson Education Singapore Pte. Ltd.
Pearson Education Canada, Ltd.
Pearson Education–Japan

Pearson Education Australia Pty. Limited
Pearson Education North Asia Ltd.
Pearson Educación de Mexico, S.A. de C.V.
Pearson Education Malaysia Pte. Ltd.

10 9 8 7 6 5 4 3 2 1
ISBN: 0-13-114989-X

We dedicate this book to the students, parents, educators, graduate students, and colleagues who helped us learn.

Preface

This book presents a unified, comprehensive, and evidence-based approach to conducting functional behavioral assessments (FBAs), designing effective function-based interventions, and implementing and monitoring those interventions. We intentionally designed it to be equally useful to students in university-based preparation programs and to professionals in schools and other natural settings who are responsible for performing these activities in their jobs. In many respects, this book is simultaneously a research-based textbook and an operations manual that presents detailed information about how to perform the necessary tasks required both by law and by the standards of good practice.

In university courses, this text will be appropriate for classes that address positive behavioral support, FBA, and advanced applications of behavior analysis. It is not intended as an introductory-level text on behavioral principles, applied behavior analysis, or behavior modification. Rather, it builds on that foundation.

For professionals already working in the field, this book will be an ideal resource for in-service training for behavioral specialists, school psychologists, counselors, administrators, general and special education teachers, and other certified personnel. It will also be an invaluable tool for practitioners who are attempting to independently improve their knowledge and skill in this area.

The process of completing an FBA and developing the function-based intervention requires professionals to perform many related tasks. We believe the best way to learn this process and the specific methods that should be employed at each step is to learn them in the sequence in which they are performed in practice. The sequence of needed steps and activities is predictable. As you will see in the Table of Contents, our book is organized to address this sequence as it naturally occurs.

As one learns this process, it is also important to clearly understand how certain fundamental principles and concepts of applied behavior analysis influence the methods we use. For this reason, we review these principles and concepts as it becomes necessary at each step in the process. This approach is intended to enhance learning by presenting these principles and concepts in context.

After an introduction to the functional approach to addressing problem behaviors, the chapters are organized into four sections. Part One covers the activities required in conducting an FBA. Chapters in this section address how to define target and replacement behaviors, gather information through structured interviews, collect direct observational data, and identify the function (or functions) of a target behavior by using an innovative tool called the Function Matrix.

Part Two explains how to develop, test, and present function-based interventions. Chapters include a Function-Based Intervention Decision Model for determining which of three intervention methods is appropriate for a given situation, explicit instructions for how to develop effective interventions using each method, and directions for how to test the intervention prior to formulating the Behavioral Intervention Plan (BIP). The section concludes with a recommended BIP format and detailed instruction as to how each part should be constructed.

Part Three addresses the essential task of implementing and monitoring function-based interventions. Chapters in this section pinpoint important factors that can "make or break" an intervention, explain how to address these factors, and show how to monitor not only the intervention, but also its implementation. Included in this material are step-by-step instructions on how to use Microsoft Excel to organize and manage data and generate useful summary charts and graphs.

Part Four reviews and integrates the entire process of function-based intervention planning through detailed case studies. Each chapter addresses one of the three intervention methods we have suggested. By following its application for a single individual, one can see how the pieces fit, from initially identifying a problem to developing, implementing, and eventually fading the intervention.

The methods we present are directly teachable and learnable, and are grounded in strongly supported, evidence-based practices that are widely accepted in the field of applied behavior analysis. Over the past several years, we have taught these methods in courses offered to both undergraduate and graduate students, and have seen that these students can easily learn and apply them. In hundreds of cases, students have been able to accurately identify a behavior's function, and then develop function-based interventions that are supported by reliable data.

When students or professionals are first learning about function-based intervention, the process can seem complicated. To facilitate learning, every chapter in Parts One to Three includes a list of expected outcomes, a summary of the steps and activities addressed in the chapter, and exercises designed to improve understanding. In addition, we present numerous examples throughout the text. Although many of these examples represent exemplary work that can serve as models, we also deliberately present negative examples of common and critical errors that can prevent success. Useful checklists, forms, diagrams, charts, graphs, and tables are also provided to assist learning and to make a seemingly complicated process understandable, manageable, and useful.

ACKNOWLEDGMENTS

As we developed the intervention methods described in Part Two of this book, we consulted with several colleagues who provided valuable feedback and suggestions. For their gracious assistance, we acknowledge and thank

Felix Billingsley, University of Washington; Glen Dunlap, University of South Florida; Lee Kern, Lehigh University; Gary Sasso, University of Iowa; George Sugai, University of Connecticut; and Frank Gresham, Louisiana State University. We also benefited from the more than able assistance provided by Rebecca Zapien, and from the helpful suggestions made by professionals who reviewed the entire manuscript. For their contributions, we thank Barbara A. Beakley, Millersville University; Kathleen Briseno, College of DuPage and Naperville Community Unit School District #203; Douglas Brooks, Miami University; James Burns, The College of St. Rose; Maureen Conroy, University of Florida; James Fox, East Tennessee State University; James Halle, University of Illinois; Victoria Hulsey, Alabama A&M University; Cathy Huaqing Qi, University of New Mexico; Laura M. Stough, Texas A&M University; and Ellie L. Young, Brigham Young University. Finally, this book would never have been written if not for the vision, insistence, encouragement, prodding, and support provided by several people at Merrill/Prentice Hall. For this, we are indebted to Allyson Sharp and Kathy Burk.

Teacher Preparation Classroom

See a demo at
www.prenhall.com/teacherprep/demo

Your Class. Their Careers. Our Future. Will your students be prepared?

We invite you to explore our new, innovative and engaging website and all that it has to offer you, your course, and tomorrow's educators! Organized around the major courses pre-service teachers take, the Teacher Preparation site provides media, student/teacher artifacts, strategies, research articles, and other resources to equip your students with the quality tools needed to excel in their courses and prepare them for their first classroom.

This ultimate on-line education resource is available at no cost, when packaged with a Merrill text, and will provide you and your students access to:

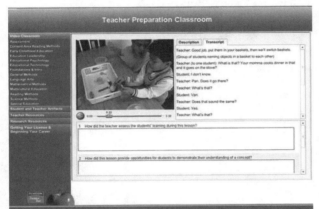

Online Video Library. More than 150 video clips—each tied to a course topic and framed by learning goals and Praxis-type questions—capture real teachers and students working in real classrooms, as well as in-depth interviews with both students and educators.

Student and Teacher Artifacts. More than 200 student and teacher classroom artifacts— each tied to a course topic and framed by learning goals and application questions— provide a wealth of materials and experiences to help make your study to become a professional teacher more concrete and hands-on.

Research Articles. Over 500 articles from ASCD's renowned journal *Educational Leadership.* The site also includes Research Navigator, a searchable database of additional educational journals.

Teaching Strategies. Over 500 strategies and lesson plans for you to use when you become a practicing professional.

Licensure and Career Tools. Resources devoted to helping you pass your licensure exam; learn standards, law, and public policies; plan a teaching portfolio; and succeed in your first year of teaching.

How to ORDER *Teacher Prep* for you and your students:

For students to receive a *Teacher Prep* Access Code with this text, instructors **must** provide a special value pack ISBN number on their textbook order form. To receive this special ISBN, please email **Merrill.marketing@pearsoned.com** and provide the following information:

- Name and Affiliation
- Author/Title/Edition of Merrill text

Upon ordering *Teacher Prep* for their students, instructors will be given a lifetime *Teacher Prep* Access Code.

Discover the Merrill Resources for Special Education Website

Technology is a constantly growing and changing aspect of our field that is creating a need for new content and resources. To address this emerging need, Merrill Education has developed an online learning environment for students, teachers, and professors alike to complement our products—the *Merrill Resources for Special Education* Website. This content-rich website provides additional resources specific to this book's topic and will help you—professors, classroom teachers, and students—augment your teaching, learning, and professional development.

Our goal with this initiative is to build on and enhance what our products already offer. For this reason, the content for our user-friendly website is organized by topic and provides teachers, professors, and students with a variety of meaningful resources all in one location. With this website, we bring together the best of what Merrill has to offer: text resources, video clips, web links, tutorials, and a wide variety of information on topics of interest to general and special educators alike. Rich content, applications, and competencies further enhance the learning process.

The *Merrill Resources for Special Education* Website includes:

- Video clips specific to each topic, with questions to help you evaluate the content and make crucial theory-to-practice connections.
- Thought-provoking critical analysis questions that students can answer and turn in for evaluation or that can serve as basis for class discussions and lectures.
- Access to a wide variety of resources related to classroom strategies and methods, including lesson planning and classroom management.
- Information on all the most current relevant topics related to special and general education, including CEC and Praxis™ standards, IEPs, portfolios, and professional development.
- Extensive web resources and overviews on each topic addressed on the website.
- A search feature to help access specific information quickly.

To take advantage of these and other resources, please visit the *Merrill Resources for Special Education* Website at

http://www.prenhall.com/umbreit

Brief Contents

Contents

15 *The Entire Process When Using Method 2: Improve the Environment* 267

16 *The Entire Process When Using Method 3: Adjust the Contingencies* 281

Functional Behavioral Assessment and Function-Based Intervention

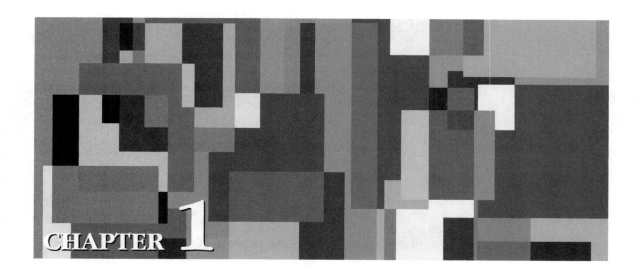

A Functional Approach to Problem Behavior

This book describes how to develop effective, efficient, and long-lasting behavioral interventions that eliminate problem behaviors, increase desirable behaviors, and change settings so desirable behaviors are more likely to occur. Functional Behavioral Assessments (FBAs) and function-based interventions provide the procedures for accomplishing this goal.

FBA AND FUNCTION-BASED INTERVENTION DEFINED

The FBA is a method for gathering information that identifies the function of problem behavior and the events that predict its occurrence (Sugai et al., 2000). By **function,** we mean the purpose the behavior serves. More specifically, we mean those events that follow the behavior and increase the likelihood that it will recur, that is, the **consequences** of the behavior. When April hits Billy at recess, does she get to use her favorite swing? When Sonia kicks Marty during silent reading, is she sent to the office? Each example indicates a consequence (i.e., getting to use the swing and being sent to the office) and a potential function of the problem behavior.

The FBA also identifies those conditions that reliably precede the occurrence of the problem behavior but are absent when it does not occur. In the example of April hitting Billy, the FBA may indicate that April only hits Billy when all swings are in use. When at least one swing is available, she simply uses it and ignores Billy. Conditions that precede problem behavior are called **antecedent conditions.** Identifying antecedent conditions not only allows one to predict when the behavior will occur, but also identifies the changes needed in the environment so the behavior does not recur. Antecedents include conditions that immediately precede the behavior (e.g., presentation of an in-class practice sheet or being asked to read aloud) and conditions more distal to the behavior (e.g., sleep deprivation or the absence of a preferred person).

A complete FBA identifies (a) a clear definition of the problem behavior, (b) the antecedent conditions that exist both when the behavior occurs and when it does not occur, (c) the consequences that maintain the behavior, (d) a clear definition of the behavior we want the student to exhibit in place of the problem behavior (i.e., the replacement behavior), and (e) a statement of behavioral function.

The term **function-based intervention** refers to the development of behavior change strategies that are based on the data gathered during the FBA and that are directly linked to the function of the behavior. The basic goal is to use the FBA information to design an intervention that decreases problem behaviors (target behaviors) while increasing desirable behaviors (replacement behaviors). The procedures for accomplishing this goal are clearly and straightforwardly described throughout this book. The outcome is an intervention that addresses the function of the behavior by (a) eliminating the consequence maintaining the problem behavior, (b) providing it or another appropriate reinforcer for the replacement behavior, and (c) removing or in some way altering the antecedent conditions that evoke the behavior. The FBA and the function-based intervention procedures provide the bulk of the information needed to complete an effective Behavior Intervention Plan (BIP), as described in Chapter 11.

WHY CONDUCT AN FBA?

Serious problem behaviors can result in injury to oneself or others. Students exhibiting problem behaviors may fail to learn needed skills, may be isolated from their peers, may find restrictions imposed on where they are allowed to go and what they are allowed to do, and may experience increasingly stringent penalties. Problem behaviors can also disrupt classroom environments so teachers and other students are distracted from their primary focus of teaching and learning. Less time spent on problem behaviors leaves more time for these endeavors.

The most important reason for completing an FBA and designing an intervention based on the function(s) identified through this process is that these interventions have proven to be more effective than interventions that simply increase reinforcement for "appropriate" behavior and penalties for problem behavior. This is the case whether the behavior is dangerous, as in the case of self-injury or aggression, or less severe, such as talking out of turn in the classroom.

Why are function-based interventions more effective? First, the "penalties" we impose may, in fact, reinforce the problem behavior. If Sonia kicks Marty so she can escape silent reading, sending her to the office more often and even suspending her will only increase the kicking behavior.

Second, the "reinforcers" we choose to increase the desirable behavior we want the student to exhibit may not be reinforcing. Reinforcers are discussed later in this chapter and throughout the book. For now, remember that what reinforces you may not be reinforcing for someone else.

Third, reinforcers may not be strong enough to overcome what is reinforcing the problem behavior, especially if a problem behavior is chronic or has proven to be intractable. The FBA provides information that allows you to identify reinforcers that address the function of the problem behavior; thus, they are more effective than those that might typically be used in the environment.

In addition, there are legal requirements for students with disabilities. The 1997 reauthorization of the Individuals with Disabilities Education Act (IDEA; PL 105–17) mandated that a school must conduct an FBA if a student has been suspended for more than 10 school days in a school year and the problem behavior was a manifestation of the child's disability. The intervention plan had to be developed based on the information collected through the FBA process. The 2004 reauthorization of IDEA, called the Individuals with Disabilities Education Improvement Act (IDEIA), increases the requirement so an FBA must be completed irrespective of whether the behavior is determined to be a manifestation of the child's disability or whether the child is removed from the current placement [(1415) (k) (1) (d) (ii)].

WHAT ARE THE FUNCTIONS OF BEHAVIOR?

In October 2001, two of the authors presented a special workshop on how to develop function-based interventions at a national conference on the subject of children with behavioral disorders. Attendance was limited to 60 people and, when the session commenced, the room was full. One of the presenters began by saying, "I have two questions for you. First, how many of you are responsible for conducting FBAs for your school or district or agency?" All but three people raised their hands. The presenter continued, "Second, how many functions of behavior are there?" Many people offered answers ranging from 4 to 30. "I have news for you that should make your job a little easier," the presenter continued. "In fact, there are only two functions of behavior—positive reinforcement and negative reinforcement."

To understand the function of a behavior, you must understand reinforcers and reinforcement. As you progress through this book and through the process of completing an FBA and developing a function-based intervention, you must be able to recognize the consequence that is maintaining problem behavior and effectively apply the appropriate reinforcement for the replacement behavior. Many textbooks (e.g., Alberto & Troutman, 2006; Cooper, Heron, & Heward, 1987; Kazdin, 2000; Martin & Pear, 2003; Miller, 2006; Sulzer-Azaroff & Mayer, 1991; Zirpoli, 2005) will provide the thorough background you need to understand how to use reinforcers most effectively. However, a few key concepts are reviewed in this section.

Reinforcers

A **reinforcer** is any event that (a) follows a behavior and (b) increases the probability of that behavior, whereas **reinforcement** involves using a reinforcer to increase the rate of behavior (Miller, 2006). If a student finishes an assignment on time (behavior) and the teacher provides extra free time (event that follows the behavior), the extra free time is a reinforcer only if the student finishes future assignments on time. This concept is important enough to repeat: Extra free time is a reinforcer because it follows the behavior and it increases the occurrence of that behavior. If the student does not finish future assignments on time, then extra free time was not a reinforcer for that behavior; that is, it did not increase the occurrence of that behavior. No matter how much we believed that it would be a reinforcer, or wanted it to be one, it was not. Table 1.1 provides more examples and non-

TABLE 1.1
Examples and Nonexamples of Reinforcement

	Example	Errors
1	Tom waits to use the water fountain.	This is only a *behavior*; the *event* that follows and an indication of an *increase* in behavior are missing.
2	Tom waits to use the water fountain and the teacher gives him a pat on the back.	An indication of an *increase* in behavior is missing.
3	Tom waits to use the water fountain and the teacher gives him a pat on the back; Tom waits patiently the next time they go to the water fountain.	No error. In this situation, a pat on the back is a *reinforcer* and the teacher has used *reinforcement*.
4	As Nathan and Shara argue over a toy, Nathan hits Shara. Shara lets go of the toy and Nathan takes it. Nathan hits peers more frequently during playtime.	No error. In this situation, the toy was a *reinforcer*.
5	As Nathan and Shara argue over a toy, Nathan hits Shara. Shara lets go of the toy and Nathan takes it.	An indication of an *increase* in behavior is missing.
6	As Nathan and Shara argue over a toy, Nathan hits Shara.	This is only a *behavior*; the *event* that follows and an indication of an *increase* in behavior are missing.
7	Lola cleans her room and her mother lets her skip another chore.	An indication of an *increase* in behavior is missing.
8	Lola cleans her room and her mother lets her skip another chore; Lola cleans her room the next evening.	No error. In this situation, skipping a chore is a *reinforcer* and the parent has used *reinforcement*.
9	Lola cleans her room.	This is only a *behavior*; the *event* that follows and an indication of an *increase* in behavior are missing.

examples of reinforcers and reinforcement. To test your understanding, you may want to cover the right-hand column of Table 1.1 to see if you can determine which examples show reinforcers and the use of reinforcement and which examples do not.

Both undesirable and desirable behaviors are subject to reinforcement. For example, if Sarah tears her math worksheets into pieces daily, then tearing math worksheets into pieces is being reinforced in some way; or if Terrance raises his hand regularly to answer questions, then hand-raising is being reinforced in some way.

In our day-to-day life, behavior is usually reinforced naturally through our interaction with the environment and the people around us. For example, eating something is reinforced by an abatement of hunger pangs. Calling a friend is reinforced by the interaction that follows. This is true for both desirable and undesirable behaviors. It is unlikely that someone would consciously encourage Sally to tear up her worksheets, but if Sally does so regularly, then she is somehow being reinforced for her behavior. It is unlikely that someone is intentionally encouraging Marcus to curse in class, but if Marcus does so regularly, cursing is somehow being reinforced.

Many people find this counterintuitive. They believe that if someone gets an item or event that most of us consider desirable, that will "reinforce" the behavior. They also believe that if an item or event is something most of us consider undesirable or aversive, it will punish the behavior. However, consider this: Each of us is an individual with different likes and dislikes, different experiences and needs, and different goals and purposes. What reinforces one student may not be reinforcing for all students and may change from day to day, or more often, depending on the conditions (the antecedents) that exist at the time the behavior occurs. Your school or classroom may have developed a wonderful list of very expensive reinforcers, but if a student's behavior does not increase after receiving one of these items, it was not a reinforcer for that student. Reinforcers must be individualized.

Preconceived notions about what is or is not a reinforcer can sabotage the FBA and the function-based intervention. A teacher or parent may not believe that reprimands or time-outs reinforce a problem behavior because they consider them undesirable consequences. However, the test of a reinforcer is whether the behavior increases, not its perceived desirability.

Positive and Negative Reinforcement

As noted earlier, there are two ways that reinforcement functions to increase or maintain behavior. These two forms of reinforcement are called positive reinforcement and negative reinforcement. Yes, negative reinforcement increases behavior. Remember, it is the fact of the behavior increasing that defines something as a reinforcer, not how the word is used in our daily life.

Positive reinforcement means you get something and the behavior that helped you get it increases. Technically, it is the contingent provision of a stimulus (e.g., a treat, object, or activity) following a behavior that results in an increase or maintenance of the frequency, duration, and/or intensity of the behavior (Skinner, 1938, 1969). For example, if you help Micah clean up his area after he throws his materials on the floor, your help provided positive reinforcement if Micah's destructive behavior increases or maintains in the future.

Negative reinforcement means that something you presumably did not like or want to do is avoided or taken away and the behavior that helped you avoid or escape that situation increases. Technically, it is the contingent removal of a stimulus following a behavior that results in an increase or maintenance of the frequency, duration, and/or intensity of the behavior (Pfiffner & O'Leary, 1987). Removing Dante from music class after he curses could be negative reinforcement if Dante's cursing continues or increases in the future. Negative reinforcement could also be the culprit if Dante avoids music class entirely by cursing on the way to class.

Understand that when interventionists discuss reinforcement, the terms positive and negative do not describe the quality or social acceptability of the student's behavior or of the reinforcer. Instead, the terms describe whether a stimulus or event was accessed (positive reinforcement) or avoided (negative reinforcement). In other words, when a behavior serves to access or gain an event or stimulus, it is being positively reinforced, even if the event or stimulus that is accessed or gained is considered by others to be undesirable. Conversely, when a behavior serves to avoid or escape an event or stimulus, it is being negatively reinforced, even if the behavior itself is very appropriate. When you conduct FBAs and design function-based interventions, you should use other terminology to differentiate between "good" and "bad" behavior (e.g., desirable and undesirable, acceptable and unacceptable, wanted and unwanted). Careful use of these terms will not only avoid confusion, but will also help in defining and solving the problem.

Types of Reinforcers

Any event that follows a behavior and increases the likelihood of the behavior can be a reinforcer. Can time with the teacher be a reinforcer? How about a cold drink? Or a kiss? These events can all be reinforcers, as long as they are delivered after a specific behavior and increase the future occurrence of the behavior. Clearly, just about anything could be a reinforcer.

Interventionists distinguish between two categories of reinforcers and several subcategories or types of reinforcers (see Figure 1.1). This is important because you need to know something about the characteristics of reinforcers within each category so you can more effectively identify a reinforcer for the replacement behavior that is comparable to the one that originally reinforced the problem behavior. In other words, when antecedent conditions remain the same, you want to provide a reinforcer for the replacement behavior that is functionally equivalent to the one provided for the problem behavior. If Paul's problem behavior gives him peer interaction, reinforcing him with access to the computer will not address the function of his behavior.

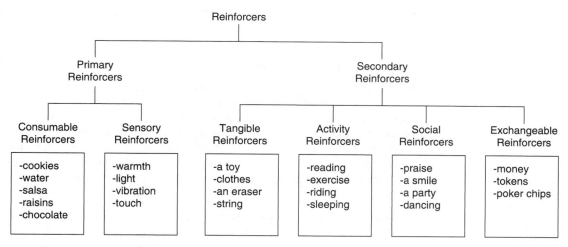

FIGURE 1.1
Types of reinforcers.

Reinforcers are identified as primary or secondary. **Primary reinforcers** are reinforcing because they meet a basic biological need. They can be broken down into the subcategories of consumable reinforcers and sensory reinforcers. Water, light, touch, and cookies are all primary reinforcers. As shown in Figure 1.1, water and cookies are **consumable reinforcers,** and light and touch are **sensory reinforcers.**

Secondary reinforcers are learned, or gain their reinforcing value, through association with primary reinforcers or other secondary reinforcers. For example, we have no biological need for a dollar bill, but it can provide access to primary reinforcers, such as a soda, or secondary reinforcers, such as a videotape. Common categories of secondary reinforcers are **tangible reinforcers** (physical objects, e.g., toys, clothes, a pencil), **activity reinforcers** (events or activities, e.g., reading, playing music, watching TV), and **social reinforcers** (activities or events that are social in nature, e.g., standing near a friend, teacher praise, a smile from a coworker).

Exchangeable reinforcers are items (e.g., money, poker chips, points for completing an assignment) that can be traded for primary or other secondary reinforcers. They provide an easy and convenient way to deliver reinforcers that might be cumbersome in some situations. For example, if Paul's problem behavior is reinforced by peer attention, you would want to reinforce him with peer attention for a replacement behavior such as participating in math instruction. However, it is usually not possible to provide peer attention throughout the school day. It would be as disruptive as the problem behavior. An exchangeable system would give Paul points for the replacement behavior that could be traded for extra free time with his friends.

Studies have shown that consequences affecting behavior most often fall under the categories of attention, tangibles, activities, and sensory stimulation.

Chapter 5 provides further discussion and a procedure for identifying the relevant type of reinforcer.

Selecting Reinforcers

When developing a function-based intervention, you must create conditions that increase the use of the replacement behavior. That is, you must identify appropriate and effective reinforcers. Once you identify the function of the problem behavior (i.e., what reinforces the problem behavior and makes it more likely to occur), you will have identified a potent reinforcer for the desirable behavior you want to replace it. However, there are two reasons you may need to more specifically and carefully identify additional positive reinforcers:

1. Some interventions will change the conditions surrounding the problem behavior to such an extent that the problem behavior is unlikely to occur and the reinforcer that was maintaining it becomes unnecessary or inappropriate. When this occurs, you need to identify strong reinforcers that will establish the replacement behavior in the student's repertoire. The development of a new behavior almost invariably requires more frequent and intense reinforcement than an established behavior.

2. You want a student's behavior to come under the control of reinforcers more naturally available in the environment—whatever those might be. In addition to providing tokens so Paul can access peer attention, you may find that Paul also responds to teacher praise, notes sent home to his mother detailing his good work, and group rewards for completing assignments correctly.

There are numerous ways to discover consequences that will increase the future likelihood of a behavior for an individual or group. These methods can be divided into procedures that are either **indirect** assessments or **direct** assessments (Hagopian, Long, & Rush, 2004). In Chapters 3 and 4, you learn more specific methods for assessing potential reinforcers.

FUNCTION-BASED INTERVENTION IN NATURAL SETTINGS

Our current approach to function-based intervention began when Carr (1977) suggested that many problem behaviors might actually be deliberate acts that people engage in because they serve a purpose. Carr suggested these behaviors might be learned and maintained (i.e., reinforced) by the consequences they produced. Perhaps people learn that inappropriate behavior generates a lot of attention from others. Perhaps these same behaviors also help them get out of doing things they do not want to do. If these behaviors are learned and maintained by the consequences they produce, then they can be considered **operant** behaviors, which are assessed and treated like any other learned behavior.

The earliest research on function-based intervention focused on developing methods designed to identify the consequences maintaining problem behaviors under controlled conditions (Iwata, Dorsey, Slifer, Bauman, & Richman, 1982). Soon after, Carr and Durand (1985) reported one of the first attempts at function-based intervention in a community setting. Working with children and adolescents with developmental disabilities who had few communication skills, these researchers identified the consequences that maintained their behaviors. Then, through the use of **functional communication training,** they taught these young people appropriate ways to gain the attention previously produced by their aggressions, tantrums, and self-injury. This work established a cornerstone of function-based intervention mentioned earlier in the chapter: the importance of teaching and reinforcing the use of appropriate **replacement** behaviors.

The first attempts at function-based intervention in school settings targeted students with special needs in segregated special education classrooms (e.g., Dunlap, Kern-Dunlap, Clarke, & Robbins, 1991; Repp, Felce, & Barton, 1988; Sasso et al., 1992). Among these early studies, the most influential was the work by Dunlap and colleagues because it created a "blueprint" for our current efforts in schools and other natural settings. Working with a 12-year-old girl with multiple disabilities and a history of severely disruptive behavior at school, these researchers first collected descriptive data through structured interviews and structured observations of her behavior. They then developed a way to directly test the functions of her behavior within the context of naturally occurring activities and routines at school. The resulting intervention, which focused on modifying her schedule and curriculum, produced dramatic and lasting improvements in her behavior.

Armed with an approach suitable for natural settings, many researchers then began to extend function-based intervention to other students in special education settings (e.g., Clarke et al., 1995; Ervin, DuPaul, Kern, & Friman, 1998; Foster-Johnson, Ferro, & Dunlap, 1994; Kern, Childs, Dunlap, Clarke, & Falk, 1994; Kern, Delaney, Clarke, Dunlap, & Childs, 2001), to students with special needs in general education classes (e.g., Todd, Horner, & Sugai, 1999; Umbreit, 1995, 1996; Umbreit & Blair, 1996), and even to typically developing children (e.g., Lewis & Sugai, 1996a, 1996b; Umbreit, Lane, & Dejud, 2004). Related work also demonstrated the effectiveness of the approach with young children in integrated child care and preschool settings both in the United States (e.g., Blair, Umbreit, & Bos, 1999; Umbreit & Blair, 1997) and in Korea, establishing the relevance and efficacy of the procedure in a country with a very different language and culture (Blair, Liaupsin, Umbreit, & Kweon, in press). Reviews of this body of work (e.g., Fox, Conroy, & Heckaman, 1998; Heckaman, Conroy, Fox, & Chait, 2000; Sasso, Conroy, Stichter, & Fox, 2001) have concluded that function-based intervention is the most effective approach for improving the behavior of students in need.

LINKING THE INTERVENTION TO THE FBA

These same reviewers also pointed out a glaring weakness in function-based intervention research: the lack of a clear set of methods for using FBA data to develop interventions. Despite numerous reports of success, researchers typically provided little if any detail about how they developed the resulting interventions.

Without clear and replicable methods for using FBA data to design effective interventions, researchers and practitioners alike are left with little guidance on how to proceed once an FBA is completed. Thus, we should not be surprised by recent research (Scott, Liaupsin, Nelson, & McIntyre, 2005; Scott et al., 2005) reporting that, even when school teams accurately identify the function of a student's problem behavior, they typically do not use information about function to develop intervention plans. This is a significant problem for two reasons: (a) The only reason to conduct an FBA is to gather the information needed to develop a corresponding function-based intervention, and (b) knowing the function of the student's behavior is of no value if the subsequent intervention fails to adequately address it.

This critical need is the reason we developed the methods specified in Chapters 6 to 8. These chapters describe a unique, straightforward technique for linking FBA results to one of three intervention methods and a Function-Based Intervention Decision Model that guides the process. During the past few years, we have taught these methods to hundreds of undergraduate and graduate students, many of whom work full time in schools, and repeatedly found that they can easily learn them and apply them effectively with students in schools.

Although much of the research cited within this text was conducted in schools, the procedures for conducting an FBA and the methods used to translate that information into an effective function-based intervention are relevant across individuals, settings, severity of behavior, and types of disability. Function-based interventions have been shown to successfully address problem behaviors within a variety of school, clinical, and community settings, with very severe (e.g., self-injury, aggression) to milder forms of problem behavior, with individuals ranging in age from preschool to adult, and with individuals with a variety of disabilities. Furthermore, these interventions have been effective regardless of whether the student has severe disabilities, mild disabilities, or no identified disabilities.

HOW THIS BOOK IS ORGANIZED

The function-based intervention process involves three broad tasks: conducting the FBA, developing and testing the intervention, and implementing the intervention. Parts 1 to 3 of this book correspond to each of these tasks, respectively. The most effective way to learn about the process and the specific methods that should be used at each step is to learn them in the sequence in which they are performed in practice. We have organized this book accordingly. Information about fundamental principles and concepts of applied behavior analysis is presented as it becomes necessary at each step in the process.

Every chapter in Parts 1 to 3 includes a list of expected outcomes, a summary of the steps and activities required to properly complete each phase of the process, and exercises designed to improve your understanding of the material that is presented. Each chapter also includes numerous examples. We deliberately provide examples of exemplary work you can use as models for your own work. However, we also provide negative examples of common and critical errors that can sabotage your efforts. Seeing both exemplary and nonexemplary work will refine your understanding and help you avoid making these same errors.

The final section of this book presents an example of the entire function-based intervention process for each intervention method we recommend. After reading Chapters 2 to 13 and completing the exercises, the material in Part 4 will help you integrate the complete process from start to finish.

REFERENCES

Alberto, P. A., & Troutman, A. C. (2006). *Applied behavior analysis to teachers* (7th ed.). Upper Saddle River, NJ: Merrill/Prentice Hall.

Blair, K. C., Liaupsin, C. J., Umbreit, J., & Kweon, G. (in press). Function-based intervention to support the inclusive placements of young children in Korea. *Education and Training in Developmental Disabilities.*

Blair, K. C., Umbreit, J., & Bos, C. S. (1999). Using functional assessment and children's preferences to improve the behavior of young children with behavioral disorders. *Behavioral Disorders, 24,* 151–166.

Carr, E. G. (1977). The motivation of self-injurious behavior—A review of some hypotheses. *Psychological Bulletin, 64,* 600–616.

Carr, E. G., & Durand, V. M. (1985). Reducing behavior problems through functional communication training. *Journal of Applied Behavior Analysis, 18,* 111–126.

Clarke, S., Dunlap, G., Foster-Johnson, L., Childs, K. E., Wilson, D., White, R., et al. (1995). Improving the conduct of students with behavioral disorders by incorporating student interests into curricular activities. *Behavioral Disorders, 20,* 221–227.

Cooper, J. O., Heron, T. E., & Heward, W. L. (1987). *Applied behavior analysis.* Upper Saddle River, NJ: Merrill/Prentice Hall.

Dunlap, G., Kern-Dunlap, L., Clarke, S., & Robbins, F. R. (1991). Functional assessment, curricular revision, and severe behavior problems. *Journal of Applied Behavior Analysis, 24,* 387–397.

Ervin, R., DuPaul, G., Kern, L., & Friman, P. (1998). Classroom-based functional and adjunctive assessments: Proactive approaches to intervention selection for adolescents with attention deficit hyperactivity disorder. *Journal of Applied Behavior Analysis, 31,* 65–78.

Foster-Johnson, L., Ferro, J., & Dunlap, G. (1994). Preferred curricular activities and reduced problem behaviors in students with intellectual disabilities. *Journal of Applied Behavior Analysis, 27,* 493–504.

Fox, J., Conroy, M., & Heckaman, K. (1998). Research issues in functional assessment of the challenging behaviors of students with emotional and behavioral disorders. *Behavioral Disorders, 24,* 26–33.

Hagopian, L. P., Long, E. S., & Rush, K. S. (2004). Preference assessment procedures for individuals with developmental disabilities. *Behavior Modification, 28,* 668–677.

Heckaman, K., Conroy, M., Fox, J., & Chait, A. (2000). Functional assessment-based intervention research on students with or at risk for emotional and behavioral disorders. *Behavioral Disorders, 25,* 196–210.

Individuals with Disabilities Education Act, 20 U.S.C. § 1401–1485.

Individuals with Disabilities Education Improvement Act of 2004, 20 U.S.C. § 1415 (k) (1) (d) (ii).

Iwata, B. A., Dorsey, M., Slifer, K., Bauman, K., & Richman, G. (1982). Toward a functional analysis of self-injury. *Analysis and Intervention in Developmental Disabilities, 2,* 3–20.

Kazdin, A. E. (2000). *Behavior modification in applied settings* (6th ed.). Belmont, CA: Wadsworth.

Kern, L., Childs, K. E., Dunlap, G., Clarke, S., & Falk, G. D. (1994). Using assessment-based curricular intervention to improve the classroom behavior of a student with emotional and behavioral challenges. *Journal of Applied Behavior Analysis, 27,* 7–19.

Kern, L., Delaney, B., Clarke, S., Dunlap, G., & Childs, K. (2001). Improving the classroom behavior of students with emotional and behavioral disorders using individualized curricular modifications. *Journal of Emotional and Behavioral Disorders, 9,* 239–247.

Lewis, T. J., & Sugai, G. (1996a). Descriptive and experimental analysis of teacher and peer attention and the use of assessment-based intervention to improve pro-social behavior. *Journal of Behavioral Education, 6,* 7–24.

Lewis, T. J., & Sugai, G. (1996b). Functional assessment and problem behavior: A pilot investigation on the comparative and interactive effects of teacher and peer social attention on students in general education settings. *School Psychology Quarterly, 11,* 1–19.

Martin, G., & Pear, J. (2003). *Behavior modification: What it is and how to do it* (7th ed.). Upper Saddle River, NJ: Prentice Hall.

Miller, L. K. (2006). *Principles of everyday behavior analysis* (4th ed.). Pacific Grove, CA: Brooks/Cole.

Pfiffner, L., & O'Leary, S. G. (1987). The efficacy of all-positive management as a function of prior use of negative consequences. *Journal of Applied Behavior Analysis, 20*(3), 265–271.

Repp, A. C., Felce, D., & Barton, L. E. (1988). Basing the treatment of stereotypic and self-injurious behaviors on hypotheses of their causes. *Journal of Applied Behavior Analysis, 21,* 281–289.

Sasso, G., Conroy, M. A., Stichter, J., & Fox, J. J. (2001). Slowing down the bandwagon: The misapplication of functional assessment for students with emotional and behavioral disorders. *Behavioral Disorders, 26,* 282–296.

Sasso, G. M., Reimers, T. M., Cooper, L. J., Wacker, D., Berg, W., Steege, M., Kelly, L., & Allaire, A. (1992). Use of descriptive and experimental analyses to identify the functional properties of aberrant behavior in school settings. *Journal of Applied Behavior Analysis, 25,* 809–821.

Scott, T., McIntyre, J., Liaupsin, C., Nelson, C. M., Conroy, M., & Payne, L. (2005). An examination of the relationship between team-based functional behavior assessment and selected intervention strategies. *Journal of Positive Behavior Interventions, 7,* 205–215.

Scott, T. M., Liaupsin, C., Nelson, C. M., & McIntyre, J. (2005). Team-based functional behavior assessment as a proactive public school process: A descriptive analysis of current barriers. *Journal of Behavioral Education, 14,* 57–71.

Skinner, B. F. (1938). *The behavior or organisms: An experimental analysis.* Oxford, England: Appleton Century.

Skinner, B. F. (1969). *Contingencies of reinforcement: A theoretical analysis.* New York: Appleton Century Crofts.

Sugai, G., Horner, R., Dunlap, G., Hieneman, M., Lewis, T., Nelson, C. M., et al. (2000). Applying positive behavior support and functional behavior assessment in schools. *Journal of Positive Behavior Interventions, 2*(3), 131–143.

Sulzer-Azaroff, B., & Mayer, R. G. (1991). *Behavior analysis for lasting change.* New York: Harcourt Brace Jovanovich.

Todd, A. W., Horner, R. H., & Sugai, G. (1999). Effects of self-monitoring and self-recruited praise on problem behavior, academic engagement, and work completion in a typical classroom. *Journal of Positive Behavior Interventions, 1,* 66–76.

Umbreit, J. (1995). Functional assessment and intervention in a regular classroom setting for the disruptive behavior of a student with attention deficit hyperactivity disorder. *Behavioral Disorders, 20,* 267–278.

Umbreit, J. (1996). Functional analysis of disruptive behavior in an inclusive classroom. *Journal of Early Intervention, 20,* 18–29.

Umbreit, J., & Blair, K. C. (1996). The effects of preference, choice, and attention on problem behavior at school. *Education and Training in Mental Retardation and Developmental Disabilities, 31,* 151–161.

Umbreit, J., & Blair, K. C. (1997). Using structural analysis to facilitate the treatment of noncompliance and aggression in a young child at-risk for behavioral disorders. *Behavioral Disorders, 22,* 75–86.

Umbreit, J., Lane, K. L., & Dejud, C. (2004). Improving classroom behavior by modifying task difficulty: The effects of increasing the difficulty of too-easy tasks. *Journal of Positive Behavior Interventions, 6,* 13–20.

Zirpoli, T. J. (2005). *Behavior management: Applications for teachers* (4th ed.). Upper Saddle River, NJ: Merrill/Prentice Hall.

Part One

Conducting the FBA

Conducting an FBA identifies two things: (a) The situations or circumstances in which a student engages in a particular problem behavior; and (b) the consequences that are reinforcing that behavior, thus leading the student to continue using it. Specific activities are required to achieve this purpose. The interventionist's task is to gather and analyze the data that make this possible.

The "information-gathering" phase of the FBA usually begins by conducting structured interviews with "informants" (i.e., people who can provide information about the student and his or her behavior in the situations that are of concern). In school settings, the most likely informants are the teaching staff who work in the student's classroom but may include other staff such as bus drivers and playground monitors. The second step in information gathering involves conducting a structured interview with the student, whenever possible.

The next activity in the information-gathering process requires the interventionist to directly observe the student engage in the problem behavior in the natural settings in which it causes concern. Direct observation enables the interventionist to witness firsthand those circumstances that exist when the problem behavior occurs and the consequences of the behavior that maintain its use by the student. Direct observation also allows the interventionist to confirm or disconfirm the information provided by the informants and the student during the interview process.

When all necessary interview and observational data have been gathered, the interventionist must then analyze this information to identify the function or functions of the student's behavior. When the interventionist can identify the situations or circumstances in which the problem behavior occurs, as well as the consequences that reinforce the behavior, the task of conducting the FBA has been completed.

Part 1 includes four chapters that provide the information and tools needed to conduct the FBA. The interview process begins by developing a sound behavioral definition of the problem (or target) behavior. If this step is done incorrectly, the error will inevitably sabotage all subsequent efforts. One cannot make sense of the information that was gathered if the informant, student, or observer was not clear about the behavior in question. Therefore, developing a good definition of the problem behavior is crucial. For this reason, Chapter 2 is devoted solely to the task of properly defining the target behavior. This chapter also provides the tools you will need to develop a solid definition of a desirable replacement behavior, which you should do as early as possible in the interview process. Chapter 3 presents the remaining information and tools you will need to conduct effective interviews with informants and the student.

With the interviews completed, you can then directly observe the student's behavior. The information and methods you will need to complete this task are presented in Chapter 4. The process of analyzing the information you have collected through interviews and observation is addressed in Chapter 5. Your analysis and conclusions must be systematic. To aid in this process, Chapter 5 presents the Function Matrix, which is a useful tool for organizing the information you have gathered and for drawing sound conclusions about the consequences that are reinforcing the target behavior.

CHAPTER 2

Identifying the Problem
Defining Target and Replacement Behaviors

OUTCOMES

After reading this chapter, you will be able to

- Describe the importance of defining the problem.
- Distinguish behaviors from nonbehaviors.
- Define a target behavior in terms that are sufficiently specific.
- Select a replacement behavior to take the place of a given target behavior.

As described in Chapter 1, the route to developing an effective function-based intervention starts with defining the behavior that is selected for intervention and deciding what the student or group should do instead. The behavior that is selected for intervention is referred to as the **target behavior.** The behavior that we want the student to perform instead is referred to as the **replacement behavior.** Defining the target behavior and selecting an appropriate replacement behavior drive the focus of interviews and observations aimed at determining why the student engages in the behavior. Appropriate definitions are essential in gathering the necessary information for designing an appropriate strategy and accurately measuring the results of the intervention. This chapter begins by presenting criteria that will help you distinguish behaviors from nonbehaviors. The remainder of the chapter concentrates on issues surrounding the definition of the target behavior and the selection of a replacement behavior.

WHAT IS BEHAVIOR?

Is walking a behavior? Is a coffee cup a behavior? Is losing weight a behavior? How about daydreaming; is it a behavior? You probably instinctively know the answers to at least the first two questions, but how did you make your decision? Before you can define a target behavior and select a replacement behavior, it is essential to understand the difference between behaviors and nonbehaviors. A basic set of criteria can be used to distinguish behaviors from nonbehaviors. **Behaviors** are actions or events that can be observed, measured, and repeated. We now look more carefully at how to use these criteria to assist in the identification of behaviors.

The first criterion of our definition states that behaviors are actions or events. This element of the definition is important for distinguishing between behaviors and the outcomes or results of behaviors. When conducting function-based interventions, we focus on reducing certain specific behaviors, while encouraging the use of other specific behaviors so we can achieve more appropriate outcomes. For instance, getting an "A" on a test is the result or outcome of any number of actions (e.g., studying, going to class, reading a chapter in a textbook). Rather than concentrating on the outcome, we are more likely to be successful in improving a student's academic performance if we promote the actual behaviors that lead to good grades.

The second criterion to consider in distinguishing behaviors from nonbehaviors is that behaviors can be seen (observed), counted (measured), and repeated (done again). The requirement that behaviors should be observable and measurable rules out many of the terms often used to describe student behavior. Some of these terms describe personal motivations (e.g., Tim is controlling), whereas other terms describe internal processes (e.g., Maria's mind wanders). Still others describe feelings (e.g., Chloe is depressed). This is not to say that personal motivations, internal processes, and feelings do not exist; it is simply that describing behavior in such terms is not specific enough for the purposes of predicting and understanding behavior. Similarly, behaviors can be repeated. A chair can be observed (seen) and measured (height, width, etc.), but it does not meet our criteria for a behavior.

Focusing only on behaviors that can be observed, measured, and repeated allows agreement among individuals regarding each occurrence of the action or event. As is further discussed in the next section, generalized descriptions of behavior, such as those mentioned previously, are often the starting point for more specific descriptions of behavior. For instance, if you ask two individuals to look at a student and tell you whether that student is "concentrating," it would likely be difficult for the observers to agree. However, the same two observers are much more likely to agree on whether a student is "looking at the work task." As is stressed throughout this text, the ability to maintain agreement among individuals regarding student behavior is a critical feature in developing effective interventions.

Behaviors can be measured in various ways. Just as a table or chair can be described in terms of length, width, height, and weight, behaviors can be described in terms of their "dimensions." The dimensions of behavior include

- Frequency/rate (how often the behavior occurs)
- Duration (how long the behavior lasts)
- Latency (how long is it before the student begins the behavior)
- Topography (the shape of the behavior; what it looks like)
- Locus (where the behavior occurs)
- Force (the strength or intensity of the behavior)

Chapter 9 presents more information about these dimensions and how to accurately measure them.

In summary, behaviors are defined as actions or events that are measurable, observable, and repeatable. In light of this definition, we now review the questions raised at the beginning of this section:

- Is walking a behavior? Yes, it is an action that can be measured, observed, and repeated.
- Is a coffee cup a behavior? No, it is not an action or event.
- Is losing weight a behavior? No, it is the outcome of behaviors such as exercising and eating healthy foods.
- Is daydreaming a behavior? No, at least not for the purpose of conducting an FBA or developing a function-based intervention. Although students may indeed daydream, it is not an event that can be observed and measured by others. Observable, measurable, and repeatable behaviors associated with daydreaming might include staring into space or gazing out the window.

DEFINING THE TARGET BEHAVIOR

A behavior that is carefully described in measurable and observable terms and that is selected for intervention is called a target behavior. The term **problem behavior** is often used synonymously with this term. However, in this text, we choose to use the term target behavior to refer to the problematic behavior that has been selected (i.e., targeted) for assessment and intervention. This term is commonly used in the field of applied behavior analysis, and is associated with a specific and useful format for describing behavior. The format for describing a target behavior includes two elements: (a) a general descriptor for the behavior; and (b) a series of specific observable, measurable, and repeatable examples. The general descriptor should be a word or short phrase that makes it easy to communicate about the target behavior with others involved in developing the function-based intervention.

The specific examples of the behavior are added to ensure two or more observers would be likely to agree when an instance of the target behavior has occurred.

Before proceeding further, it is important to recognize the pivotal nature of properly defining the target behavior. If the definition of the target behavior is faulty, then the information gathered through interviews and observations is immediately questionable. One cannot be sure that different respondents are referring to the same behavior when they answer interview questions. Similarly, one cannot be certain that observers are recording occurrences of the same behavior. Appropriately defining the target behavior improves communication and accuracy, and prevents the needless waste of time spent gathering ambiguous information. If you are not sure whether the interview and observational data pertain to the same exact behavior, you must determine this before you can make use of that information.

Following are two examples of properly defined target behaviors. Each description begins with the general descriptor and is followed by three or four specific examples of the behavior:

Example A: The target behavior is destruction of classroom property, which includes behaviors such as drawing in books, tearing up worksheets, and breaking pencils.

Example B: The target behavior is self-stimulation, which is defined as hand flapping, rocking, stomping while seated, and head nodding.

As mentioned earlier in this chapter, the information necessary to define the target behavior is most often gathered during interviews with teachers, parents, other relevant staff, and the student. As is discussed in Chapter 3, this information can be collected using structured interview protocols and supplemented through the use of unstructured or semistructured discussions. Regardless of the methods used to assemble the information that defines the target behavior, the goal is to create a description of the behavior that is useful for both communicating with others and collecting observational data (addressed in Chapter 4).

When working with teachers or others to develop a target behavior definition, the most important task is to identify the specific examples that typify the behavior. You can then develop a general descriptor that encompasses all examples. For instance, in Example A, a teacher may have originally described the student as "disrespectful." In this case, an interviewer would ask questions to clarify what the student's disrespectful behavior "looks like" (drawing in books, tearing up worksheets, and breaking pencils). In addition, the interviewer might ask if all instances of disrespect involved destruction of property. If so (and provided there is agreement from other sources), the interviewer has the information necessary to define the target behavior. If not, then the interviewer should continue to elicit examples that appear to be related to the target behavior. Whether these additional examples belong in the target behavior definition is discussed later in this chapter.

TABLE 2.1
Examples of Target Behaviors

Student	General Descriptor	Specific Examples	Error
Ex 1: Tara	The target behavior is destruction of property,	which includes pushing books to the floor, tearing up worksheets, and breaking pencils.	No error.
Ex 2: Luis	(No general descriptor necessary.)	The target behavior is pushing peers in line while waiting for lunch.	No error.
Ex 3: Mercedes	The target behavior is aggression toward staff,	which includes *making staff members angry and irritated.*	Specific examples include *outcomes* of behavior.
Ex 4: James	The target behavior is daydreaming,	which includes *thinking about anything other than work.*	Specific examples include *covert* behaviors that would be difficult to measure.
Ex 5: Marcia	The target behavior is disrespect to staff,	which includes cursing at staff, refusing to follow directions, and *tardiness.*	Specific examples include behaviors that may not belong to the same *response class.*

Because development of a target behavior definition is a key step toward creation of a function-based intervention, it is important at this point in the process to recognize and avoid errors that can ruin the usefulness of the target behavior definition. Table 2.1 presents two properly formatted definitions, as well as examples of three of the most frequent errors encountered during the development of a target behavior definition. A discussion of each example follows.

Example 1 presents a properly formatted definition. The target behavior for Tara is defined as destruction of property, which includes behaviors such as pushing books to the floor, tearing up worksheets, and breaking pencils. It should be noted that there is at least one exception to following this format for describing target behaviors, as shown in Example 2. In this example, the only presenting problem is that Luis pushes other children in line while waiting for lunch. There may be instances in which a single behavior appears to be the only presenting problem. In such cases, there is no need to create a general descriptor. However, you may want to approach these situations with healthy skepticism. In other words, be careful to explore whether a single example sufficiently describes the range of the target behavior. During the interview process, you should determine whether other behaviors (hitting, kicking) occur under the same conditions and whether the same behavior occurs under any other conditions (pushing in the hall, pushing while waiting in line to use the bathroom).

As was described earlier in this chapter, actual behaviors are often confused with the outcomes of behavior. In Example 3, the general descriptor of

Mercedes's behavior (aggression toward staff) is acceptable. However, the remainder of the definition presents outcomes of behavior (e.g., making staff angry and irritated) rather than actual behaviors. Returning to the criteria for distinguishing a behavior from a nonbehavior will allow you to sniff out outcomes masquerading as actual behaviors. Although it may be true that Mercedes is "making staff angry and irritated," this is not an observable and measurable action performed by the student. To correct this error in the target behavior description, we should ask the question: What does Mercedes *do* to anger and irritate staff (e.g., use crude language, make threats, throw furniture)?

Another common error in developing a target behavior description is to select specific behaviors that are hidden or **covert.** It can be acceptable to choose a general descriptor that describes a covert behavior, as long as you choose specific behavioral examples that would allow you to observe and measure when the covert behavior is occurring. For instance, in Example 4, daydreaming is an acceptable general descriptor of the behavior, but you would not be able to observe and measure whether a student was thinking about anything other than work. However, as mentioned earlier, daydreaming could be associated with observable and measurable behaviors such as looking out the window, staring into space, or sitting motionless with eyes open.

One final common error occurs when the specific examples that are included in the definition do not belong to the same response class. Behaviors that serve the same function are considered to belong to the same **response class.** In other words, two behaviors that look very different can produce similar results. In a classroom, the behaviors of "drumming on a desk" and "calling out" belong to the same response class if both serve the function of gaining the teacher's attention. If we identify a series of behaviors that serve the same function, then a single intervention is likely to have an effect on all behaviors in the response class. In the previous example, teaching a student to "raise his or her hand and wait to be called on" could help reduce both "drumming on the desk" and "calling out" if they both serve to gain teacher attention.

A response class error is not especially problematic at this point in the process. Simply be aware that you may need to revise the target behavior definition once you determine the function. At that time, you should review the target behavior definition to consider whether the behaviors of concern actually belong to the same response class. If they do not, then you can revise the definition and determine whether another intervention is required for the behaviors that do not fit within the response class for the current target behavior. For example, after initial interviews with her teacher, you might define Marcia's disrespect to staff (Example 5) as including examples such as cursing at staff, refusing to follow directions, and tardiness. If the function of Marcia's disrespectful behavior allows her to avoid classroom activities, then the specific examples currently in the target behavior definition may appear to serve that function. However, if you determine that the function of Marcia's disrespectful behavior is to access staff attention, tardiness would likely be dropped from the definition because it does not function to provide access to teacher attention.

SELECTING A REPLACEMENT BEHAVIOR

By defining the target behavior, you have identified a behavior that should be decreased in frequency or intensity, or eliminated from the student's repertoire altogether. We should keep in mind, however, that if a student is not engaging in the target behavior, then he or she must do something in its place. If a student is no longer throwing pencils and books in math class, will he or she make noises, walk around the classroom, or do math? If a student is no longer running down the hall, will he or she be skipping, spinning, rolling, or walking? Some of these alternatives are acceptable, whereas others are not. Identifying what the student should do is the next step in the process of developing a function-based intervention. If we take the initiative of selecting, teaching, and promoting an appropriate behavior, then we are more likely to see that behavior replace the target behavior. The behavior we choose to take the place of the target behavior is called the replacement behavior.

The selection of a replacement behavior requires access to information about both the student and the environment. This information is generally collected via interviews with the student's teachers, other adults and staff, and the student. You might also gain valuable information during direct observations that will help you refine the target behavior. You learn more about these methods of gathering information in Chapters 3 and 4. The remainder of this chapter focuses on describing criteria for selecting an appropriate replacement behavior. In brief, these criteria suggest that an appropriate replacement behavior should

- Be stated in terms of what you want the student to do
- Be something the student can do or can learn to do
- Be supported by the natural environment

Criteria for Selecting an Appropriate Replacement Behavior

One characteristic of an appropriate replacement behavior is that it describes a behavior in terms of what you want the student to do. A mistake that is often made is to define the replacement behavior as the absence of behavior; if the target behavior is "talking out of turn," then the replacement behavior is not "not talking out of turn." Instead, the replacement behavior should positively state the new behavior. For the previous target behavior, you might choose "raise a hand and wait to be called on to speak." The error of defining the replacement behavior as the absence of the target behavior is an example of using the "Dead Man's Rule" (i.e., the idea that if a dead man could meet the criteria, then it is not a behavior). A dead person definitely does "not talk out of turn."

The next task in selecting a replacement behavior is to ensure it is a behavior that a student can perform or can learn to perform. Obviously, it is important to consider whether there is any sensory or physical impairment that might prevent the student from using the replacement behavior. The directive "raise a hand and wait to be called on to speak" might not be appropriate for a student with certain motor or speech difficulties. Less obvious is the issue of determining whether the student can learn to perform the behavior. For example, Toby is a student who is disruptive during silent reading. Specific examples of his behaviors include making noises, talking with peers, and walking around the room. What the teacher wants the student to do instead is to "engage in silent reading." At this point, the question that should be raised is whether Toby can read at a sufficient level to engage in the selected replacement behavior. If he cannot, then the teacher should either select an alternate replacement behavior or develop a function-based intervention that includes adjusting the reading materials or assessing and teaching reading skills. In Chapters 6 to 8, you learn to incorporate environmental adjustments and academic instruction into function-based intervention plans.

You may have noted situations in which a student was enticed to perform a new behavior through a contingency that had nothing to do with the actual behavior (a soda for keeping hands to self), only to find that once the additional reinforcement (the soda) was removed, the student stopped performing the behavior. The failure to consider that the natural environment must contain reinforcement for the replacement behavior is one reason such problems are likely to occur.

At times, it may be necessary to use contrived or extrinsic reinforcers to promote the initial use of a new behavior. **Contrived reinforcers** are those consequences that maintain a behavior but that are not natural to a situation (e.g., trinkets or treats for completing a reading assignment). **Extrinsic reinforcers** are consequences that maintain behavior but that are under someone else's control (e.g., a teacher or parent). However, if we want the new behavior to persist once contrived or extrinsic reinforcers are removed, we should begin by selecting a replacement behavior that is reinforced by the natural environment.

One way to increase the likelihood that you will select a behavior that is supported by the natural environment is to choose a behavior that students with the same developmental characteristics often use in a similar situation. In other words, if a student's peers frequently use a behavior, then reinforcement for that behavior must exist somewhere in the environment.

Of course, this assumes all school environments incorporate reinforcement for appropriate behavior. Unfortunately, this is not always the case. In some settings, the most logical and appropriate replacement behavior may be one that is not frequently reinforced. When working with a student who is in such a situation, there are two choices. First, from numerous possible replacement behaviors, you might choose the one that is most likely to be reinforced. Second, you might choose what appears to be the most appropriate

TABLE 2.2
Examples of Replacement Behaviors

Student	Target Behavior	Replacement Behavior	Error
Ex 1: Sara	Disrupting class during group discussions, which includes talking out and talking with peers	Sitting quietly and raising a hand to be called on during group discussions	No error: The replacement behavior is (a) what we want the student to do, (b) something the student can do, and (c) supported by the natural environment.
Ex 2: James	Off-task activities during math class, which include behaviors such as rearranging materials, sharpening pencils, and digging in a backpack	A grade of "A" in math class	The replacement behavior is an outcome or product of behavior.
Ex 3: Luis	Pushing peers while waiting in line	Not pushing peers while waiting in line	The replacement behavior describes the absence of behavior.
Ex 4: Morgan	Hitting staff, which includes open hand slaps and closed-fist hits	?	No error, but identification of the function of the target behavior will be necessary before selecting a replacement behavior.

replacement behavior and take steps to develop reinforcement for use of the behavior in the environment. Your decision may be based on whether it is likely that the student's environment can be altered to include reinforcement for the new behavior. The information you gather during interviews and observations (Chapters 3 and 4) will help you make this decision. In addition, in Chapters 6 to 8, you learn to incorporate enrichment of the student's environment into your function-based intervention plan.

We now review the information in this section by examining an acceptable replacement behavior and the common mistakes to avoid when selecting a behavior to promote in place of the target behavior. Table 2.2 presents a list of examples that include the target behaviors, the resulting replacement behaviors, and, in some cases, the errors that have been made.

In Example 1, Sara has been exhibiting problem behavior during group discussions. After interviews and observations, it is determined that the target behavior is "disrupting class during group discussions, which includes talking out and talking with peers." The chosen replacement behavior is "sitting quietly and raising a hand to be called on." Through general inspection and information gained during interviews and observations, we can quickly assess whether this replacement behavior is appropriate. First, the behavior is stated in terms that clarify what the student should do. Second, Sara has been seen to sit quietly and raise her hand in other situations, so we are sure it is something she can do. Third, our interviews and observations confirm that the teacher does verbally praise other students who use the same behaviors, so they are supported by the natural environment.

Applying these criteria to any replacement behavior is relatively simple and will generally result in selection of an appropriate replacement behavior. However, care should be taken to further ensure the replacement behavior is well defined. Common mistakes include choosing a replacement behavior that is actually an outcome or product of behavior or creating a statement that reflects the absence of behavior. An additional problem can occur when it is not possible to select a replacement behavior until you have more information on how the behavior functions for the student under the given conditions. Each issue is discussed using the remaining examples in Table 2.2.

As is the case when creating a target behavior definition, it is important to avoid selecting a replacement behavior that is the outcome of behavior. In many instances, simply adhering to the goal of ensuring you are describing what you want the student to do will help you avoid this problem. However, when considering Example 2, it could certainly be said that because James is off-task during math class, what we want him to do is to get an "A" in math. The error here is that a good grade in a class is actually an outcome of a set of behaviors that is likely to include studying, reading, and completing assignments. If we look more closely at the activities during which James is off-task, we might choose to promote one of or all behaviors that might lead him to earn a passing grade. In other words, if you find that you have mistakenly chosen a product of behavior, a suitable replacement behavior can often be selected from the set of behaviors that leads to the desired outcome.

Example 3 presents an error in the selection of a replacement behavior that often occurs when we simply think in terms of "opposites" and end up with a statement that describes the absence of the target behavior. As described earlier in this chapter, if a student ceases to engage in one behavior, he or she must be doing something else. The goal in choosing a replacement behavior is to select the most appropriate "something else" for the given conditions. If you recall the case of Luis, the target behavior is "pushing peers while waiting in line." If we were to act too quickly in determining what we want him to do instead, we might choose "not pushing peers while waiting in line." This replacement behavior also violates the "Dead Man's Rule"; that is, a dead man could certainly "not push peers." Again, working more methodically and considering the criteria for an acceptable replacement behavior is likely to resolve this error. Behaviors that Luis can do and that are supported by the natural environment might include standing with his hands to himself, reading a book, or talking quietly with peers. Information gathered during interviews and observations would help determine which of these replacement behaviors is appropriate in Luis's situation.

At this point in the process, you should make every effort to identify an appropriate replacement behavior if you can. In most cases, this will not be difficult. However, in some cases, it is not possible to identify an appropriate replacement behavior until you have determined the function served by the problem behavior. In Example 4, consider Morgan, a young student with developmental disabilities who hits people. Before you determine the right replacement behavior for hitting, you would first have to know why it is happening (i.e., what reinforcer is maintaining it). If Morgan is hitting to receive attention from others, the replacement behavior might be to use appropriate ways of gaining attention and interacting with others (e.g., tapping their arm, looking at them, saying or signing something). However, if Morgan were hitting to avoid certain activities, such as having to perform a long task, we might choose appropriately requesting a break (e.g., using the sign for "break") as the replacement behavior. In cases such as these, you should simply state that the appropriate replacement behavior cannot be identified until the function of the target behavior has been determined.

SUMMARY

Defining the target behavior and selecting a replacement behavior are the first critical steps in developing a function-based intervention. Both target behaviors and replacement behaviors should fit the description of a behavior; they should be actions or events that are observable, measurable, and repeatable. In addition, target behaviors and replacement behaviors have specific characteristics. The target behavior describes the action that is targeted for intervention and is usually formatted as a general descriptor followed by specific examples of the behavior. A replacement behavior is a positively worded statement that describes what you want the student to do as an alternative to the target behavior. An appropriate replacement behavior should identify what the student is supposed to do, be a behavior that the student can do or can learn to do, and be likely to be reinforced by the natural environment.

Steps for Defining Target and Replacement Behaviors
Steps and Activities for Implementation

Defining the target behavior:

1. Gather information about the presenting problem or problems from various sources.
2. If there are multiple examples of the target behavior, develop a general descriptor that encompasses the range of specific examples.
3. Review the definition to ensure it
   a. describes actual behavior rather than an outcome of behavior.
   b. describes an observable, measurable, and repeatable behavior.

Selecting a replacement behavior:

1. Based on the target behavior definition, choose a replacement behavior that

a. states what the student is to do.
b. is something the student can do or can learn to do.
c. is a behavior that is supported by the natural environment.
2. Review the definition to ensure it
a. describes actual behavior rather than an outcome of behavior.
b. describes an action or activity rather than the "absence" of behavior.

After you determine the function of the target behavior:

1. Review the target behavior definition to ensure it includes only behaviors that belong to the same response class.

2. Review the replacement behavior to ensure it fits logically with the function of the behavior.

EXERCISES

1. List three things that you believe are behaviors and three that are non-behaviors. Next to each, write (a) whether it is an action or event; and (b) whether it is observable, measurable, and repeatable.
2. A target behavior description includes a general descriptor of the behavior that is followed by specific examples. For the following general descriptors, provide some specific examples of the behavior:
   a. Disruptive
   b. Aggressive toward peers
   c. Off-task
3. A replacement behavior describes what the student should do in place of the target behavior. For each target behavior description you completed in Exercise 2, select a likely replacement behavior. Make sure your replacement behaviors identify what the student should do, describe a behavior the student can do or can learn to do, and are supported by the natural environment.

CHAPTER 3

Functional Behavioral Assessment
Interviews

OUTCOMES

After reading this chapter, you will be able to

- Understand the reasons for conducting functional assessment interviews.
- Use a specific format and procedure for completing functional assessment interviews with teachers, parents, and students.

In Chapter 2, you learned to identify and operationally define target and replacement behaviors. In brief, you have selected what you believe to be a keystone problem behavior that—if altered—has the potential to improve the quality of a student's life. For example, if a student has high rates of disruptive behavior (e.g., verbal aggression), this has the potential to impede the student's ability to get along with other students and his or her teacher and, over time, may result in academic underachievement due to lost instructional time (Lane, 2004; Walker, Ramsey, & Gresham, 2004). You have also identified a replacement behavior (e.g., asking for assistance or expressing discontent) that, if used instead of the target behavior, may enhance educational and social outcomes. Furthermore, you have also learned both importance of and procedures for operationally defining both the target and the replacement behaviors.

In this chapter, you learn a specific format and procedure for completing functional assessment interviews with all participants: teachers, parents, and students. The goals of the functional assessment interviews are to (a) solidify your choice of target and replacement behaviors, (b) obtain information about the circumstances or events that set the stage for the target behavior (antecedents or stimuli), and (c) obtain information about the circumstances or events that follow the target behavior that influence the extent to which it will recur.

Interviews are typically conducted with teachers, paraprofessionals, and other school site personnel. However, it is important to remember that parents and students may also provide valuable insight regarding the occurrence and nonoccurrence of the target behavior. Therefore, it is important to carefully consider who should participate in functional assessment interviews: teachers? paraprofessionals? students? parents? In many cases, you will need to interview only one or two people (e.g., teacher, classroom aide). In other cases, you may need to interview several staff (e.g., teachers, aides, library staff, the principal), as well as the student's parents. In every case, you will want to interview the student if he or she is able to provide meaningful information. When interviewing students, be sure to give them some flexibility in responding. For example, let them know that it is okay to skip questions. Also, for younger children (e.g., preschool-age students), it may be necessary to modify the interview to reflect a nonacademic day.

In general, interviews should be conducted with the student and with all significant persons who have sustained interactions with the student or who have experience with the behavior of interest. However, as previously mentioned, in cases where the student is not able to participate in the interviews (e.g., students who have limited cognitive ability or limited communication skills, and/or students who are quite young), it may be particularly important to interview the parents because they may be able to provide information typically provided by students.

After completing functional assessment interviews, you will observe directly in the natural settings (e.g., hallways, cafeteria, playground) in which the behavior is causing concern. These direct observations (see Chapter 4) provide additional information that help you confirm (or disconfirm) the information obtained during the interviews. Then, you will use that information to identify the likely function(s) of the target behavior (see Chapter 5). The goal of the interviews and direct observations is to identify the antecedents and consequences associated with the target behavior so an intervention—based on the function of the behavior—can be designed, implemented, and evaluated (see Dunlap, Foster-Johnson, Clarke, Kern, & Childs, 1995; Dunlap & Kern, 1996; Ervin, DuPaul, Kern, & Friman, 1998; Lane, Umbreit, & Beebe-Frankenberger, 1999; Umbreit, 1995; Umbreit, Lane, & Dejud, 2004).

As you will see, the functional assessment interview is the first step in a series of tools and procedures used to determine why the target behavior is occurring. There are currently a number of highly reputable functional assessment interviews available for use: the Preliminary Functional Assessment Survey (Dunlap et al., 1993), the Functional Analysis Interview Summary Form (O'Neill et al., 1997), the Teacher Interview Form for Functional

Behavioral Assessment: Behavioral Excess Problem, Teacher Interview Form for Functional Behavioral Assessment: Behavioral Deficit Problem (Witt, Daly, & Noell, 2000), and the Student-Assisted Functional Assessment Interview (Kern, Dunlap, Clarke, & Childs, 1994).

One key to selecting an interview is to ensure the interview contains the questions necessary to identify the function of the target behavior. We encourage you to use whichever tool contains the requisite questions; however, we have found two instruments, the Preliminary Functional Assessment Survey (Dunlap et al., 1993) and the Student-Assisted Functional Assessment Interview (Kern et al., 1994), to be highly useful in our work due to the relevance, thoroughness, and brevity of each tool. This chapter provides a specific format and procedure for completing functional assessment interviews and examples that include all participants (e.g., teachers, parents, students) in the functional assessment process. After providing general recommendations for conducting interviews, we will provide detailed descriptions of both the Preliminary Functional Assessment Survey and the Student-Assisted Functional Assessment Interview. We also provide the results of sample interviews with teachers, parents, and students as they relate to a hypothetical case study.

GENERAL RECOMMENDATIONS FOR CONDUCTING FUNCTIONAL ASSESSMENT INTERVIEWS

Prior to beginning the interviews, it is important to consider issues of schedule, location, and privacy. It will be necessary to schedule a sufficient block of time to conduct an uninterrupted interview. Although the length of the interview can be dependent on a number of variables (e.g., how talkative the informant is with the interviewer, the degree of comfort between the informant and the interviewer, how many informants are being interviewed at the same time), we recommend that a period of 30 to 45 minutes be scheduled. Contact the desired informants (teacher, paraprofessionals, and/or parents) ahead of time to set an appointment at a convenient time and location. Call to confirm the appointment the day before the interview, and arrive with a blank interview form, an extra copy for each respondent to examine or keep, and two to three writing utensils. Also, dress professionally, that is, in a manner that conveys respect and does not draw unnecessary attention.

When considering the location, it is important to select a location that affords privacy so other persons cannot hear the contents of the interview. No one should be in close proximity to the interview location (e.g., teachers' lounge). We recommend a conference room or an empty classroom. However, when interviewing a student, it would be best to ensure a school official is close by (e.g., in a nearby office).

Finally, remember that the interview will produce essential, personal information that must be treated with confidentiality. You will be recording the informant and student responses directly on the forms during the interview process. Ensure the completed interview is legible and kept in a safe location (e.g., locked filing cabinet) to ensure privacy.

INFORMANTS INTERVIEW

The Preliminary Functional Assessment Survey

Initial Information. At the beginning of the interview, complete the initial demographic information requested. Record the student's name, gender, and age. Although some teachers may know the student's age, others may not. Therefore, it would be wise to ask for the student's birthday. After recording the date of the interview, list the respondents. It is imperative that the interview actually be conducted with the teacher, paraprofessional, and/or parent, rather than asking them to fill out the interview on their own. By conducting the interview in person, you will be able to provide queries to ensure behavior-specific information is obtained. For example, if a parent or teacher lists "laziness" as a target behavior, you could ask "and what does that look like at home?" or "and what does that look like in your classroom?" These types of questions will help guide the informant to provide specific information about the behaviors of concern (e.g., "He completes his chores, but does so in a really sloppy way" or "He finishes the classwork, but his printing is really sloppy").

Interviews with school site personnel and parents are often conducted individually; however, it is possible to interview more than one person (e.g., teacher and paraprofessional) at the same time. Prior to conducting group interviews, obtain sufficient information to ensure interviewing two or three people simultaneously would not impede the process. For example, if there is a personality conflict between the teacher and paraprofessional, individual interviews are recommended. Similarly, interviewing the parent and the teacher at the same time may not be the best option if the teacher feels that he or she cannot be as direct in the presence of the parent. Your goal is to obtain the information necessary to determine the function of the behavior. Consequently, it is important to ensure the interview process is structured to facilitate the flow of information (see Figure 3.1; Dunlap et al., 1993).

Question 1: List and describe behavior(s) of concern. In Chapter 2, you learned to define target and replacement behaviors. You now apply this knowledge in handling Question 1. This step is essential because, if there are problems with the definitions of the target or replacement behaviors, your interview information will be suspect. When teachers, parents, or students give information about the target behavior, what behavior are they talking about? If there is any confusion about this, the interview information might be meaningless and unusable. Therefore, you must begin with adequate response definitions, and the respondents must clearly understand the behavior(s) that are being addressed. Ask the teachers to list the specific behaviors of concern. As mentioned in Chapter 2, if the teacher says "he's lazy," redirect the teacher to define the behavior by prompts such as "and what does Jimmy do that makes you feel that he's lazy?" or "and what does laziness look like?"

Question 2: Prioritize these behaviors (which is the most important)? After you have listed and defined the behaviors discussed in Question 1, the

Positive Behavioral Support

. . . for Children
and their Families

TIME STARTED: ________________

PRELIMINARY FUNCTIONAL ASSESSMENT SURVEY

Instructions to PBS Staff: The following interview should be conducted with the student's teacher. Prior to the interview, ask the teacher whether or not the Classroom Aide should participate. If yes, indicate both respondents' names. In addition, in instances where divergent information is provided, note the sources attributed to specific information.

Student:______________________ Subject #:____________________

Age:_____ Sex: M_____ F_____

Interviewer:___________________ Date:_______________________

Respondent(s):____

1. List and describe behavior(s) of concern.
   a.
   b.
   c.
   d.
   e.
2. Prioritize these behaviors (which is the most important?)
   a.
   b.
   c.
   d.
3. What procedures have you followed when the behaviors first occurred?
   a.
   b.
   c.
   d.
   e.

FIGURE 3.1
Preliminary Functional Assessment Survey.

Note. From *Preliminary Functional Assessment Survey*, by G. Dunlap, L. Kern, M. dePerczel, S. Clarke, D. Wilson, K. E. Childs, R. White, and G. D. Falk, 1993, Unpublished document, Division of Applied Research and Educational Services, University of South Florida, Tampa. Reprinted by permission.

4. What do you think causes (or motivates) the behavior?

   a.

   b.

   c.

   d.

   e.

5. When do these behaviors occur?

   a.

   b.

   c.

   d.

   e.

6. How often do these behaviors occur?

   a.

   b.

   c.

   d.

   e.

7. How long has this/these behavior(s) been occurring?

   a.

   b.

   c.

   d.

   e.

8. Is there any circumstance under which the behavior does not occur?

   a.

   b.

   c.

   d.

   e.

9. Is there any circumstance under which the behavior always occurs?

   a.

   b.

   c.

FIGURE 3.1 (*continued*)

d.

e.

10. Does the behavior occur more often during certain times of the day?

a.

b.

c.

d.

e.

11. Does the behavior occur in response to the number of people in the immediate environment?

a.

b.

c.

d.

e.

12. Does the behavior occur only with certain people?

a.

b.

c.

d.

e.

13. Does the behavior occur only during certain subjects?

a.

b.

c.

d.

e.

14. Could the behavior be related to any skills deficit?

a.

b.

c.

d.

e.

15. What are the identified reinforcers for this student?

a.

(continued)

b.

c.

d.

e.

16. Is the student taking any medication that might affect his/her behavior?

a.

b.

c.

d.

e.

17. Could the student's behavior be signaling some deprivation condition (e.g., thirst, hunger, lack of rest, etc.)?

a.

b.

c.

d.

e.

18. Could the behavior be the result of any form of discomfort (e.g., headaches, stomachaches, blurred vision, ear infection, etc.)?

a.

b.

c.

d.

e.

19. Could the behavior be caused by allergies (e.g., food, materials in certain environments, etc.)?

a.

b.

c.

d.

e.

20. Do any other behaviors occur along with this behavior?

a.

b.

c.

FIGURE 3.1 (*continued*)

---

d.

e.

21. Are there any observable events that signal the behavior of concern is about to occur?

a.

b.

c.

d.

e.

22. What are the consequences when the behavior(s) occur?

a.

b.

c.

d.

e.

TIME COMPLETED:

TOTAL TIME:

---

next step is to prioritize the behaviors. This is a vital step because the intervention must address behaviors that are socially valid from the consumers' perspectives (this is discussed in more detail in Chapter 12). In brief, a socially valid intervention is one that targets socially important goals, uses socially acceptable treatment procedures, and produces socially important outcomes (Kazdin, 1977; Lane & Beebe-Frankenberger, 2004). If the problem behavior targeted for intervention is rather trivial, it is unlikely that the intervention will be implemented as designed; consequently, it is unlikely the intervention will produce the desired outcomes. Therefore, it is critical that the intervention target meaningful behaviors that are apt to be viewed as "important" from the consumers' (teachers', parents', and students') perspectives.

Question 3: What procedures have you followed when the behaviors first occurred? This question seeks to identify previous intervention efforts. It is useful to know what staff have done in the past to improve the student's behavior, especially if these interventions have been unsuccessful. Encourage the respondents to be specific and ask how they documented their intervention efforts. Too often, interventions get implemented, but not as planned—with low treatment integrity (see Chapter 12 for a discussion of treatment integrity; Lane, Beebe-Frankenberger, Lambros, & Pierson, 2001).

Question 4: What do you think causes (or motivates) the behavior? Next, ask the teacher, paraprofessional, and/or parent what he or she thinks motivates the target behavior. In other words, what do they think the student is getting or avoiding when he or she demonstrates this behavior? Consider Jimmy, who frequently argues with his teacher when it is time to be in small reading groups. Mrs. Pinkleton may encourage Jimmy to join the group and may even raise her voice when talking with him. However, if Jimmy continues to argue with her, Mrs. Pinkleton simply sends him to the vice principal. These details provide important information. In this case, the target behavior is arguing, and the two possible motives for the behavior that you would suspect are teacher attention and escape from the reading task.

Question 5: When do these behaviors occur? Next, ask the informant when the target behavior occurs. Does it surface during a specific content area or during a certain time of the day? Your goal is to identify an overall pattern of responding. The answer to this question is important because it will help you identify the conditions in which the behavior occurs. It will also help you determine when direct observations of behavior (discussed in Chapter 4) should occur.

Question 6: How often do these behaviors occur? This next question examines the issue of frequency. The goal is to determine if this is a high- or low-frequency behavior. Although low-frequency, high-intensity behavior such as hitting another child is clearly problematic, behaviors that take place often and distract from the instructional activities (e.g., talking out of turn, being out of seat, humming) can be upsetting for teachers as well (Walker & Severson, 1992).

Question 7: How long has this/these behavior(s) been occurring? Once the frequency of the behavior is determined, the next step is to determine how long the behavior has been occurring. Is this a new behavior in response to a stressful set of circumstances (e.g., parents having marital problems), or is this a persistent pattern of responding (e.g., struggling to participate in group activities all year)?

Question 8: Is there any circumstance under which the behavior does not occur? This question will help identify any circumstances under which the behavior does not take place. By learning more about these circumstances, it is possible to determine what stimuli or antecedents do not set the stage for the behavior to occur. This information can be used to inform the development of interventions in the environments in which the behavior does occur.

Question 9: Is there any circumstance under which the behavior always occurs? Similarly, this question will also inform intervention development by identifying circumstances in which the behavior occurs consistently. For example, if a student suddenly and consistently "feels sick" when it is time to go to recess, this is an indication that something in the recess environment (e.g., teasing by peers, being alone) is prompting some "escape" behavior. The student's "sick" feeling is in response to something aversive in the recess environment (the antecedent).

Question 10: Does the behavior occur more often during certain times of the day? The answer to this question will help you determine specific times of the day when the behavior is most likely to occur. For example, the behavior may often take place immediately before or after lunch, or prior to leaving school for the day. Identifying when the behavior is most likely to occur will, at the very least, provide direction on when to conduct direct observations of behavior (see Chapter 4).

Question 11: Does the behavior occur in response to the number of people in the immediate environment? Some behaviors, particularly those performed to obtain attention from others, are more likely to occur when there are relatively high numbers of people in the room. In essence, the student exhibiting the problem behavior is more likely to demonstrate the behavior (e.g., making sarcastic comments to the teacher) when there is a greater chance that students will respond with laughter (e.g., during whole-class instruction as compared with small-group instruction). In contrast, the behavior may occur only when the student is working individually with a teacher or paraprofessional. Either way, the answer to this question will provide additional information about the circumstances that set the stage for the target behavior to occur.

Question 12: Does the behavior occur only with certain people? Similarly, this question will help identify whether the target behavior is more likely to occur in the presence of specific individuals (e.g., music teacher, bus driver). If so, it would be wise not only to conduct direct observations in these settings, but also to conduct functional assessment interviews with these people.

Question 13: Does the behavior occur only during certain subjects? This question is similar to Question 10 in the sense that its purpose is to obtain information about when the behavior occurs. Specifically, this question will determine if the behavior is more likely to occur in a given content area such as math, reading, science, or writing. If so, this may indicate a problem with instructional level (i.e., it is possible that the instructional activities are either too easy or too difficult; cf. Gickling & Armstrong, 1978; Gunter, Denny, Jack, Shores, & Nelson, 1993; Umbreit et al., 2004).

Question 14: Could the behavior be related to any skills deficit? If the student has a skill deficit such as poor decoding skills, limited acquisition of basic math facts, or inadequate social skills, it is possible that the target behavior could be a signal of this skill deficit. This has important consequences for the interventions that are discussed in Chapters 6 to 8. In brief, if the student has a skill deficit (also referred to as an acquisition deficit or a "can't do problem") as opposed to a performance deficit (or a "won't do problem"; Gresham, 2002), the intervention needs to address the skill deficit by actually teaching the student the missing skill (Witt et al., 2000). In other words, there is not a problem of motivation—rather, the skill is simply not part of the student's repertoire.

Question 15: What are the identified reinforcers for this student? When attempting to change a student's behavior, interventions will involve increasing rates of reinforcement for the desired behavior while decreasing or eliminating reinforcement for the target behavior. Consequently, it is imperative to know what is reinforcing for a given student. It is also important to recognize that what is reinforcing for one student may not be reinforcing for all students (see Chapter 1). Therefore, this question attempts to identify those items (e.g., candy, stickers, or pencils), events (e.g., lunch with the teacher), or opportunities (e.g., skip one homework assignment or a go to the front of the lunch line) that are reinforcing to the student from the teacher's perspective. Clearly, teachers may not be privy to some reinforcers for students, but they can provide initial insight on how to reinforce the desirable replacement behavior and eliminate reinforcement for the undesirable behavior. After obtaining information from the teacher's perspective, it would be wise to confirm this information by (a) conducting observations and (b) speaking directly to the student to identify reinforcers.

Question 16: Is the student taking any medication that might affect his/her behavior? Some medication, such as medications prescribed for attention deficit hyperactivity disorder (ADHD) (American Psychiatric Association, 1994), have known, intended effects on student behavior. However, these and other medications may also have unintended effects on behavior (e.g., nausea, drowsiness, constipation). Due to these intended and unintended effects on behavior, it is important that informants provide accurate information about any medications a student is taking. Then, it is necessary to find out (a) dosage, (b) when the medication is taken, (c) who is responsible for administering the medication (e.g., school nurse, parent), (d) to what extent the medication is taken as prescribed (fidelity of treatment), (e) how long the student has been taking the medication (e.g., has the student been taking the medication for a few months? weeks? days?), (f) whether the student has experienced frequent medication changes, and (g) whether there are any potential interaction effects with other medications if the student is taking more than one medication.

Question 17: Could the student's behavior be signaling some deprivation condition (e.g., thirst, hunger, lack of rest, etc.)? Just as most seasoned teachers or parents will tell you, behavior is seldom "typical" or "desirable" when a student has stayed up too late watching television, skipped breakfast, or did not get enough water to drink on a hot day. The intent of this question is to determine whether the target behavior under investigation could be due to any of these conditions or any other deprivation conditions that could be prompting an undesirable behavior.

Question 18: Could the behavior be the result of any form of discomfort (e.g., headaches, stomachaches, blurred vision, ear infection, etc.)? Just as a student's problem behaviors may indicate some type of deprivation, these behaviors can also indicate other forms of discomfort, such as ear infections, respiratory problems, poor vision, headaches, and/or stomachaches. This question will help identify such forms of discomfort that may be prompting or escalating the target behavior.

Question 19: Could the behavior be caused by allergies (e.g., food, materials in certain environments, etc.)? It is possible that students could have allergies that they may or may not be aware of that are influencing their behavior. Some such allergies could be food-based (e.g., peanuts, dairy, strawberries), whereas others may be more environmental (e.g., pollens, grass, trees). When collecting this information, it would be ideal to interview those adults who have known the student over a sustained period of time or at least those who have access to medical information.

Question 20: Do any other behaviors occur along with this behavior? Some behaviors co-occur with other behaviors. For example, if thumb sucking is the behavior of concern, it is possible that the target behavior only occurs or often occurs in the presence of another behavior. Perhaps the student only sucks his or her thumb during naptime when he or she is rubbing the satin corner of his or her favorite blanket. These behaviors—thumb sucking and blanket rubbing—are part of the same response class, meaning that they serve the same function (occur for the same reason; Sulzer-Azaroff & Mayer, 1991). If we can identify those behaviors that tend to co-occur with the target behavior, it may be that we can design an intervention that will address the function of both behaviors.

Question 21: Are there any observable events that signal the behavior of concern is about to occur? In some instances, there are indications that the target behavior is about to take place (Colvin, 1993; Walker et al., 2004). For example, it may be that the student who explodes into frequent tantrums in the classroom that include verbally aggressive comments to other students (e.g., "You suck! I hate you!") and physical aggression toward objects (e.g., throwing chairs) actually shows signs of escalating behaviors before these forms of verbal and physical aggression take place. For some students, signs of agitation include increases in behavior such as darting eyes, moving hands frequently (e.g., finger or pencil tapping), and starting and stopping tasks frequently. For other students, signs of agitation include decreases in behavior such as not interacting with others, nonconversational language, and failure to participate in any instructional activity. Although very different sets of behaviors, both are indicative of an escalating behavioral concern that, if not interrupted, could lead to the target behavior (e.g., aggression; Walker et al., 2004). As has been shown in some research (e.g., Kern, Childs, Dunlop, Clarke, & Falk, 1994), it is sometimes possible to intervene and prevent the "signal" behaviors from occurring, which, in turn, prevents the eventual occurrence of the target behavior.

Question 22: What are the consequences when the behavior(s) occur? The final question pertains to the consequences or the events that follow the target behavior and influence the probability that it will recur. For example, if the target behavior is telling jokes in class and the consistent consequence associated with "joke telling" is peer, teacher, and/or parent laughter, the maintaining consequence may be attention. If a student is consistently disruptive during small-group, oral reading activities, the disruptive behavior may be signaling a problem with task difficulty.

Closing Information. At the close of the interview, review each question to ensure all questions have been answered thoroughly. Conclude the interview by asking the respondent if he or she has any concluding comments.

Also, be sure to record any additional information that you deem relevant to the interview experience. Finally, record the time the interview was completed and compute the total time spent interviewing the respondent by subtracting the start time from the finish time.

Concluding Components

As you become more familiar with the 22 questions, you will be able to record responses as information becomes available. For example, if you are asking the respondent whether the student's behavior could be signaling a deprivation condition (Question 17) and he or she states that the child frequently skips breakfast and then complains about headaches before nutrition break, you could record the information about headaches in Question 18 (Could the behavior be the result of any form of discomfort?).

However, regardless of how thorough the interview, it is essential that the interview be followed up with direct observation (A-B-C; Bijou, Peterson, & Ault, 1968) sessions to confirm the information gleaned from the interview regarding the antecedent (A) conditions that set the stage for the target behavior (B) to occur and the consequences (C) that maintain the target behavior. However, prior to conducting these observations, it is important to interview the student to identify the antecedents, behavior, and consequences from his or her perspective.

STUDENT INTERVIEW
Student-Assisted Functional Assessment Interview

The Student-Assisted Functional Assessment Interview (Kern et al., 1994) contains four sections: initial information, open-ended questions, evaluation of the content areas, and Likert-type questions, all of which are designed to identify the (a) antecedents that prompt the target behavior, (b) nature of the target behavior itself, (c) consequences that increase or decrease the target behavior from recurring, and (d) reinforcers for the student (see Figure 3.2). Each section is described in detail as follows.

Initial Information. Begin by recording the student's name, date of the interview, and the time at which the interview begins. Next, record both the name of the target behavior determined in the previous informant interview(s) and the operational definition.

Open-Ended Questions. There are five open-ended questions asking the student for his or her perceptions of the target behavior.

Question 1: When do you think you have the fewest problems with _____ (target behavior) in school? Why do you not have problems during this/these time(s)? This question speaks to the nonoccurrence of the target behavior. The goal of this question is to identify the circumstances under which the target behavior does not occur in an effort to identify

STUDENT ASSESSMENT

Student:

Date:

Administration Time: _____

Target Behavior:

_____

1. When do you think you have the fewest problems with _____ (target behavior) in school?

Why do you not have problems during this/these time(s)?

2. When do you think you have the most problems with _____ (target behavior) in school?

Why do you have problems during this/these time(s)?

3. What causes you to have problems with _____ (target behavior)?

4. What changes could be made so you would have fewer problems with _____ (target behavior)?

5. What kinds of rewards would you like to earn for good behavior or good school work?

Rate how much you like the following subjects:

	Don't like at all		Fair		Like very much
Reading	1	2	3	4	5
Math	1	2	3	4	5
Spelling	1	2	3	4	5
Handwriting	1	2	3	4	5
Science	1	2	3	4	5
Social Studies	1	2	3	4	5
English	1	2	3	4	5
Music	1	2	3	4	5
P.E.	1	2	3	4	5
Art	1	2	3	4	5

FIGURE 3.2
Student-Assisted Functional Assessment Interview.

Source: "Student-Assisted Functional Assessment Interview," by L. Kern, G. Dunlap, S. Clarke, and K. E. Childs, in *Diagnostique* (now *Assessment for Effective Intervention*), *19*, pp. 37, 38. Copyright © 1994 by the Council for Educational Diagnostic Services. Reprinted with permission of the publisher.

What do you like about _____?

What do you like about _____?

What do you like about _____?

What do you like about _____?

What do you like about _____?

What do you like about _____?

What don't you like about _____?

Is there any type of _____ you have ever done that you've liked?

What could be done to improve _____?

What do you like about _____?

What do you like about _____?

What do you like about _____?

What don't you like about _____?

Is there any type of _____ you have ever done that you've liked?

What could be done to improve _____?

What do you like about _____?

What do you like about _____?

What do you like about _____?

What don't you like about _____?

Is there any type of _____ you have ever done that you've liked?

What could be done to improve _____?

STUDENT ASSESSMENT

STUDENT: _____

DATE: _____

INTERVIEWER: _____

1. In general, is your work too hard for you?	always	sometimes	never
2. In general, is your work too easy for you?	always	sometimes	never
3. When you ask for help appropriately, do you get it?	always	sometimes	never

FIGURE 3.2 (*continued*)

4. Do you think work periods for each subject are too long?	always	sometimes	never
5. Do you think work periods for each subject are too short?	always	sometimes	never
6. When you do seatwork, do you do better when someone works with you?	always	sometimes	never
7. Do you think people notice when you do a good job?	always	sometimes	never
8. Do you think you get the points or rewards you deserve when you do good work?	always	sometimes	never
9. Do you think you would do better in school if you received more rewards?	always	sometimes	never
10. In general, do you find your work interesting?	always	sometimes	never
11. Are there things in the classroom that distract you?	always	sometimes	never
12. Is your work challenging enough for you?	always	sometimes	never

the antecedents and consequences that prompt and reinforce other, more appropriate behavior instead. For example, if shouting out (target behavior) rarely happens during math instruction, the student may provide valuable information as to why shouting out does not take place during this time (e.g., "The teacher calls on everyone who raises his or her hand.").

Question 2: When do you think you have the most problems with _____ *(target behavior) in school?* Why do you have problems during this/these time(s)? This question speaks to the occurrence of the target behavior. The goal of this question is to determine, from the student's perspective, when the target behavior is most likely to occur and the reasons why these conditions are more likely to set the stage for the target behavior (e.g., "This teacher hardly ever calls on me when I do raise my hand.").

Question 3: What causes you to have problems with _____ *(target behavior)?* This question allows students to provide their opinion on the causes of the target behavior. In terms of shouting out behavior, it may be that the student is eager to share his or her knowledge of the subject matter and that the teacher, despite asking students to raise their hand, does not call on those students who follow the rules. It may be that the best way to be heard and responded to by the teacher is simply to call out the answer.

Question 4: What changes could be made so you would have fewer problems with _____ (target behavior)? The goal of this question is to obtain input on how to manipulate either the antecedents or consequences to change the probability that the target behavior will occur. For example, if the teacher would (a) remind all students to raise their hand before making a comment or asking a question, (b) ignore students who call out, and (c) respond only to students who raise their hands and wait to be called on, then the rate of shouting out behavior would likely decrease.

Question 5: What kinds of rewards would you like to earn for good behavior or good school work? This question seeks to identify reinforcers for desirable performances behaviorally and academically. Often, reinforcers are determined solely from the teacher's, paraprofessional's, or parent's perspective. Yet, these adults may not be privy to the full range of student reinforcers. Therefore, it is important to not overlook the obvious—ask students what they like in terms of tangible and activity reinforcers. As previously mentioned, this self-report information can be confirmed through direct observations. For example, the student might tell you that he or she loves to eat and that he or she would really like to have a bag of chips or a package of cookies as a reinforcer. However, your observation might suggest that he or she rarely opens the chips or cookies at lunchtime. In this case, you might want to include other types of reinforcers as you plan your intervention.

Evaluation of Content Areas. After the previous questions have been addressed, the next step is to evaluate how much students like the subjects they take in school. This is done by rating all subjects that the student takes (see Figure 3.2) on a 5-point, Likert-type scale ranging from—*Don't like at all* (1) to *Fair* (3) to *Like very much* (5).

Next, a series of follow-up questions are asked about the subjects that the student likes (e.g., What do you like about _____?) and subjects that the student does not like (e.g., What don't you like about _____? Is there any type of _____ you have ever done that you've liked? What could be done to improve_____?). The goal of both sets of questions is to identify the conditions of academic subjects that are and are not reinforcing for the student. For example, it may be that the student appears to enjoy those subject areas in which the teacher employs partner or group activities as opposed to only individual activities. It may be that the student enjoys group discussion but really struggles to sit through a lecture-type format. Likewise, the student may enjoy having an option as to which activities to participate in first and dislike those situations where there is no "choice" built into the subject.

Likert-Type Questions. The final section contains 12 questions that are rated on a Likert-type scale ranging from *always* to *sometimes* to *never* to identify further characteristics of the subject, instructional strategies, and support that are and are not desirable from the student's perspective. Questions

1 and 2 inquire as to the difficulty of the tasks (too easy or too hard). Question 3 asks if the student receives help if he or she asks appropriately. Questions 4 and 5 ask about the appropriateness of the work period (too long or too short). Just as task difficulty plays a role in student behavior, so does task length. It may be that the student is capable of completing the activities but that the work period is too long. In this situation, it may be useful to break up the activities into shorter segments (e.g., rather than having a 30-minute circle time in the morning, shift to two 15-minute sessions with one in the early morning and one before recess).

Question 6 asks whether the student does better if someone works with him or her during seatwork activities. Questions 7 to 9 pertain to reinforcement, asking whether recognition is given for desired performance and whether the student would prefer higher rates of reinforcement. Question 10 asks about the extent to which the work is interesting to the student, and Question 11 asks whether there are things in the classroom that are distracting. If the latter is found to be true, an antecedent-based intervention in which the distracters are removed or at least minimized would be logical (e.g., removing mobiles that are hanging from the ceiling or displaying student work at the rear of the classroom so as not to compete for student attention when the teacher is talking at the front of the classroom). The final question asks if the work is challenging enough for the student. Often, the first thought is that the work is too difficult, but misbehavior can also indicate that assignments are too easy. If a student can already do long division, a worksheet with 25 long-division problems can seem monotonous.

Concluding Components

As we discussed previously, no matter how strong the interview, additional information will need to be obtained with direct observations of student behavior (see Chapter 4) to confirm or disconfirm the information obtained during the interview process. Nonetheless, the student interview can provide valuable information that is often not available from the adult perspective.

SUMMARY

As evidenced in this chapter, functional assessment interviews are an important first step in a series of tools and procedures used to determine why the target behavior is occurring. Although there are a range of interviews available for use, the Preliminary Functional Assessment Survey (Dunlap et al., 1993) and the Student–Assisted Functional Assessment Interview (Kern et al., 1994) are two user-friendly, empirically validated tools that have met with demonstrated success in identifying the antecedents (A) that precede a target behavior, the nature of the behavior (B) itself, and the consequences (C) that maintain the target behavior.

In the following chapters, you will learn about observational techniques that may be used to confirm and further develop information gleaned from the functional assessment interviews (see Chapter 4). Then, in Chapter 5, you will learn about the Function Matrix, a tool for organizing and interpreting functional assessment data.

Steps in Conducting Functional Assessment Interviews

The following list of steps and activities summarize the process for conducting functional assessment interviews:

1. Schedule the interviews with the informants (teachers, paraprofessional, and students) at a time convenient for them that allows for a 30- to 45-min, uninterrupted period of time in a private location.
2. Confirm the appointment the day prior, and arrive at the school with copies of the instrument and two to three writing utensils.
3. Familiarize yourself with the instrument(s) prior to each interview.
4. Conduct the full interview by asking all questions and querying, as appropriate.
5. Allow the informant or student to ask questions at the conclusion of the interview.

EXERCISES

1. Read Jason's PFAS in Figure 3.3. What information is missing? What type of queries would you ask to obtain this information?
2. Read Jason's SFAI in Figure 3.4. What information is missing? What type of queries would you ask to obtain this information?
3. Create a procedural checklist for the steps that need to be taken before conducting the functional assessment interview(s).

Positive Behavioral Support

. . . for Children
        and their Families

TIME STARTED: _____ *3:10* _____

PRELIMINARY FUNCTIONAL ASSESSMENT SURVEY

Instructions to PBS Staff: The following interview should be conducted with the student's teacher. Prior to the interview, ask the teacher whether or not the Classroom Aide should participate. If yes, indicate both respondents' names. In addition, in instances where divergent information is provided, note the sources attributed to specific information.

FIGURE 3.3
Jason's Preliminary Functional Assessment Interview.

Student: ___Jason___   Subject #: _____

Age: _8_   Sex: M _X_   F _____

Interviewer: ___Carlos___   Date: _10/2/2005_

Respondent(s): _Mrs. Rice (teacher) and Mrs. Appleton (paraprofessional)_

1. List and describe behavior(s) of concern.

    a. being out of seat without permission during work time

    b. doing something he is not supposed to do

    c. talking to other students when he is supposed to be working

    d.

    e.

2. Prioritize these behaviors (which is the most important?)

    a. being out of seat without permission during work time

    b. talking to other students when he is supposed to be working

    c. doing something he is not supposed to do.

    d.

3. What procedures have you followed when the behaviors first occurred?

    a. talking to him

    b. talking to his parents

    c. keeping him in during recess

    d. sending him to the office

    e.

4. What do you think causes (or motivates) the behavior?

    a. being lazy

    b.

    c.

    d.

    e.

5. When do these behaviors occur?

    a. during math and reading

    b.

    c.

    d.

    e.

(continued)

6. How often do these behaviors occur?

    a. almost every time these subjects are taught

    b.

    c.

    d.

    e.

7. How long has this/these behavior(s) been occurring?

    a. since school started in September

    b.

    c.

    d.

    e.

8. Is there any circumstance under which the behavior does not occur?

    a. during free time

    b. during science and social studies

    c. during art

    d.

    e.

9. Is there any circumstance under which the behavior always occurs?

    a. during independent time in reading, when he's working in his workbook

    b. during independent time in math, when working in his math workbook

    c.

    d.

    e.

10. Does the behavior occur more often during certain times of the day?

    a. just during those two subjects

    b.

    c.

    d.

    e.

11. Does the behavior occur in response to the number of people in the immediate environment?

    a. no, it's pretty consistent — doesn't matter if his friends are in class or absent

FIGURE 3.3 (*continued*)

b.

c.

d.

e.

12. Does the behavior occur only with certain people?

    a. not really

    b.

    c.

    d.

    e.

13. Does the behavior occur only during certain subjects?

    a. yes, just during math and reading — but only during independent time

    b.

    c.

    d.

    e.

14. Could the behavior be related to any skills deficit?

    a. I don't think so. Jason is really smart.

    b.

    c.

    d.

    e.

15. What are the identified reinforcers for this student?

    a. He likes to read.

    b. He likes time on the computer.

    c. He likes to help other students with their work.

    d.

    e.

16. Is the student taking any medication that might affect his/her behavior?

    a. no — he doesn't take any meds

    b.

    c.

    d.

    e.

(continued)

17. Could the student's behavior be signaling some deprivation condition (e.g., thirst, hunger, lack of rest, etc.)?

    a. I'm not sure

    b.

    c.

    d.

    e.

18. Could the behavior be the result of any form of discomfort (e.g., headaches, stomachaches, blurred vision, ear infection, etc.)?

    a. he's never complained about any of those things

    b.

    c.

    d.

    e.

19. Could the behavior be caused by allergies (e.g., food, materials in certain environments, etc.)?

    a. His mom said he has a peanut allergy. But, I've never seen him eat any peanut products

    b.

    c.

    d.

    e.

20. Do any other behaviors occur along with this behavior?

    a. Well, he just gets out of his seat a lot.

    b. He walks around the room, talks to his friends.

    c. Sometimes he will go help another kid who is stuck. But, then I tell him to go sit back down. Then, I look over and he's out of his seat again.

    d.

    e.

21. Are there any observable events that signal the behavior of concern is about to occur?

    a. I don't know.

    b.

    c.

    d.

    e.

FIGURE 3.3 (*continued*)

22. What are the consequences when the behavior(s) occur?

    a. I just send him back to his seat.

    b. If it happens more than a few times, then I keep him in during recess and make him finish his work. The funny thing is that he finishes it in about 5 minutes and rushes out to recess. But, the answers are all right, so I can't really complain about that.

    c.

    d.

    e.

    TIME COMPLETED:___*3:44*___
    TOTAL TIME:___*34 min*___

FIGURE 3.3 (*continued*)

STUDENT ASSESSMENT

Student: Jason

Date: 10/5/2005

Administration Time: 3:00 to 3:17; 17 min

Target Behavior: being off-task (out of seat; walking around the room)

1. When do you think you have the fewest problems with ___off-task___ (target behavior) in school?

During the fun stuff—science, social studies, art, PE

Why do you not have problems during this/these time(s)?

Because I like those subjects and they are fun.

2. When do you think you have the most problems with ___off-task___ (target behavior) in school?

During workbook time—in math and reading

Why do you have problems during this/these time(s)?

Because it's boring. I could do that stuff 2 years ago.

3. What causes you to have problems with ___off-task___ (target behavior)?

I guess is just seems like baby work. I'd rather be doing something else. You know, harder work, but I can't. So I try to help the other kids.

4. What changes could be made so you would have fewer problems with ___off-task___ (target behavior)?

FIGURE 3.4
Jason's Student-Assisted Functional Assessment Interview.

Well, I'll like to do stuff that's harder—stuff that I haven't done before.

5. What kinds of rewards would you like to earn for good behavior or good school work?

I'd like to help some of the other kids or maybe spend some time on the computer.

Rate how much you like the following subjects:

	Don't like at all		Fair		Like very much
Reading	1	②	3	4	5
Math	1	②	3	4	5
Spelling	1	2	3	④	5
Handwriting	1	2	3	④	5
Science	1	2	3	4	⑤
Social Studies	1	2	3	4	⑤
English	1	2	3	4	⑤
Music	1	2	3	④	5
P.E.	1	2	3	4	⑤
Art	1	2	3	4	⑤

What do you like about _____ Science _____ ?

I like getting to do the experiments and reading about the chemicals and stuff.

What do you like about _____ Social Studies _____ ?

I like learning about the United States. I really like doing stuff with maps and stuff like that.

What do you like about _____ Music _____ ?

It's pretty fun to sing and be loud. I'm either going to be a rapper or scientist. Or maybe I'll be both.

What do you like about _____ PE _____ ?

I like playing basketball and dodge ball. I don't really like running laps, though.

What do you like about _____ Art _____ ?

I liked it when we made paper and I like to draw.

What do you like about _____ Handwriting _____ ?

I like learning how to write in cursive. That's really fun.

What don't you like about _____ Math _____ ?

Well, I don't like working in the workbooks.

Is there any type of _____ Math _____ you have ever done that you've liked?

FIGURE 3.4 *(continued)*

Yeah. Last year my teacher let us work ahead if we did a good job. And we got to work in teams to learn our math facts. It was really fun. My team was doing fifth-grade work by the end of the year.

What could be done to improve _____ Math _____?

Do what my last year teacher did. Everybody doesn't need to be on the same page.

What do you like about _____ Spelling _____?

I am a really good speller. I usually get 100% on my spelling tests on Friday.

What do you like about _____?

What do you like about _____?

What don't you like about _Reading_?

I like to read stuff I like. I just don't like reading these dumb stories in the workbook. They're like baby stuff. I can get all the questions right. I just think the stories are lame.

Is there any type of _Reading_ you have ever done that you've liked?

Yeah. Last year, my teacher let me work ahead in the book. So, like if the rest of the class was on lesson 20, I might be on lesson 32 or something like that. Then, after I did the question, I got to help other kids if they had questions or I could read a book in the classroom library. That was better because the work was more for me. And I liked that I got to choose when I got to do stuff.

What could be done to improve _____ Reading _____?

Just do the stuff I told you my last year's teacher use to do.

What do you like about _____?

What do you like about _____?

What do you like about _____?

What don't you like about _____?

Is there any type of _____ you have ever done that you've liked?

What could be done to improve _____?

STUDENT ASSESSMENT

STUDENT: _____ Jason _____

DATE: _____ 10/5/2005 _____

INTERVIEWER: _____ Carlos _____

1. In general, is your work too hard for you?   always   sometimes   (never)

(continued)

2. In general, is your work too easy for you?	always	(sometimes)	never
3. When you ask for help appropriately, do you get it?	(always)	sometimes	never
4. Do you think work periods for each subject are too long?	always	(sometimes)	never
5. Do you think work periods for each subject are too short?	always	sometimes	(never)
6. When you do seatwork, do you do better when someone works with you?	always	(sometimes)	never
7. Do you think people notice when you do a good job?	always	(sometimes)	never
8. Do you think you get the points or rewards you deserve when you do good work?	always	(sometimes)	never
9. Do you think you would do better in school if you received more rewards?	always	(sometimes)	never
10. In general, do you find your work interesting?	always	(sometimes)	never
11. Are there things in the classroom that distract you?	always	(sometimes)	never
12. Is your work challenging enough for you?	always	(sometimes)	never

FIGURE 3.4 (*continued*)

REFERENCES

American Psychiatric Association (1994). *Diagnostic and statistical manual of mental disorders* (4th ed.). Washington, DC: Author.

Bijou, S. W., Peterson, R. F., & Ault, M. H. (1968). A method to integrate descriptive and experimental field studies at the level of data and empirical concepts. *Journal of Applied Behavior Analysis, 1,* 175–191.

Colvin, G. (1993). *Managing acting-out behavior.* Eugene, OR: Behavior Associates.

Dunlap, G., Foster-Johnson, L., Clarke, S., Kern, L., & Childs, K. E. (1995). Modifying activities to produce functional outcomes: Effects on the problem behaviors of students with disabilities. *Journal of the Association for Persons with Severe Handicaps, 20,* 248–258.

Dunlap, G., & Kern, L. (1996). Modifying instructional activities to promote desirable behavior: A conceptual and practical framework. *School Psychology Quarterly, 11,* 297–312.

Dunlap, G., Kern, L., dePerczel, M., Clarke, S., Wilson, D., Childs, K. E., White, R., & Falk, G. D. (1993). *Preliminary Functional Assessment Survey.* Unpublished document, Division of Applied Research and Educational Services, University of South Florida, Tampa.

Ervin, R. A., DuPaul, G. J., Kern, L., & Friman, P. C. (1998). Classroom-based functional and adjunctive assessments: Proactive approaches to intervention selection for adolescents with attention deficit hyperactivity disorder. *Journal of Applied Behavior Analysis, 31,* 65–78.

Gickling, E., & Armstrong, D. (1978). Levels of instructional difficulty as related to on-task behavior, task completion, and comprehension. *Journal of Learning Disabilities, 11,* 559–566.

Gresham, F. M. (2002). Social skills assessment and instruction for students with emotional and behavioral disorders. In K. L. Lane, F. M. Gresham, & T. E. O'Shaughnessy (Eds.),

Interventions for children with or at risk for emotional and behavioral disorders (pp. 242–258). Boston: Allyn & Bacon.

Gunter, P., Denny, R. K., Jack, S., Shores, R., & Nelson, C. M. (1993). Aversive stimuli in academic interactions between students with serious emotional disturbance and their teachers. *Behavioral Disorders, 18,* 265–274.

Kazdin, A. E. (1977). Assessing the clinical or applied significance of behavior change through social validation. *Behavior Modification, 1,* 427–452.

Kern, L., Childs, K. E., Dunlap, G., Clarke, S., & Falk, G. D. (1994). Using assessment-based curricular intervention to improve the classroom behavior of a student with emotional and behavioral challenges. *Journal of Applied Behavior Analysis, 27,* 7–19.

Kern, L., Dunlap, G., Clarke, S., & Childs, K. E. (1994). Student-assisted functional assessment interview. *Diagnostique, 19,* 20–39.

Lane, K. L. (2004). Academic instruction and tutoring interventions for students with emotional/behavioral disorders 1990 to present. In R. B. Rutherford, M. M. Quinn, & S. R. Mathur (Eds.), *Handbook of research in emotional and behavioral disorders* (pp. 462–486). New York: Guilford Press.

Lane, K. L., & Beebe-Frankenberger, M. E. (2004). *School-based interventions: The tools you need to succeed.* Boston: Allyn & Bacon.

Lane, K. L., Beebe-Frankenberger, M. E., Lambros, K. L., & Pierson, M. E. (2001). Designing effective interventions for children at-risk for antisocial behavior: An integrated model of components necessary for making valid inferences. *Psychology in the Schools, 38,* 365–379.

Lane, K. L., Umbreit, J., & Beebe-Frankenberger, M. (1999). A review of functional assessment research with students with or at-risk for emotional and behavioral disorders. *Journal of Positive Behavioral Interventions, 1,* 101–111.

O'Neill, R. E., Horner, R. H., Albin, R. W., Sprague, J. R., Storey, K., & Newton, J. S. (1997). *Functional assessment and program development for problem behavior: A practical handbook* (2nd ed.). Boston: Brooks/Cole.

Sulzer-Azaroff, B., & Mayer, G. R. (1991). *Behavior analysis for lasting change.* Fort Worth, TX: Holt, Rinehart and Winston.

Umbreit, J. (1995). Functional assessment and intervention in a regular classroom setting for the disruptive behavior of a student with attention deficit hyperactivity disorder. *Behavioral Disorders, 20,* 267–278.

Umbreit, J., Lane, K. L., & Dejud, C. (2004). Improving classroom behavior by modifying task difficulty: The effects of increasing the difficulty of too-easy tasks. *Journal of Positive Behavior Interventions, 6,* 13–20.

Walker, H. M., Ramsey, E., & Gresham, F. M. (2004). *Antisocial behavior in school with infotrac: Evidence-based practices.* Belmont, CA: Wadsworth.

Walker, H. M., & Severson, H. H. (1992). *Systematic Screening for Behavior Disorders (SSBD): User's guide and technical manual.* Longmont, CO: Sopris West.

Witt, J. C., Daly, E. M., & Noell, G. (2000). *Functional assessments: A step-by-step guide to solving academic and behavioral problems.* Longmont, CO: Sopris West.

CHAPTER 4

Functional Behavioral Assessment
Direct Observation

OUTCOMES

After reading this chapter, you will be able to

- Explain the A-B-C Model and its uses and limitations.
- Explain the concept of the antecedent.
- Explain the concept of the consequence.
- Identify appropriate times to collect A-B-C data.
- Identify or construct an A-B-C data collection form.
- Identify the necessary amount of A-B-C data that should be collected.

At this point in the FBA process, you have identified and defined the target behavior and, if possible, a replacement behavior. You have also conducted structured interviews with informants (e.g., teaching staff, parents) and, when appropriate, with the student. Now, it is important to directly observe the student engaging in the target behavior in the classroom and/or other school environment in which it is causing concern.

This chapter discusses how to conduct direct observations and how to collect direct observational data in natural contexts such as the classroom or other school environments. The methods described here apply to conducting direct observations in any natural context, including those outside the school (e.g., the home or other community settings), although the emphasis in this chapter is on conducting direct observations in school settings. Specifically, this chapter covers the Antecedent-Behavior-Consequence (A-B-C) Model, the purpose and limitations of this model, the nature of the antecedent and the consequence, and how to collect A-B-C data. The chapter concludes with a summary of the steps and activities required to collect A-B-C data, as well as exercises designed to give you experience and improve your understanding of the A-B-C data collection process.

THE A-B-C MODEL

The A-B-C Model, described to some extent in Chapter 1, is the basic model used in the field of behavior analysis (see Figure 4.1). It has formed the basis for all behavior analysis and applied behavior analysis for more than 70 years. The model can be traced to the early work of B. F. Skinner, starting as early as 1930 (summarized by Skinner in his first major book, *The Behavior of Organisms: An Experimental Analysis,* published in 1938).

When behaviorists analyze behavior, they do so in a deliberate and particular way. Specifically, they examine a behavior in relation to two things: the context in which it occurs (referred to as the "antecedent"), and the events that follow it and affect its future occurrence (referred to as the "consequence"). Put simply, behaviorists attempt to identify (a) the conditions that exist when a behavior occurs and (b) the consequences of the behavior that influence whether it will recur. Consequences that cause the behavior to recur in a particular situation are called **reinforcers.** Consequences that cause a behavior not to recur, or to occur less often, are called **punishers.**

Consider the behavior of Jimmy, a 9-year-old student in a fourth-grade class. In Jimmy's class, the teacher often asks the students questions. The children are supposed to raise their hands and wait to be called on before answering a question (replacement behavior). The teacher is concerned that Jimmy, unlike the other children, answers questions without raising his hand and waiting to be called on (target behavior). With these behavioral definitions, we can now directly observe in the classroom. Our first task is to determine the conditions in which the target behavior is occurring. In Jimmy's case, answering out of turn occurs when he is in the classroom with the other students and the teacher asks a question. These conditions comprise the antecedent. Our second task is to identify the consequences that influence

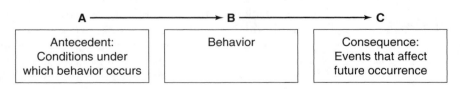

FIGURE 4.1
The Antecedent-Behavior-Consequence (A-B-C) Model.

whether Jimmy will continue to answer out of turn or, instead, raise his hand and wait to be called on like the other children.

Through direct observation in the classroom, we observe that, when Jimmy answers out of turn, the teacher acknowledges his answer and then reminds him that he is supposed to raise his hand first and wait to be called on. However, the teacher never enforces this requirement. She always acknowledges Jimmy's answer. To explain Jimmy's behavior (i.e., answering out of turn), we simply identify the antecedent conditions in which it occurs and the consequences that affect its future occurrence. In Jimmy's case, talking out of turn occurs when he is in class and the teacher asks a question (antecedent), and it occurs because of the consequence (i.e., the teacher always acknowledges his answer). Furthermore, we can predict that Jimmy's inappropriate behavior will continue as long as the antecedents and consequences remain the same. If the teacher ignored Jimmy's answer and, instead, called only on those children whose hands were raised, we would also predict that Jimmy would then start to raise his hand and wait to be called on like the other children.

This simple example illustrates how we apply the A-B-C Model to explain Jimmy's inappropriate behavior in the classroom. Whenever we attempt to understand or explain why a behavior occurs, we first define the behavior of concern. Then, we identify the antecedent conditions in which it occurs and the consequences that affect its future occurrence.

In conducting an FBA, structured interviews are completed before collecting A-B-C data. Although interviews often provide useful information for assessment and intervention, it is still necessary to follow them by directly observing problematic behaviors as they occur naturally. Data generated by direct observation have the potential to confirm the information provided by respondents during interviews. These data also have the potential to shed additional light on the situation. In some cases, A-B-C data also reveal important antecedents and consequences that the respondents have not previously recognized.

Consider what occurred with Reggie (Umbreit & Blair, 1996), an 11-year-old boy with severe disabilities. At school, Reggie routinely engaged in problematic behaviors such as hitting, screaming in a high-pitched voice, falling down on the floor and refusing to get up, running away, and spitting. During interviews, his teachers reported that these behaviors occurred because Reggie was trying to gain their attention. However, they also reported that Reggie received attention from staff "almost constantly." These two reports appeared to be contradictory. Why would Reggie routinely misbehave to gain attention if attention was "constantly available"?

To better understand this situation, the researchers directly observed Reggie in several different school environments (classrooms, hallways and walkways, office, library, gym) and collected A-B-C data. Their findings revealed that Reggie's teachers were missing something important. In fact, Reggie did receive attention in two situations: first, whenever he was receiving direct instruction; and second, whenever he engaged in one of the problematic behaviors. However, Reggie received almost no attention in any noninstructional situation in which he was behaving appropriately. Put simply, doing the "right" thing did not pay off.

This finding was a revelation to the teaching staff. Once they understood that most of Reggie's appropriate behaviors were not followed by attention, a consequence that would make him more likely to behave appropriately again, they also realized that Reggie engaged in problematic behaviors because they did result in gaining attention, which, in turn, made these behaviors more likely to recur. The information gathered through A-B-C data collection not only shed new light on the teachers' responses during the interviews, but it also provided useful data for designing an effective intervention.

Purpose and Limitations of the A-B-C Model

Before attempting to apply the A-B-C Model to analyzing behavior, it is important to clearly understand the model's purpose and its limitations. The specific purpose of the A-B-C Model is to enable one to predict and control behavior. The terms "prediction" and "control" require some explanation because they are often misunderstood. As part of the A-B-C Model, the term **prediction** has the same meaning as when it is used generally; put simply, it means that one is able to identify beforehand what is likely to occur in the future. Thus, by analyzing a behavior in relation to its relevant antecedents and consequences, one is able to identify behavior that is likely to occur in the future. The previous example of Jimmy provides a good example of this. As long as Jimmy's teacher continues to acknowledge his answers, even though he has not raised his hand or waited to be called on, he will continue to answer out of turn.

In contrast, the term **control** requires some explanation because, when it is used as part of the A-B-C Model, the common dictionary definition of the term does not apply. Rather, the term has a technical definition, which is to alter the probability or influence the likelihood that a particular behavior will or will not occur. The ideas of "force" or "coercion" do not apply to the concept of behavioral "control."

The following example illustrates the important distinction between the common and technical definitions of the term "behavioral control." Several years ago, the mayor and the police chief in a large Southwestern city developed a plan to reduce traffic problems and improve traffic safety. Based on data collected by the city, the mayor and the police chief determined that the majority of traffic accidents occurred at four particular intersections. They also determined that traffic accidents were most likely to occur at these intersections during the morning and evening rush hours (i.e., between 7 a.m. and 9 a.m. in the morning, and between 4 p.m. and 6 p.m. in the evening). Finally, they determined that drivers at these intersections routinely "ran" red lights (i.e., entered the intersection after the light had turned red). Armed with this information, the mayor and the police chief concluded that the "running" of red lights was a likely contributor to the high frequency of traffic accidents. They also reasoned that, if they could reduce the number of drivers who ran red lights, they could also reduce the number of traffic accidents, thereby improving traffic safety. Reducing the number of traffic accidents would inevitably save lives, prevent injuries, and eliminate considerable financial expense.

To address this problem, the mayor and the police chief developed a plan to station two motorcycle police officers at each of the four intersections during the rush hours. The two police officers at each intersection were to position themselves on opposite corners so (a) they could easily see anyone running a red light and (b) drivers could easily see the police officers. To make drivers aware of their plan, the mayor and the police chief held a press conference and announced the details. The information was featured in both the city's newspapers and on all the city's television news reports.

On the first morning the plan was implemented, although thousands of cars passed through these intersections during rush hour, not one driver ran a red light and there were no traffic accidents. The police did not issue a single ticket. The same thing occurred during the evening rush hour and on subsequent days when police were stationed at these intersections.

The fact that no one entered an intersection after the light turned red is an excellent example of **behavioral control.** No one was "forced" to stop when the light turned red or "coerced" into driving safely. Nevertheless, everyone did. By stationing police officers at these high-risk intersections, the city exerted extraordinary control over the behavior of thousands of drivers. If we apply the technical definition of the word "control" as it is used in the A-B-C Model, we see that the presence of the police officers altered the probability that a particular behavior would occur.

The expressed purpose of the A-B-C Model—to enable prediction and control of behavior—also defines its limitations. First, the model applies only to the analysis of behavior. It does not apply to feelings, moods, or any other nonbehavioral phenomena. Second, the model was never intended to explain emotions, attributions, perceptions, or opinions. Third, the model was never intended to compete with or be part of alternative, nonbehavioral theories that attempt to explain various aspects of the human experience. The A-B-C Model has one specific purpose: to enable the prediction and control of behavior as these terms are defined technically. Put simply, the model enables one to predict what a person is likely to do under certain circumstances and to influence the likelihood that the person will or will not behave that way again.

The "Antecedent"

Before attempting to collect A-B-C data, you need to have a clear understanding of the concept of the "antecedent." To be exact, the **antecedent** refers to the entire set of conditions in which a behavior occurs. Put simply, the antecedent refers to the context (or "circumstances" or "situation") in which a person behaves. The antecedent is not *only* the specific stimulus (or event) that immediately precedes the behavior. It also includes other variables that comprise the existing conditions when a behavior occurs and that influence its occurrence. There has been considerable confusion about this point in recent years. However, a review of the writings of founders of our field (e.g., B. F. Skinner, Sidney W. Bijou) reveals that they never considered the antecedent to include only the specific stimulus that immediately preceded the behavior (e.g., Bijou & Baer, 1961; Skinner, 1938). Rather, they considered the antecedent to be the "conditions" in which a behavior occurs.

The following example illustrates this point. Assume that you are driving down a busy street and approaching a major intersection. As you approach the intersection, the traffic light is green. However, when you reach a point approximately 200 feet before the intersection, the light turns from green to yellow. What will you do when the light turns yellow? Will you press the brake so you can slow down and stop at the intersection, or will you press the accelerator so you can get through the intersection before the light turns red? Knowing only the information presented so far, most people (if they are honest) admit that they will accelerate so they can get through the intersection. So far, in this example, we know only about the behavior of interest (pressing the accelerator or the brake) and the stimulus that immediately precedes the behavior (the light turning yellow). However, the situation can include many important variables other than the color of the light. For example, what would you do if there were a policeman stationed at the intersection watching traffic? (Hint: Most people would press the brake rather than the accelerator.) What would you do if there was no policeman and you were late for an important meeting? (Hint: Most people would accelerate, that is, just the opposite of what they would do in the previous example.) Consider some other possibilities. What would you do if you had just passed a serious accident at the previous intersection? What would you do if you had recently been in a serious accident? Finally, what would you do if one more traffic ticket would cause a drastic increase in your automobile insurance rates?

As you can see from these examples, different conditions are likely to result in different behavior. It is not sufficient to consider only the yellow light, the specific stimulus that immediately preceded the behavior. In the same respect, direct observation of a problematic behavior in a classroom requires you to consider more than the specific stimulus that immediately preceded the behavior. Direct observation requires that you consider the antecedent conditions that exist when a target behavior occurs. The conditions that need to be considered are those that could have an impact on the occurrence of the target behavior. Information from the structured interviews conducted as part of the FBA process, prior to direct observation, is likely to be helpful in identifying these conditions.

In recent years, some behaviorists have shown a growing interest in the concept of the "setting event" (Kantor, 1959) and in a related concept, the "establishing operation" (Michael, 1993). Kantor (1959) identified the **setting**

event as a variable other than the specific preceding stimulus that alters the typical interaction between antecedent, behavior, and consequence. Along similar lines, in an attempt to improve understanding of parts of Skinner's (1957) analysis of verbal behavior, Michael (1993) identified the **establishing operation** as a variable that altered the value of a reinforcer. In both cases, these theorists were attempting to include consideration of conditions beyond the simple examination of a single, specific antecedent stimulus that immediately precedes a behavior.

If one defines the antecedent in the restrictive, specific stimulus sense, then it is also absolutely necessary to include consideration of the setting event or establishing operation. However, if one considers the antecedent to be the conditions under which a behavior occurs, as Skinner did, it can be argued that additional concepts, such as the setting event and establishing operation, have already been incorporated into the analysis. Our position is that it is preferable to define the antecedent, for the purpose of collecting A-B-C data, as including all relevant contextual conditions that may influence the behavior.

The "Consequence"

The consequence of a behavior is the event (or events) that follows the behavior and affects its future occurrence. As mentioned earlier, if a particular consequence makes a particular behavior more likely to recur, that consequence is called a *reinforcer* for that behavior in that situation. In contrast, if a particular consequence makes a particular behavior less likely to recur, that consequence is called a *punisher* for that behavior in that situation. Unfortunately, many teachers and school systems have come to equate the word "consequence" with punishment. In reality, consequences that are reinforcing offer teachers and school systems one of the most powerful and effective ways to improve behavior. Failure to recognize this fact has led many teachers and schools to rely heavily on "behavior management" systems in which staff become very skilled at catching children being bad, but very ineffective at "catching children being good," a technique that Becker (1971) described. This same misunderstanding of "consequences" has resulted in many teachers and school systems failing to recognize that most problematic behaviors in the classroom occur because they are regularly receiving some form of reinforcement (which is discussed in considerable detail in Chapter 5).

When collecting A-B-C data, the goal is to identify those consequences that follow the behavior that make it more likely to recur. Thus, the objective, even when observing problematic behavior, is to identify the consequences that are reinforcing the behavior. When collecting A-B-C data, the task is to identify the specific events that are reinforcing the behavior. At a later point (discussed in Chapter 5), you will need to identify the functional properties of these events (i.e., the specific effect they have on the behavior). In this regard, it is important to recognize that two identical events can have very different effects on behavior. Consider the example of a teacher reprimanding a student. If the "reprimand" makes the student less likely to misbehave in the future, then it is a mild form of punishment. However, consider the possibility that the student "misbehaves" because it is a very effective way to gain the teacher's attention, regardless of whether it is positive attention or negative attention. In this example, if the "reprimand" makes it more likely the student will misbehave again, then it actually functions not as punishment, but as reinforcement.

Now that you have a clear understanding of the concepts of the antecedent and the consequence, we can turn to the task of how to collect A-B-C data.

HOW TO COLLECT A-B-C DATA

As part of the FBA process, we collect direct observational (A-B-C) data because it produces information that helps in identifying the function of a problematic behavior (discussed in detail in Chapter 5). The method we recommend for collecting A-B-C data, as part of an FBA, uses the same principles that Bijou, Peterson, and Ault (1968) identified when they first described the approach. However, the method differs in one important respect. In the original method, observers recorded all interactions that occurred during an observation without particular emphasis on any specific target or problematic behavior. Bijou et al. compiled a narrative, continuous recording of all behavior that occurred during a session. After the observation, the researchers applied the A-B-C Model to the narrative transcript that had been produced. They were then able to examine any behavior that occurred during the session by identifying the antecedent conditions that immediately preceded it, and the consequences that immediately followed.

An understanding of this process reveals an important point about A-B-C data analysis, namely, that any particular behavior or event has both antecedents and consequences. Furthermore, an event that follows a particular behavior (i.e., is its consequence) is also the antecedent for the next behavior that occurs. Thus, one particular behavior is not just a behavior—it is a consequence for the previous behavior that occurred, as well as an antecedent for the next behavior. Antecedents and consequences become defined as such because of their relationship to a particular behavior.

Although Bijou et al.'s (1968) methodology involved recording a comprehensive, continuing account of various behaviors as they occurred during an observation, it is not always necessary to have such a complete accounting. When conducting an FBA, our primary concern is the occurrence of a particular target or problematic behavior. Therefore, the method we recommend uses the same methods and principles that Bijou et al. first described, except the data are collected only with regard to the specified target behavior. Thus, during an observation period, we would record occurrences of a target behavior and its relevant antecedents and consequences. We would not record the occurrence of any other behaviors or their antecedents or consequences.

The remainder of this section directly addresses the important issues of when to observe, how to observe, and how much to observe.

When to Observe

Conducting an FBA can take some time. You certainly do not want to do anything that would make the process take any longer than necessary. Prior attention to selecting productive periods for observation should save time and improve efficiency. Fortunately, information provided during the structured interviews gives a head start to knowing when to observe.

As a general approach, we recommend beginning with the biggest problems. This means that you should focus your initial FBA efforts on the problematic behavior (or behaviors) that are the most serious. In most cases, problematic behaviors in the classroom do not present a serious threat of harm or injury. (If such behaviors do exist, they should be addressed immediately.) Normally, however, the "biggest" problem behaviors are those that most disrupt an environment. For example, Reggie (mentioned earlier) began screaming in a high-pitched voice within 1 min after entering a general education classroom. Reggie continued screaming until he was removed from the class, at which point he immediately stopped. This was a regular pattern for Reggie, not an isolated behavior. It is safe to say that, in most classrooms, the presence of a child who is screaming in a high-pitched voice would be considered disruptive to the environment. Regardless of the particular circumstances you face, starting with the "biggest" problem first is usually the most productive approach.

In line with this approach, you want to observe when the target behavior is most likely to occur. Responses to some of the interview questions can be very helpful in this regard. For example, one of the questions in the Preliminary Functional Assessment Survey (Dunlap et al., 1993) asks, "Is there any circumstance under which the behavior always occurs?" Another question asks, "Is there any circumstance under which the behavior does not occur?" Other questions ask whether the behavior's occurrence is related to the time of day, the number of people in the immediate environment, certain people, or certain subjects. In addition, the Student-Assisted Functional Assessment Interview (Kern, Dunlap, Clarke, & Childs, 1994) asks the student, "When do you think you have the fewest problems with (the target behavior) in school?" and "When do you think you have the most problems with (the target behavior) in school?" Close attention to the answers to these questions is likely to help you identify the best time to observe in the classroom. Once you have identified a likely time, check it with the teaching staff to see if they agree that an observation at that time is likely to be productive.

One of our colleagues, Dr. James Fox from East Tennessee State University, has reduced all the questions mentioned earlier to one summary question: "If I wanted to see this behavior happen, what is the one thing you (the teacher) could do to make it happen?" Dr. Fox is not suggesting that teachers should provoke children; rather, he is simply asking teachers a question so he can obtain some important information. Common responses include "Give him a math problem," "Ask him to read out loud," or "Have him sit next to Joey." Responses such as these give important information that you can use to identify productive times to observe.

When selecting observation times, the other important considerations are to identify (a) how long the observation period should be and (b) how many times you need to observe. Frequently, the naturally occurring length of a classroom activity will determine the length of the observation. For example, if the target behavior occurs most frequently during math lessons, and the lessons normally last for 30 min, then an observation length of 30 min would seem to make sense. However, consider that the math lesson typically involves 10 min of teacher instruction, followed by 20 min of independent work by the students. Based on responses during the structured interviews, you might determine that the target behavior is most likely to occur during the independent work portion of the lesson and very unlikely to occur during the 10 min of teacher instruction. In this case, your observation would start once the independent portion of the lesson began (i.e., in this case, it would cover the last 20 min of the lesson).

Sometimes a single observation session will give you all the information you need. Sometimes additional sessions will be needed. It is not possible to know beforehand exactly how many times you will need to observe. Information presented in the next section provides an important guideline for making this decision once you have begun to collect A-B-C data. Many people prefer to observe on at least two occasions to ensure the behavior and circumstances they are recording are typical. This is a good practice, especially if you have any concerns about the representativeness of your A-B-C data. It is also helpful to ask the teaching staff and student if what you observed was typical or unusual.

How to Observe

Before collecting A-B-C data, you will need to determine where you will position yourself. If the observation is to take place in the classroom, you will need to determine where you should sit. If the observation is to occur in another school environment, such as the gym or playground, you will need to determine where you should stand or sit. In selecting a position for observation, you will need to make sure that you can (a) see and hear clearly so you can record accurately and (b) have as little influence as possible on the naturally occurring behavior that you intend to observe. A discussion of this matter with the teaching staff before the observation should help you identify an acceptable place from which to observe.

Your presence may alter the behavior that occurs when you observe. Because your objective is to observe naturally occurring interactions, you will want to take precautions to minimize the impact of your presence on the behavior that occurs during the observation session. Put simply, you should be as unobtrusive as possible. If the observation is to take place in

```
┌─────────────────────────────────────────────────────────────┐
│                   A-B-C Observation Form                      │
│  Student: _____                     │
│  Target Behavior: _____ │
│                                                               │
│  Date: _____        Time: _____            │
│  Location: _____                 │
│                                                               │
│  Observer: _____                │
│  ┌──────────────────┬──────────────────┬──────────────────┐   │
│  │    Antecedent    │     Behavior     │   Consequence    │   │
│  ├──────────────────┼──────────────────┼──────────────────┤   │
│  │                  │                  │                  │   │
│  │                  │                  │                  │   │
│  │                  │                  │                  │   │
│  │                  │                  │                  │   │
│  │                  │                  │                  │   │
│  └──────────────────┴──────────────────┴──────────────────┘   │
└─────────────────────────────────────────────────────────────┘
```

FIGURE 4.2
Sample A-B-C Observation Form for data collection.

a particular classroom, and you have often been in that classroom, the students may pay little attention to your presence. However, if the observation is to take place in a classroom in which the students do not know you, or in which you have rarely been present, your presence is likely to draw their attention. One approach to handling this situation is to have the teacher introduce you to the whole class and provide a vague explanation as to why you are there (e.g., "Miss Jones is here because she wants to see how we do math in our class"). Even with a vague explanation, some students are still likely to attend to your presence for a short while. For this reason, you may want to enter the classroom 10 to 15 min prior to the start of your data collection. This time period will give the students a chance to forget about your presence, especially if you avoid directly looking at or interacting with any of them.

If you have previously conducted a structured interview with the student you are observing, it is likely that the student will know exactly why you are there. In these cases, your presence for a period of time prior to starting data collection will be particularly important. As mentioned earlier, you should always ask the teaching staff after the observation whether the behavior you observed was typical.

Once the time for data collection begins, you will need some way to organize your observations. Many people use a prepared form, such as the one shown in Figure 4.2, whereas others prefer to construct their own form. They do this by taking a blank sheet and making three columns. Each column has a heading. The far left-hand column would have the heading "Antecedent." The middle column would have the heading "Behavior." The far right-hand column would have the heading "Consequence." Each time the behavior occurs, you would write down in the "Antecedent" column the conditions that preceded the target behavior. In the "Behavior" column, you would write down the student's specific action. In the "Consequence" column, you would write down the specific event that followed the occurrence of the target behavior. In Jimmy's case, described earlier, the A-B-C Observation Form would have several occurrences of "talking out of turn" in the "Behavior" column. The "Antecedent" column would have something like "Teacher asks a question," whereas the "Consequence" column would have something like "Teacher accepts answer and then repeats class rule." To save time and space, you should consider abbreviating your notations (e.g., "T accepts, then reminds").

In addition to the A-B-C data, your observation form should include certain identifying information. For record-keeping purposes, it is important to identify who conducted the observations, who was observed, and what specific target behavior was observed. It is also important to identify the date, time, length, and location of the observation session. This information can prove useful if data are reviewed later.

An option when collecting A-B-C data is to record each occurrence on a separate index card (Carr et al., 1994). The same information is provided on each card. This method allows you to later "sort" instances of behavior according to the function of the behavior (addressed in Chapter 5).

When recording data, it is important to ensure you record actual behavior, not interpretations of the behavior (Zirpoli, 2005). For example, if Susie screams, it would be correct to record "Susie screams" in the "Behavior" column. It would not be correct to record "Susie is scared." Similarly, in the "Consequence" column, it would be appropriate to record "Teacher answers question" rather than "Teacher gets annoyed." Finally, it is important to realize that A-B-C data collection requires the observer's full attention (Cooper, Heron, & Heward, 1987). This type of data collection cannot be conducted while carrying out other activities in the classroom.

How Much to Observe

As mentioned earlier, the A-B-C Model enables the prediction and control of behavior. In turn, the specific purpose of A-B-C data collection and analysis is to enable the identification of the specific antecedent conditions under which a particular behavior occurs, and the specific consequences that follow the behavior and affect its future occurrence. Therefore, your goal in collecting A-B-C data is to identify a consistent pattern of antecedents, behavior, and consequences. How much data are needed to accomplish this goal? How many occurrences of the target behavior must be observed before your task is completed? It is not possible to identify a specific number of occurrences that must be observed. The overriding guideline that determines how much data you need can be found in the goal of the activity: You need to collect enough data to identify a consistent pattern of antecedents, behavior, and consequences. Less data would be insufficient; more data would be unnecessary. For example, in some cases, 5 to 8 occurrences will be sufficient. In other cases, 15 to 20 or more occurrences may be needed. Keeping a clear eye on the activity's purpose—the identification of a consistent pattern of antecedents, behavior, and consequences—should make it possible to readily determine when you have completed the task.

SUMMARY

The A-B-C Model is the basic model that unifies the field of behavior analysis, including the part of the field known as applied behavior analysis. The model enables the prediction and control of behavior. "Prediction" occurs through examining the occurrence of a particular behavior in relation to (a) the antecedent conditions under which it occurs and (b) the consequences that follow the behavior and affect its future occurrence. "Control," as defined technically (i.e., arranging conditions to alter the probability that a behavior will occur), involves arranging antecedent and/or consequent conditions so certain behavior is likely to occur and other behavior is unlikely to occur.

As part of the FBA process, conducting direct observations in which A-B-C data are recorded enables one to observe a target behavior as it occurs naturally, and to identify the antecedent conditions that "trigger" or set the occasion for the behavior and the consequences that reinforce it. In the FBA process, direct observations are conducted after first defining the target behavior and, if possible, the replacement behavior, and after conducting structured interviews with informants and, when appropriate, the student. A-B-C data have the potential to confirm information obtained during the structured interviews. These data also have the potential to shed new light on important variables about which the respondents may not be aware.

The goal of A-B-C data collection is to identify a consistent pattern of antecedents, behavior, and consequences. It is not possible to determine ahead of time how many occurrences of the target behavior will be needed to identify this consistent pattern. Therefore, the overriding guideline for determining when sufficient data have been collected is that one needs to continue with the activity until a consistent pattern has been identified.

At this point, it will be useful to examine examples of A-B-C data collected with real students in actual classroom situations. The next section presents several examples and includes positive examples (i.e., models of the task being done well), as well as a negative example in which several mistakes were made.

Examples of A-B-C Data Collection

This section includes four examples of A-B-C data collected in classrooms. First is a positive example of A-B-C data collected in a single session in a single classroom. This is followed by a negative example of the same observation session, except that it includes a number of recording errors. The last two examples each present data recorded with a single student but in multiple sessions in different classrooms.

Example 1

Figure 4.3 presents data on Phyllis M., a 16-year-old 11th-grade student. The data were collected in her Math class. The target behavior was defined as "talking during instructional time that is not related to instruction." As can be seen in Figure 4.3, the observer, Lisa J., correctly supplied all necessary identifying information (her name; the student's name; the target behavior being observed; and the date, time, and location of the observation). Note that the observer also recorded the student's age in parentheses after her name. In this particular case, the observer also chose to identify the exact time of each occurrence of the target behavior, which is noted in the far left-hand column of the A-B-C Observation Form. The observer also recorded the antecedent that preceded each occurrence of the target behavior and the consequence that immediately followed. In each case, the observer's notations were descriptions of behavior, not interpretations of behavior. After five occurrences of the target behavior, a clear pattern of antecedents and consequences emerged. Using these A-B-C data, the next step would be to identify the function of each consequence of the target behavior. This step in the FBA process is described in detail in Chapter 5.

Example 2

Figure 4.4 presents a negative example of A-B-C data for the same observation session described in Example 1. It shows several errors one can make

---

A-B-C Observation Form

Observer: <u>Lisa J.</u>   Student: <u>Phyllis M. (16)</u>

Target Behavior: <u>Talking during instructional time (not related to instruction)</u>

Date: <u>February 15</u>   Time: <u>10:30–10:50</u>   Location: <u>Grade 11 Math Class</u>

Time	Antecedent	Behavior	Consequence
10:31	Student comment	Talks	Teacher warning
10:35	Student behavior	Talks	Teacher warning
10:37	Student comment	Talks	Teacher warning
10:42	Student comment	Talks	Teacher warning
10:49	Student comment	Talks	Teacher warning

FIGURE 4.3
Positive example of A-B-C data collection in a single session.

A-B-C Observation Form

Observer: _____   Student: <u>Phyllis M. (16)</u>

Target Behavior: <u>Talking during instructional time (not related to instruction)</u>

Date: _____   Time: 10:30–10:50   Location: _____

Time	Antecedent	Behavior	Consequence
10:31	Student comment	Talks	teacher irritated
10:35	Student behavior	Talks	teacher irritated
10:37	Student comment	Talks	teacher irritated
10:42	Student comment	Talks	teacher irritated
10:49	Student comment	Talks	teacher irritated

FIGURE 4.4
Negative example of A-B-C data collection in a single session.

when recording A-B-C data. First, the observer failed to identify him- or her-self and also failed to identify the date and the location of the observation. It is important that you record all required identifying information. With the limited information provided in Figure 4.4, it would be difficult to later de-termine who conducted the observation and when it occurred. Equally im-portant, it would be almost impossible to determine what subject matter was being taught when the data were recorded. An additional error occurred in the observer's notations in the "Consequence" column. After each occur-rence of inappropriate talking, the observer described the consequence as "teacher irritated." This is a good example of the mistake of recording an in-terpretation of behavior, rather than describing the behavior itself. Based on the data presented in Figure 4.4, we have good information about who was observed, the target behavior, the time of the observation, the time that each target behavior occurred, and the antecedent that preceded each occurrence of the target behavior. Unfortunately, we cannot determine (a) who recorded the data, (b) when the observation was conducted, (c) the location or activ-ity in which the data were collected, or (d) the teacher's response (i.e., the consequence) when the target behavior occurred.

Example 3

Figure 4.5 is a positive example of A-B-C data collected about the behavior of Roger, a 15-year-old boy in ninth grade. The target behavior of concern was that Roger used any available implement to draw graffiti on the classroom furniture. Because this behavior occurred in multiple classrooms throughout the day, data were collected in three different classes (i.e., English, Math, and Life Skills). All necessary identifying information is recorded at the top of the

A-B-C Observation Form

Observer: <u>Chris C.</u>   Student: <u>Roger (15)</u>   Target Behavior: <u>Drawing graffiti on furniture</u>
<u>instructional time</u>

Date: <u>February 15</u>   Time: <u>9:30–10:15;</u>   Location: <u>9th Grade English,</u>
<u>10:25–11:10;</u>   <u>Math,</u>
<u>12:15–1:00</u>   <u>Life Skills</u>

Antecedent	Behavior	Consequences
English class: students seated at desks listening to instructions	Roger takes out a pen and begins to write on desk	T asks Roger to put the pen away
Later, same English class: students are discussing a poem	Roger takes out the same pen and begins to add to his name on the desk	T takes pen away from Roger
Math class: students working on fraction problems	Roger uses scissors to scratch his name on the chair	T gives Roger verbal warning and takes scissors away
Later, same Math class: students are correcting their work	Roger uses a pencil to color in the scratches made by the scissors in the chair	T reprimands Roger, gives a behavior incident report, and sends Roger to the office
Life Skills lesson: students are watching a video	Roger scribbles with pen on the back of the person's chair in front of him	T sends Roger out of the video viewing and requires him to return after class to clean off the graffiti

FIGURE 4.5
Positive example of A-B-C data collection in multiple sessions and classrooms.

A-B-C Observation Form. Furthermore, the data recorded in each column of the form are descriptions, not interpretations, of the behavior that occurred.

Example 4

Figure 4.6 is a final positive example of A-B-C data collection. These data pertain to 14-year-old Marco, a ninth-grade student who, during instructional activities, often puts his head down on the desk or leans it against a window. This target behavior occurs during several different classes. Therefore, A-B-C data were collected in three different classes (i.e., Math, Social Studies, and English). Each class session lasted 50 min. In collecting the A-B-C data, the observer (Philip W.) included the necessary identifying information and, because of the multiple observations, combined the entries for time and location. The data that were recorded describe behavior, rather than interpretations of behavior. With the A-B-C data recorded here, in addition to the data from structured interviews collected earlier, the observer is now in position to begin determining the function of Marco's behavior.

A-B-C Observation Form

Observer: <u>Philip W.</u>   Student: <u>Marco (14)</u>   Target Behavior: <u>Puts head down on desk or window during instruction</u>

Date: <u>February 15</u>   Time/Location: <u>9th grade Math (9–9:50); Social Studies (10–10:50); English (11–11:50)</u>

Antecedent	Behavior	Consequence
Math class: T passing out assignment; students sitting at their desks.	Marco has his head on the desk looking away from the teacher.	T asks Marco to sit up.
T going over examples on the board.	M curls over and puts his head back on the desk.	T asks Marco to sit up.
Another child is reiterating example from the board to her classmates.	M puts his head down on the desk.	T motions to paraeducator to sit next to M and make him sit up.
Other children working on their assignment (order of operations worksheet). T perusing the classroom.	M is leaning against the window looking outside.	T instructs M to begin assignment or he will receive a behavior incident report.
40 min into the class; other students continue to work.	M stops work and puts his head back on the desk.	T writes behavior incident report; tells paraeducator to escort M to Time-Out.
Social Studies: class is watching a video.	M puts head down on the desk.	T tells M to sit up and take notes on video.
30 min later; video still showing.	M puts head down on the desk; goes to sleep.	M allowed to sleep.
English class: teacher reading another student's essay.	M leans head on the window and looks outside.	T tells M to sit up and pay attention.
T reviewing editing symbols with the class.	M puts head down on the desk; doodles.	Paraeducator tells M to sit up.
Other students are editing their essays.	M puts head down; goes to sleep.	T writes a behavior incident report and sends M to the Principal.

FIGURE 4.6
Positive example of A-B-C data collection in multiple classes.

Steps and Activities Required in Collecting A-B-C Data

The following list summarizes the steps and activities involved in collecting A-B-C data as part of the FBA process.

Before the data collection session occurs:

1. Identify the "biggest" problem and address it first.

2. Identify an appropriate time and location in which to collect data.

3. Determine the length of each observation period.

4. Identify an appropriate place to position yourself in the classroom (or other environment).

5. Identify when you should enter the classroom and when you should begin collecting A-B-C data.

6. Identify an appropriate form on which to record A-B-C data.

7. Complete the necessary identifying information at the top of the observation form (data recording sheet).

During data collection:

1. Minimize and, if possible, completely avoid interactions with anyone in the classroom.

2. For each occurrence of the target behavior, record the relevant antecedents and consequences. Make sure to record descriptions of actual behavior, not interpretations of behavior.

3. Continue collecting A-B-C data until you can identify a consistent pattern of antecedents, behavior, and consequences.

EXERCISES

1. A-B-C data can be collected and analyzed for any behavior, including behaviors that are appropriate. Collect A-B-C data on a particular appropriate behavior in a classroom setting. Apply the information, and follow the steps presented in this chapter. Be sure to identify and define a behavior that is discrete and that is likely to occur several times during an observation session. Avoid selecting a continuous behavior (e.g., "on-task" behavior). Continuous behaviors can vary widely in duration (i.e., one occurrence may last for 10 seconds, whereas the next occurrence may last for 10 minutes). In fact, a single occurrence of a continuous behavior could last throughout the entire observation session, thus producing very little useful information.

2. Repeat Exercise 1, but target a problematic behavior rather than an appropriate behavior.

REFERENCES

Becker, W. C. (1971). *Parents are teachers: A child management program*. Chicago: Research Press.

Bijou, S. W., & Baer, D. M. (1961). *Child development: Vol. 1: A systematic and empirical theory*. New York: Appleton-Century.

Bijou, S. W., Peterson, R. F., & Ault, M. H. (1968). A method to integrate descriptive and experimental field studies at the level of data and empirical concepts. *Journal of Applied Behavior Analysis, 1,* 175–191.

Carr, E. G., Levin, L., McConnachie, G., Carlson, J. I., Kemp, D. C., & Smith, C. E. (1994). Functional assessment: Describe. In *Communication-based intervention for problem behavior* (pp. 31–62). Baltimore: Paul H. Brookes.

Cooper, J. O., Heron, T. E., & Heward, W. L. (1987). *Applied behavior analysis*. Upper Saddle River, NJ: Merrill-Prentice Hall.

Dunlap, G., Kern, L., dePerczel, M., Clarke, S., Wilson, D., Childs, K. E., White, R., & Falk, G. D. (1993). *Preliminary Functional Assessment Survey*. Unpublished document, Division of Applied Research and Educational Services, University of South Florida, Tampa.

Kantor, J. R. (1959). *Interbehavioral psychology*. Granville, OH: Principia Press.

Kern, L., Dunlap, G., Clarke, S., & Childs, K. E. (1994). Student-Assisted Functional Assessment Interview. *Diagnostique, 19,* 29–39.

Michael, J. (1993). Establishing operations. *The Behavior Analyst, 16,* 191–206.

Skinner, B. F. (1938). *The behavior of organisms: An experimental analysis*. New York: Appleton-Century.

Skinner, B. F. (1957). Verbal behavior. Upper Saddle River, NJ: Prentice Hall.

Umbreit, J., & Blair, K. C. (1996). The effects of preference, choice, and attention on problem behavior at school. *Education and Training in Mental Retardation and Developmental Disabilities, 31,* 151–161.

Zirpoli, T. J. (2005). *Behavior management: Applications for teachers and parents* (4th ed.). Upper Saddle River, NJ: Merrill/Prentice Hall.

CHAPTER 5

Determining the Function of the Behavior
Using the Function Matrix

OUTCOMES

After reading this chapter, you will be able to

- Explain how specific principles of behavior are used to determine the function of a target behavior.
- Use data collected through interviews and observations to determine the function of a target behavior.
- Determine whether a target behavior serves a single function or multiple functions.
- Use the Function Matrix to systematically determine the function of a target behavior.
- Write a statement that describes the function of a target behavior.

Now that you have all the information you need, you are ready to complete the final step in the FBA: determining the function of the target behavior. This chapter leads you through two important steps in discovering the function of the target behavior: (a) using data to arrive at a determination of function, and (b) developing a simple statement that accurately describes the function of the behavior. We describe a tool called the Function Matrix that simplifies the task of reviewing the data collected during interviews and observations, and ensures consideration of each possible function of the target behavior. We also present a format for creating a statement that describes the function of the target behavior. The chapter concludes with three examples that provide further insight into the important task of discovering the function of the target behavior.

Chapter 1 provided an introduction to some principles of applied behavior analysis that are key to determining function. These terms and concepts included *positive reinforcement, negative reinforcement, access, escape, reinforcers, antecedents, consequences,* and *function.* We discuss these concepts again as we describe how they are used to develop an understanding of the function of a target behavior. However, this chapter does not redefine these principles in depth. If you have not read Chapter 1 or if you think you would benefit from a review of these concepts, consider re-examining Chapter 1 before reading further.

DETERMINING THE FUNCTION OF THE BEHAVIOR
Why Bother?

Chapter 1 introduced the importance of understanding the function of the target behavior in developing an effective intervention. In short, knowing the function of a behavior helps you carefully construct an effective intervention, rather than dealing with it by simply choosing among many popular behavior management strategies that may or may not be appropriate. Consider the situation endured by Mr. Hawthorne. A student in his third-grade class, Andy, frequently curses at peers during group math activities. This behavior disrupts other students who are either shocked or laugh at Andy. It also results in Andy failing to complete assignments when he is sent to the office. Mr. Hawthorne decides he cannot tolerate this behavior, so he implements a technique he has seen another teacher use successfully. Every time Andy curses, Mr. Hawthorne "fines" him 5 minutes of recess time. Unfortunately, over the next few weeks, Andy's cursing does not abate, even though he is sitting out of recess entirely almost every day. Somewhat frustrated by this outcome, Mr. Hawthorne wonders what sort of strategy he should try next.

Rather than "grasping at behavior management techniques," Mr. Hawthorne would be more likely to choose or develop an effective intervention if he considers that Andy's cursing serves a *function.* That is, Andy's cursing occurs in response to certain situations or *antecedents* and is *reinforced* or maintained by the *consequences* he experiences. Mr. Hawthorne also needs to understand how Andy's behavior is being reinforced and what the reinforcers are. With this information, he could approach the problem directly and effectively. Mr. Hawthorne could make sure Andy's cursing no longer provided the reinforcer he was seeking, that a new more useful behavior would be promoted, and that antecedent conditions in the classroom were conducive to Andy's use of the replacement behavior. In summary, unless you base your intervention on the function of the target behavior, the intervention components that you select for a student may or may not be effective or may even be counterproductive.

Using Data

As you might have guessed from the previous example, Mr. Hawthorne needs to gather a variety of information to make a decision about the function of Andy's cursing. The steps described in Chapters 2 to 4 were designed to collect this information.

The interview and direct observation data should identify the antecedents that precede the target behavior and the consequences that immediately follow the target behavior. To continue the example of Andy's cursing, an interview conducted with Mr. Hawthorne might indicate that a common antecedent to the cursing is peers whispering in his ear or talking quietly to him. The interview might also indicate that the consequences that follow most of the cursing incidents are similar; the peers laugh or act shocked, and Andy is sent to the office. Direct observations can confirm and add depth to this information.

To determine the function of Andy's behavior, you also need information about the specific type and nature of the reinforcer. As was described in Chapter 1, there are only two ways that a behavior is reinforced (i.e., through positive reinforcement or negative reinforcement). To decide whether positive or negative reinforcement maintains Andy's behavior, simply ask whether the behavior (a) allows access to something (positive reinforcement) or (b) allows escape from something (negative reinforcement).

The next thing you need to know is the something (i.e., what specifically is the individual accessing or escaping through the use of the target behavior?). Reinforcers can be organized in various ways. In Chapter 1, reinforcers were categorized as those that meet a biological need (primary reinforcers) or those that gain their reinforcing value through association with existing reinforcers (secondary reinforcers). However, for the purpose of determining the function of behavior, we can divide all reinforcers into three simple categories: (a) attention, (b) tangibles and/or activities, and (c) sensory. All reinforcers that individuals seek to gain (positive reinforcement) or escape (negative reinforcement) fall into one of these three categories.

In the case of Andy's cursing, our data collection revealed that peer laughter and shock are the consequences of his behavior. These consequences fit the category of attention.

In schools and other community settings, reinforcers that fit the category of **attention** include consequences that access staff or peer interaction (e.g., the teacher providing assistance, peers laughing) or consequences that avoid staff and peer interactions (e.g., the teacher ceasing to ask questions, peers stopping their teasing). The category of **tangibles/activities** generally includes consequences in which an individual gains access to items (e.g., toys, music CDs, work materials, food) or avoids those items. This category also includes activities that are either accessed (e.g., computer time, cleaning the board, playing a group game) or avoided (e.g., academic tasks, group work, cleaning the workspace). Although tangible items and activities seem like quite different categories, we group them together for a simple reason: Although people may engage in activities that do not include any tangible items, they always access tangible items so they can do something with them. They also avoid tangible items because of the activities connected with them. Finally, **sensory** reinforcers include consequences people seek (e.g., warmth, touch, pleasant sounds) and avoid (e.g., pain, discomfort, noise).

The Function

Once you have data, you are ready to determine the function of the target behavior. As described earlier, determining function involves reviewing the interview and observation data, and deciding whether the target behavior provides access (positive reinforcement) or escape (negative reinforcement). Once that is determined, you also need to identify what is being gained or avoided. Because there are two functions of behavior and three types of reinforcers, there are six unique possibilities you might identify:

1. Positive reinforcement (access)—attention
2. Negative reinforcement (escape)—attention
3. Positive reinforcement (access)—tangibles/activities
4. Negative reinforcement (escape)—tangibles/activities
5. Positive reinforcement (access)—sensory stimulation
6. Negative reinforcement (escape)—sensory stimulation

When you can identify at least one of these combinations of function and reinforcer to explain the recurring chains of antecedents, behaviors, and consequences, you have arrived at a determination of the function of the target behavior. Figure 5.1 provides examples of recurring A-B-C chains of behavior that would fit into each category of function. Aside from simply using one of the previous six phrases to describe function of the target behavior, you should also create a **statement of function** that clearly communicates the function of the target behavior. Later in this chapter, we present a format for correctly writing a complete statement of function.

We now return briefly to Andy's target behavior of cursing. Assume Mr. Hawthorne gained some basic knowledge about determining the function of a target behavior. To determine function, he would need to look at interview and observational data and ask whether Andy's cursing appears to access something or avoid something, and what the something is. He asks the behavioral consultant (whose knowledge is also new and somewhat incomplete) to collect some interview and observational data. The data reveals repeated instances in which the peers quietly say something to Andy (the antecedent), Andy curses (the target behavior), and peers laugh or look

Positive Reinforcement—Attention
In the classroom, Peter argues with the teacher and peers laugh.
On the playground, Sara dances and takes off clothing and peers come over to her.
During circle time, Terrance punches peers, they turn to him, and he talks with them.
Negative Reinforcement—Attention
During group games on the playground, Reneta argues with peers and then does not have to interact with them.
During classroom group discussions, Latitia complains of illnesses and the teacher stops asking her questions.
After arriving early and waiting in the lunchroom with peers for school to start, Martin fights with peers to stop them from teasing him.
Positive Reinforcement—Tangibles/Activities
During free play, Mica hits peers and takes their toys.
In the lunchroom, Abby curses at peers and they give her part of their lunch.
In the classroom, Karen tantrums until the teacher gives her what she asks for.
Negative Reinforcement—Tangibles/Activities
In social studies class, Jaques argues with the teacher until she lets him out of work.
During PE, Baylee stays in the locker room and misses most of class.
After being dismissed for the bus, Darren stops to talk with peers and staff to avoid riding the bus.
Positive Reinforcement—Sensory Stimulation
During transitions between classes, Marcus leaves campus to smoke a cigarette and is tardy to classes.
Negative Reinforcement—Sensory Stimulation
In the lunchroom, Todd leaves before being dismissed to escape from the noise.

FIGURE 5.1
Examples of combinations of function and reinforcer.

shocked and then leave Andy alone (the consequence). Because Andy's behavior results in peers leaving him alone (escape), and the type of reinforcer is peer comments (attention), Mr. Hawthorne determines that the function of the behavior is negative reinforcement—attention. In effect, Andy appears to use cursing to get peers to leave him alone.

Mr. Hawthorne and the behavioral consultant then craft a simple intervention. They plan to move Andy away from the peers who are making the comments and, at the end of each class session that does not include cursing, reinforce Andy with verbal praise for doing such a good job in class. Things go well at first; Andy does not curse for a day or two and sits quietly at his desk during independent activities. However, much to Mr. Hawthorne's dismay, Andy begins to engage in a new behavior—taunting peers from a distance. The peers then confront Andy, Andy is verbally abusive, and Mr. Hawthorne sees no other recourse than removing Andy from the classroom.

After several days of these problems, Mr. Hawthorne is more frustrated than ever and wonders where he went wrong.

Perhaps because they are new to doing FBAs or because it can be difficult for novices to deal with complex data, Mr. Hawthorne and the behavioral consultant have fallen prey to one of the additional complexities of functional assessment. They did in fact correctly determine one of the functions of the target behavior. What they failed to realize is that a target behavior can serve more than one function.

Multiple Functions

To put the issue simply, a single behavior can serve several functions. If a behavior serves multiple functions, and you create an intervention that addresses only one function of the behavior, the intervention will probably be only partly successful. Figure 5.2 shows how a single behavior or class of behaviors can serve multiple functions in one environment. A single behavior or class of behaviors can also serve one function (or set of functions) in one environment and another function (or set of functions) in another environment.

Bill (the student who is the subject of Figure 5.2) may destroy materials when presented with independent math work and when presented with group math tasks. In the former case, the function of destroying materials may be to escape work that he cannot do (negative reinforcement—activities). In the group work, the function of the same behavior may be to escape work

Positive Reinforcement (Access)—Attention
During math, Bill *destroys materials* and peers look and laugh.
Negative Reinforcement (Escape)—Attention
During math, Bill *destroys materials* and peers leave him alone.
Positive Reinforcement (Access)—Tangibles/Activities
During math, Bill *destroys materials*, and the teacher comes to his desk and helps him with his work.
Negative Reinforcement (Escape)—Tangibles/Activities
During math, Bill *destroys materials*, is sent from the classroom, and does not have to do his work.
Positive Reinforcement (Access)—Sensory Stimulation
During math, Bill *destroys materials* because it sounds interesting.
Negative Reinforcement (Escape)—Sensory Stimulation
During math, Bill *destroys materials* so the teacher will send him to the corner chair, where it is quieter.

FIGURE 5.2
A single behavior serving multiple functions across one environment.

he cannot do (negative reinforcement—activities) and to get the attention of peers (positive reinforcement—attention). In some situations, a single replacement behavior and adjustments to the environment may adequately replace a target behavior and address its multiple functions across antecedents. In Bill's case, providing him with additional instruction in math, preparing him for upcoming group work, and allowing him access to peers only when he properly maintains classroom materials might form the basic elements of an intervention to deal with the multiple functions of his property destruction. In other cases, the range of functions may require incorporating more adjustments and more than one replacement behavior in a student's function-based intervention plan.

We now return a final time to Andy's case and make the assumption, once again, that Mr. Hawthorne and the district behavioral consultant learn more about function-based intervention planning and the issue of multiple functions. As they review the A-B-C data a second time for recurring antecedents and consequences, they notice another common consequence—Andy's cursing results in him being removed from the room, and he often does not have to complete his work. So, not only does Andy appear to use cursing to escape the comments of peers, he also curses to escape work tasks (negative reinforcement—activities). Mr. Hawthorne now sees why his first intervention did not work; moving Andy away from peers provided a better option for escaping attention, but it did not deal with the fact that Andy was also trying to escape work tasks.

Certainly, the issue of multiple functions adds another level of complexity to the process of determining the function of a target behavior. However, in the next section of this chapter, we present a tool that will help you assess single and multiple functions. This tool will also help you conceptualize how positive reinforcement, negative reinforcement, and specific reinforcers make up the process of determining function, and provide a format for working systematically to review and categorize behavior patterns in your A-B-C data.

THE FUNCTION MATRIX
A Useful Tool

Given all we have covered so far, it is easy to see why individuals new to FBAs might make errors. Determining behavioral function requires the consistent application of several related, and often confused, principles of applied behavior analysis. It also calls for reviewing a large volume of data in which repeated patterns of behavior can easily be overlooked. The issue of multiple functions adds to the complexity of the task. It would obviously be helpful to have a tool that could be used to make decisions about the function of a behavior.

We have developed a tool, the Function Matrix (see Figure 5.3), that is useful in dealing with the difficulties described herein. The Function Matrix conceptually organizes the underlying concepts involved in determining the relationship between antecedents, consequences, and a target behavior. It also

FIGURE 5.3
The Function Matrix.

	Positive Reinforcement (Access Something)	Negative Reinforcement (Avoid Something)
Attention		
Tangibles/ Activities		
Sensory		

provides a structure for considering the six combinations resulting from the two functions of behavior and the three categories of reinforcers. Finally, application of the Function Matrix ensures the possibility of multiple functions is fully considered. This section describes how to use the Function Matrix.

We have taught the use of the Function Matrix for several years in our courses on function-based intervention planning. Students, including many professionals, have found the Function Matrix to be very useful and have experienced a high degree of success in accurately determining the function of target behaviors. We strongly recommend using this tool as a regular part of the function-based intervention planning process.

The Layout

The Function Matrix presents the principles necessary to determine function as part of a grid that has three columns and four rows. The first column lists the three categories of reinforcers that may be maintaining the target behavior: attention, tangibles/activities, and sensory stimulation. The two functions of behavior (positive reinforcement and negative reinforcement) are found in the two far right columns. Figure 5.4 demonstrates how the grid design of the Function Matrix results in the six combinations of functions and reinforcers:

1. Positive reinforcement—attention
2. Negative reinforcement—attention
3. Positive reinforcement—tangibles/activities
4. Negative reinforcement—tangibles/activities
5. Positive reinforcement—sensory stimulation
6. Negative reinforcement—sensory stimulation

As we have stressed throughout this chapter, determining the function of a behavior requires carefully reviewing your interview and observational data for recurring patterns of behavior that include the target behavior, and then deciding whether the target behavior provides access or escape to a specific reinforcer. The Function Matrix simplifies this process by allowing the user to systematically consider each possible combination of function and reinforcer type. Furthermore, by dealing with each combination individually, the user is aided in identifying whether multiple functions are responsible for maintaining the target behavior.

	Positive Reinforcement (Access Something)	Negative Reinforcement (Avoid Something)
Attention	Positive Reinforcement—Attention	Negative Reinforcement—Attention
Tangibles/ Activities	Positive Reinforcement—Tangibles/Activities	Negative Reinforcement—Tangibles/Activities
Sensory	Positive Reinforcement—Sensory Stimulation	Negative Reinforcement—Sensory Stimulation

FIGURE 5.4
The Function Matrix: resulting combinations.

Using the Function Matrix

A relatively simple and systematic process is employed in using the Function Matrix. Starting with the grid box in the upper left-hand corner of the table, which represents the function and reinforcer combination of positive reinforcement and attention, ask yourself whether the interview and observational data suggest that the student is using the target behavior to access (or get) attention. If the answer is Yes, put a checkmark or "X" in the grid box. If the answer is No (i.e., the interview and observation data do not support the idea that access to attention is maintaining the target behavior), then move to the next grid box. Which grid box you choose next is unimportant, as long as you repeat the previous process for each remaining grid box. Remember to use this process for all six grid boxes to identify all functions of the behavior. The three cases at the end of this chapter provide further examples of the use of the Function Matrix to identify target behaviors maintained by individual and multiple functions.

Once you have used the Function Matrix to consider each possible combination of function and reinforcer, you should write one or more summary statements that describe the function or functions of the target behavior.

WRITING A STATEMENT OF FUNCTION
Purpose of the Statement of Function

The goal of writing a statement of function is twofold: (a) to provide information relevant to making effective intervention decisions, and (b) to clearly communicate the function of the behavior to other persons in crafting and implementing the intervention. When properly developed, a statement of function should contain much of the information you will need to move forward with the creation of a function-based intervention.

In developing the intervention, you may work with a wide variety of individuals, including general and special educators, administrators, school psychologists, therapists, parents, and, in some cases, the student. The statement of function should be carefully created so it is useful in both developing the

FIGURE 5.5
Complete statement
of function for Billy.

> When peers in a group make comments about his lunch, Billy is physically aggressive (hits with a closed fist and kicks) to avoid peer attention. That is, Billy is either removed from the lunchroom or peers stop making comments (negative reinforcement—attention).

intervention and clarifying the function of the behavior to persons with various educational backgrounds. To meet these needs, we suggest formatting your statement of function to include (a) the antecedent, (b) the student, (c) the target behavior, (d) the function(s) of the behavior, and (e) any brief additional information that may aid other professionals in understanding the statement. Figure 5.5 provides a complete statement of function for a student named Billy. The recommended elements of a function statement are described next.

Antecedent

Although it is easy to associate particular environments with the occurrence of a problem behavior (i.e., when in the lunchroom, Billy hits to avoid peer attention), making this mistake could lead to an inappropriate intervention (i.e., removing Billy from the environment). To avoid this problem, think in terms of antecedents, rather than location. Remember that the antecedent occasions, or sets the stage, for behavior. Billy's hitting is not occasioned by the lunchroom, but by the specific antecedents that are present in the lunchroom. When crafting a statement of function, the goal is to identify the antecedents in the environment that are present prior to occurrences of the behavior. Focusing on the elements of the antecedent in the environment allows us to later consider whether these antecedents may need to be altered to create a well-designed intervention. In the case of Billy, closer inspection of interview and observational data may reveal that his hitting occurs when peers in a group make comments about his lunch.

Student

This element of a statement of function is generally self-explanatory. The student is named to personalize the statement and ensure correct communication with others who may refer to your work or assist in making intervention decisions. In this scenario, the student is Billy.

Behavior

The identification of the target behavior was described in Chapter 2. As you recall, a target behavior is an observable, measurable, and repeatable action that is considered to be the focus of the intervention. Correctly describing a target behavior calls for naming the student and providing a general descriptor of the behavior followed by one or more specific examples (e.g.,

Billy is physically aggressive, which includes hitting with a closed fist and kicking). Up to this point in the FBA process, the target behavior will have been used to focus the collection of observational and interview data. The target behavior is included in the statement of function to provide a referent for the description of function.

Function

If you used the Function Matrix to evaluate the commonalities in the data collected through interviews and direct observations, then you can use your findings to complete this element of the function statement. In the case of Billy, the function was identified as "negative reinforcement—attention." If you identified multiple functions for the target behavior, you should describe each function.

Additional Information

At this point, the statement of function should clearly describe how the behavior functions, in the presence of specific antecedents, to either access or escape a particular type of reinforcer. However, it may be useful to add brief statements that clarify elements of the function statement. Adding information can keep important details in the forefront during the development of a function-based intervention. Such information might clarify the antecedent, the specific reinforcer, or the function of the behavior. Adding information to the statement of function is optional and should be included only if it promotes the development of the function-based intervention and furthers the goals of clearly communicating the function of the behavior to other professionals.

EXAMPLES

This section includes three examples that demonstrate the use of the Function Matrix. Although there are certainly more than three possible outcomes, these examples should provide you with the background needed to apply the Function Matrix in any given situation.

Example 1: Negative Reinforcement—Activities
Tia is a 10th-grade student with autism and limited verbal skills. Her teacher is concerned about her destructive behavior, which consists of tipping over her chair or desk in the classroom. You interview Tia's special education teacher and a classroom assistant. The teacher is concerned about the behavior because it is dangerous and results in time being lost from engagement in academic tasks. A review of both interviews suggests that Tia's behavior occurs when she is working on tasks with a specific classroom assistant. The special education teacher and assistant note that the consequence for this behavior has been a reprimand from the assistant and the requirement that Tia place the chair or desk back in its original position. The

teacher suggests that the behavior does not occur during her interactions with Tia because she allows frequent breaks from the task. The assistant is new to the classroom and does not have much experience dealing with students who have autism. The fact that Tia has a very limited set of functional words for communication prevents you from interviewing her.

You observe in the special education classroom at times when Tia is scheduled to work with the classroom assistant. During three observations, you witness four occurrences of the behavior. Prior to each instance of flipping over a chair or desk, you note that Tia has been engaged in an academic task with the classroom assistant for at least 15 min. Immediately after each occurrence, the assistant scolds Tia and they both spend several minutes putting the furniture back into place and gathering the task materials.

Armed with your collected data, you consider the following questions posed by the Function Matrix: Does the interview and observational data suggest that the behavior is maintained by

1. Access to attention? No. Tia has the classroom assistant's attention prior to the behavior and the behavior does not result in additional attention from the special education teacher.
2. Escape from attention? No. The classroom assistant continues to provide attention as she scolds Tia and assists her in cleaning up.
3. Access to tangibles or activities? No. There were no instances in which Tia's behavior provided access to an item or activity.
4. Escape from tangibles or activities? Yes. Prior to each instance of the behavior, the classroom assistant and Tia have been focusing on the given task for 15 min. After each incident, Tia and the classroom assistant stop working on the task and instead spend several minutes restoring the environment.
5. Access to sensory stimulation? No. There are no data to suggest Tia's behavior allows her to access sensory stimulation.
6. Escape from sensory stimulation? No. The data do not support the idea that Tia's destructive behavior provides escape from sensory stimulation.

Your complete Function Matrix resembles Figure 5.6. Given the insight gained through data collection and use of the Function Matrix, you create

	Positive Reinforcement (Access Something)	Negative Reinforcement (Avoid Something)
Attention		
Tangibles/Activities		X
Sensory		

FIGURE 5.6
Example 1: Function Matrix for Tia.

the following statement of function: When working on a task for more than 15 min, Tia engages in destructive behavior (tips over her chair or desk) to avoid an activity. In other words, when Tia is destructive, she gets a break from the work task (negative reinforcement—tangible/activity).

Example 2: Negative reinforcement—Attention

Bernard is a sixth-grade boy who has few friends. He has been referred for his tendency to exhibit aggressive verbal behavior in unsupervised settings. This behavior includes yelling at peers and making threatening comments. Interviews with two teachers suggest that Bernard's behavior occurs immediately after peers tease him. These teachers also agree that, in most cases, the consequence of Bernard's behavior is that the peers stop teasing. Your interview with Bernard confirms the antecedent and the consequence; Bernard tells you that other students make fun of his weight and his clothes and that he yells or says things to scare them so they will stop. After reviewing the interview data, you decide that you would have the best opportunity to observe this behavior during lunch and transition periods.

You observe on three occasions during the time that Bernard leaves class, goes to lunch, and returns to class. During these A-B-C observations, you record two instances of Bernard's verbally aggressive behavior. In both cases, you observe that, prior to the behavior, peers are facing Bernard and talking, although you cannot hear the words clearly. You also observe that, immediately after the behavior, the peers leave the area.

As you review your data in relation to the Function Matrix, you ask a series of six questions. Does the interview and observational data suggest that the behavior is maintained by

1. Access to attention? No. There were no instances in which Bernard's behavior was associated with gaining additional attention.

2. Escape from attention? Yes. Interviews with the teachers and with Bernard point out that peers leave Bernard alone after he is verbally aggressive. Your observational data confirm the interview findings.

3. Access to tangibles or activities? No. There were no instances in which Bernard's behavior provided access to an item or activity.

4. Escape from tangibles or activities? No. Bernard's aggressive verbal behavior does not appear to allow him to escape a task or activity.

5. Access to sensory stimulation? No. There are no data to suggest Bernard's behavior allows him to access sensory stimulation.

6. Escape from sensory stimulation? No. The data do not support the idea that Bernard's verbal aggression provides escape from sensory stimulation.

Your analysis results in a Function Matrix that looks like Figure 5.7. Using your collected data and the results from considering the Function Matrix, you develop the following statement of function: When peers make fun of him, Bernard is verbally aggressive (yells and makes threatening comments) to avoid peer attention. That is, when Bernard is verbally aggressive, peers tend to leave him alone (negative reinforcement—attention).

	Positive Reinforcement (Access Something)	Negative Reinforcement (Avoid Something)
Attention		X
Tangibles/Activities		
Sensory		

FIGURE 5.7
Example 2: Function Matrix for Bernard.

Example 3: Multiple Functions

Charlie is a 9-year-old boy in the second grade. Given his problems with handwriting, Charlie's classroom teacher has referred him for special education services, although Charlie has not yet been identified as eligible for services. Charlie's teacher is also worried about his off-task behavior. This behavior includes talking with peers, walking around the room, repeatedly restarting assignments, and rooting around in his desk or backpack. The teacher is concerned that Charlie is off-task far more often than other students and that the behavior is interfering with his ability to learn and complete his work.

The teacher describes two different situations in which Charlie's behavior occurs. First, she notes that Charlie's off-task behavior tends to occur shortly after he is presented with a task that calls for extended writing, such as developing three or more complete sentences around a single theme. The teacher explains that this behavior seems to result in Charlie's failure to complete his work. Second, she suggests that, in other situations, the off-task behavior tends to occur when Charlie is seated next to certain classroom peers whom the teacher reports are Charlie's friends. When Charlie does attempt to socialize with his friends during class, they often happily reciprocate.

Your interview with Charlie confirms the teacher's perceptions and adds other details. Charlie reports that PE and being with his friends are probably his favorite activities in school and that he most dislikes the morning writing tasks that students are expected to complete each day. Charlie recognizes his off-task behavior as a problem only in that he "gets in trouble" more than other students.

You conduct observations on three separate occasions during morning classroom routines, a time when the teacher reports much of the off-task behavior occurs. You witness several occurrences of off-task behavior during each observation. As suggested by the teacher, you observe that the antecedents of Charlie's off-task behavior include the presentation of handwriting tasks and proximity to specific peers. You also discern that the consequences do indeed include failure to complete work and social responses from peers around him.

FIGURE 5.8
Example 3: Function Matrix for Charlie.

	Positive Reinforcement (Access Something)	Negative Reinforcement (Avoid Something)
Attention	X	
Tangibles/Activities		X
Sensory		

Armed with the Function Matrix, you begin the process of systematically considering your data in light of the following six questions. Does the interview and observational data suggest that the behavior is maintained by

1. Access to attention? Yes. Both interviews and observations confirm that off-task behavior occurs when Charlie sits near certain peers and that peers reciprocate Charlie's off-task social advances.

2. Escape from attention? No. There were no instances in which Charlie's off-task behaviors provided escape from peer or staff attention.

3. Access to tangibles or activities? No. There were no instances in which Charlie's behavior provided access to an item or activity.

4. Escape from items or activities? Yes. Multiple sources of data show that Charlie's off-task behaviors tend to occur when he is presented with tasks that require extended handwriting. The data also include evidence that the consequence of Charlie's behavior is failure to complete assignments.

5. Access to sensory stimulation? No. There are no data to suggest Charlie's behavior allows him to access sensory stimulation.

6. Escape from sensory stimulation? No. No data are present that support the idea that Charlie's off-task behavior provides escape from sensory stimulation.

The Function Matrix produced from your evaluation of the data resembles Figure 5.8. Given the results, you create two function statements:

a. When seated near certain peers, Charlie engages in off-task behavior (including talking with peers, walking around the room, repeatedly restarting assignments, and rooting around in his desk or backpack) to access peer attention.

b. When asked to complete tasks that require extended handwriting, Charlie engages in off-task behavior (including talking with peers, walking around the room, repeatedly restarting assignments, and rooting around in his desk or backpack) to escape the activity. In other words, Charlie engages in off-task behaviors to gain peer attention and to avoid handwriting tasks, which are difficult for him (positive reinforcement—attention and negative reinforcement—tangible/activity).

SUMMARY

Determining the function of the target behavior is the final step in the FBA and a critical step in the function-based intervention planning process. Understanding the function of a target behavior leads to the selection of appropriate intervention components and the creation of interventions that are likely to be effective. To determine the function of a target behavior, you must carefully consider your interview and observational data, looking for repeated patterns of antecedents and consequences that are associated with the target behavior. The function of the target behavior is revealed when we understand whether the target behavior is maintained by positive or negative reinforcement (or both), and we can categorize the reinforcers into three basic categories: attention, tangibles/activities, and sensory stimulation. Although a target behavior may have a single function, it is also important to determine whether it serves multiple functions. The task of determining function(s) can be simplified through the use of the Function Matrix. Once the function has been determined, it is helpful to develop a summary statement that describes the function or functions in a format that can be easily communicated to other professionals.

Steps for Determining the Function of the Target Behavior

1. Gather your interview and direct observation data.
2. Obtain a copy of the Function Matrix.
3. Systematically apply the Function Matrix. Ask whether the target behavior appears to be maintained by
   a. Positive reinforcement—attention
   b. Negative reinforcement—attention
   c. Positive reinforcement—tangibles/activities
   d. Negative reinforcement—tangibles/activities
   e. Positive reinforcement—sensory stimulation
   f. Negative reinforcement—sensory stimulation
4. Write a statement that summarizes each function.

EXERCISES

1. List three behaviors you engage in every day. For instance, you might choose jogging, washing dishes, and brushing your teeth. Use the Function Matrix to determine whether these behaviors serve individual or multiple functions in your life.
2. Write at least three correctly formatted statements of function that describe the results of Exercise 1.

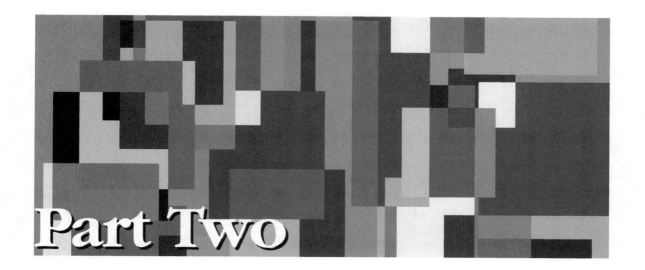

Part Two

Developing and Testing the Intervention

The importance of linking the intervention to FBA results is well documented. We know that FBA results provide the best foundation for selecting specific and individualized behavior change strategies for students who exhibit problem behavior. These strategies are successful because they address the consequences maintaining, and environmental factors influencing, behavior. Strategies selected without the benefit of a formal or informal assessment of the relationship between consequences, behavior, and antecedents are often unsuccessful because they do not address the behavior's function. In fact, they may inadvertently reinforce the problem behavior. Consider the example of Gary, a third-grade student.

Gary was observed to hit other students on an almost daily basis during reading instruction. The teacher tried reprimands, enlisting help from his mother, removing him to a quiet area of the classroom, sending him to the office, and social skills instruction. Gary's problem behavior remained unchanged. An FBA revealed that hitting other students allowed Gary to escape reading. The previous interventions (i.e., sending him out of the room, reprimands that interrupted his reading, and seating Gary in a different area of the room to "think about his behavior") actually provided an escape from reading and increased the likelihood that the problem behavior would occur. Without meaning to, the staff was reinforcing Gary's hitting. Social skills instruction, although providing Gary with needed skills, did not address the function of the behavior. Therefore, it did not decrease Gary's hitting.

In practice, designing interventions that address the relationships described in the FBA can be complicated and difficult. Summary statements about the behavior and the conditions under which it occurs do not always logically lead to the most appropriate intervention. Successful interventions require a systematic and specific methodology that links assessment results to strategies that ensure all factors affecting the behavior are addressed. Testing the intervention developed from the FBA provides a safeguard—verification that you have successfully identified the function and that the intervention accurately addresses that function.

In Chapters 2 to 5, you completed the first three steps needed to design and implement a function-based intervention. You completed an FBA by defining target and replacement behaviors, gathering information using interviews and observations, and identifying the function of the target behavior.

This section includes six chapters that are designed to teach you the next steps. You will learn to develop function-based interventions in Chapters 6 to 8, identify an appropriate measurement system in Chapter 9, test the intervention(s) in Chapter 10, and complete a BIP in Chapter 11.

CHAPTER 6

Intervention Method 1
Teach the Replacement Behavior

OUTCOMES

After reading this chapter, you will be able to

- Use the Function-Based Intervention Decision Model.
- Link the results of the FBA to an appropriate intervention method.
- Develop an intervention when the FBA results indicate the student cannot perform the replacement behavior.

A successful function-based intervention is developed using the results of the FBA. For example, if Andrea hits and pushes other students (target behavior) to gain the teacher's attention (positive reinforcement—attention), an intervention based on the FBA would provide teacher attention for the replacement behavior. Using another form of reinforcement, such as tokens for items in a school store or allowing a break, will not be effective because it does not address the function of the target behavior.

This chapter describes a specific straightforward technique for directly linking interventions to the identified function of the problem behavior. The technique sends the interventionist back to the assessment information through a series of questions that identify which of three methods will most directly address the behavioral function, decrease the problem behavior, and increase the replacement behavior. Specifically, this chapter introduces and describes the Function-Based Intervention Decision Model, identifies the three methods that must be considered when designing an intervention plan, and presents examples and discussion of the first of these methods, which is appropriate when the assessment indicates a need to teach the replacement behavior.

FUNCTION-BASED INTERVENTION METHODS
Categorizing Intervention Methods

The research describing successful function-based interventions divides intervention methods and strategies into a few basic categories. For example, Dunlap and Kern (1996) identified two categories: (a) teaching alternative (replacement) behaviors that are functionally equivalent to the problem behavior, and (b) changing the environment when assessment data indicate conditions (antecedents) that evoke or in some manner exert control over the behavior. These categories focus on manipulation of antecedent conditions; however, consequence manipulations are inherent within the strategies.

Other groupings not only include the two categories identified by Dunlap and Kern (1996), but also list consequence manipulation as a separate choice. For example, the Office of Special Education Programs (OSEP) Center on Positive Behavior Interventions and Support notes that intervention plans should include the following categories of intervention: (a) adjustments to the environment that reduce the likelihood of problems, (b) teaching replacement skills and building general competencies, and (c) manipulating consequences to promote positive behaviors and deter problems (Sugai et al., 2000).

These three basic categories comprise the methods used in the Function-Based Intervention Decision Model presented in this chapter. They are Method 1: Teach the replacement behavior, Method 2: Improve the environment, and Method 3: Adjust the contingencies. A brief description of each method is provided as follows. Detailed descriptions are provided later in this chapter and in Chapters 7 and 8.

Method 1: Teach the Replacement Behavior. Teaching skills that provide *alternatives* to problem behavior is a powerful tool for producing behavior change. Strategies described within Method 1 provide instruction to ameliorate deficits in the student's academic, adaptive, and social behavior that prevent him or her from functioning effectively in the environment in which the behavior occurs. Examples include instruction in communication, social skills, prerequisite academic skills, and self-management skills.

Method 2: Improve the Environment. In Method 2, the practitioner assesses the extent to which antecedent events that elicit problem behavior provide the most effective environment in which teaching and learning can occur. Strategies described within this method focus on eliminating or modifying aversive events so they are no longer aversive and making positive reinforcement more readily available for appropriate behavior. Examples include implementing environmental systems that provide clear and specific incentives, rules, and choices; modifying routines, physical arrangements, and organization; increasing time spent on instruction; and using effective teaching strategies.

Method 3: Adjust the Contingencies. The contingency describes the relationship of the behavior to the consequence (i.e., how often the behavior is reinforced). Strategies included within this method focus on contingency manipulations that eliminate the consequence that formerly maintained the target behavior (i.e., the specific problem identified in the FBA) and provide it for the replacement behavior. Antecedent adjustments might include a simple reminder that the contingencies have changed.

Selecting a Method and Strategy

At this point, you should already have defined the target of the intervention (the problem behavior) and the replacement behavior. If you have not defined the replacement behavior, you must do so now. Remember to choose a replacement behavior that builds the student's capacity to function in the environment, as described in Chapter 2. Next, review the assessment information to answer two simple questions that will help you decide which of the three intervention methods will facilitate identification of the most appropriate function-based intervention (see Table 6.1):

1. *Can the individual perform the replacement behavior?* If the individual cannot perform the replacement behavior, the plan must delineate strategies for teaching the behaviors the individual is expected to exhibit.

2. *Do the antecedent conditions represent effective practices for the environment in which the behavior occurs?* If the environment (e.g., instruction, routines, organization, arrangement) is not the most effective, the plan must identify strategies to make it so.

You must always ask and answer both key questions. The answers will lead you to the correct method or combination of methods for developing

---

TABLE 6.1
Key Questions

1. Can the student perform the replacement behavior?
    a. If the answer is "No," use Method 1: Teach the replacement behavior, and
    b. Ask the next question.
2. Do the antecedent conditions represent "effective educational practice"?
    a. If the answer is "No," use Method 2: Improve the environment.
    b. If the answer to both questions is "Yes," use Method 3: Adjust the contingencies.
    c. If the answer to both questions is "No," use Method 1: Teach the replacement behavior and Method 2: Improve the environment.

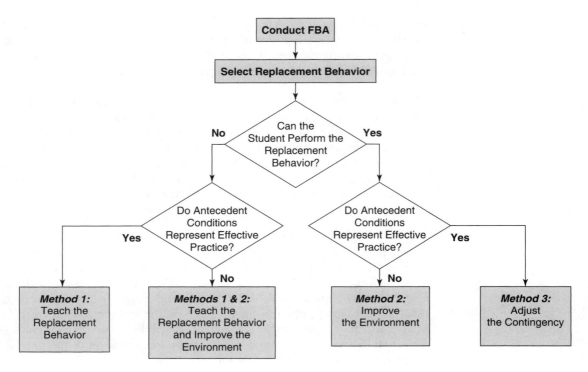

FIGURE 6.1
Function-Based Intervention Decision Model.

the function-based intervention. As shown in the Function-Based Intervention Decision Model (see Figure 6.1), four options are possible:

1. If the answer to question 1 is "No," the student cannot perform the replacement behavior, and if the answer to question 2 is "Yes," the antecedent conditions represent effective practice, use only Method 1. Method 1 delineates three strategies: (a) adjust the antecedent conditions so new behavior can be learned and aversive conditions avoided, (b) provide reinforcement that establishes the replacement behavior in the individual's repertoire, and (c) eliminate reinforcement for the target behavior if it recurs. Teaching new behaviors changes the antecedent conditions and should eliminate those that set the occasion for the target behavior to occur. Additional antecedent changes may be included in the intervention plan to ensure the individual has the opportunity to exhibit the new skill. A more detailed description of Method 1 strategies is provided later in this chapter.

2. If the answer to question 1 is "Yes," the student can perform the replacement behavior, and if the answer to question 2 is "No," the antecedent conditions do not represent effective practice, use only Method 2. Method 2 delineates three strategies: (a) adjust the environment to

eliminate conditions that elicited the target behavior, (b) provide reinforcement for the replacement behavior, and (c) eliminate reinforcement for the target behavior if it recurs. Decisions about what changes are appropriate come from the details of the interview, observation, and review of student records completed during the FBA and from the literature describing effective practice in schools and/or for specific disabilities. (However, if you are not in a school, some of the suggestions for what constitutes effective practice will still apply, and other ideas can be found in research literature in your area of expertise.) A more detailed description of Method 2 strategies is provided in Chapter 7.

3. If the answer to questions 1 and 2 is "Yes," the student can perform the replacement behavior and the antecedent conditions represent effective practice, use Method 3. Method 3 suggests strategies that manipulate the contingencies that reinforce the target behavior. Method 3 delineates three strategies: (a) adjust the reinforcement contingencies so consequences that previously reinforced the target behavior are provided for the replacement behavior, (b) withhold those consequences when the target behavior occurs, and (c) adjust the antecedents so the replacement behavior is more likely to occur. A more detailed description of Method 3 strategies is provided in Chapter 8.

4. If the answer to questions 1 and 2 is "No," the student cannot perform the replacement behavior and the antecedent (classroom) conditions do not reflect effective practice, you need to use both Method 1 and Method 2. The extra components required to include Method 2 are usually small additions to the function-based intervention you will have already constructed using Method 1. An example of an intervention that includes both Method 1 and Method 2 strategies is presented in Chapter 7.

By using the Function-Based Intervention Decision Model, you should be able to identify at least one intervention method that is appropriate for the student, behavior, and circumstances you are addressing.

Other Considerations

Use of Multiple Strategies Across Methods. Strategies within each method always address all three terms of the contingency statement. That is, interventions adjust both antecedents (A) and consequences (C) to change the behavior (B).

First, consequences are always manipulated or adjusted so the replacement behavior is reinforced and the target behavior is not. Reinforcement for the new behavior must be as effective, efficient, and as robust as it was for the target behavior. If the contingencies are not adjusted, the replacement behavior will be unable to compete with a target behavior that has a long history of producing the reinforcer more quickly and more efficiently (Horner & Day, 1991).

You must also withhold reinforcement when the target behavior occurs. This is called an **extinction procedure.** It is very important that you withhold the same reinforcer that originally reinforced the target behavior (Iwata, Pace, Cowdery, & Miltenberger, 1994). If attention originally maintained a student's off-task behavior, attention is the reinforcer that must be withheld whenever the student is off-task. If the student's off-task behavior had been maintained by some other reinforcer, such as escaping from a task (negative reinforcement— activity) or gaining a preferred activity (positive reinforcement—activity), then those reinforcers would be withheld whenever off-task behavior occurred. The point is that you must be very careful that the extinction procedure withholds the reinforcer that originally maintained the target behavior.

Second, antecedent adjustments are always included as part of the intervention. Antecedent manipulations are the primary focus of Methods 1 and 2. In Method 1, the student learns a new behavior, which means new circumstances and materials; in Method 2, the environment is changed to provide the most effective conditions for eliciting appropriate behavior. Although the focus of Method 3 is on manipulation of consequences, it also includes strategies that adjust the environment to further strengthen the replacement behavior. Again, the replacement behavior must be more effective than the target behavior and, therefore, more likely to recur. Antecedent changes recommended in Method 3 may seem relatively minor when compared with those used in Methods 1 and 2 (e.g., reminding the student of the new contingency and behavior).

Application to Differing Functions.   The basic strategies described within each method can be applied to behavior whether the function is positive or negative reinforcement. For example,

1. Alex screams and is given food (positive reinforcement—tangible). Using Method 1, we would teach the replacement behavior of asking for food.

2. When asked to complete worksheets for 60 minutes or longer, Errol throws his instructional materials on the floor and is sent to the office (negative reinforcement—activity). Using Method 2, we would restructure the environment so worksheet activities were minimized and more active instruction provided.

3. Wilma cries when placed in a group of three or more people and is sent to a "cooling down" area (negative reinforcement—attention). Using Method 1, we would teach Wilma to ask to go home or to remove herself to an area with fewer people.

4. Deion engages in long discussions with his friends when they are placed in the same work group (positive reinforcement—attention). Using Method 2, we would move Deion to another group that does not include his friends.

These examples demonstrate the flexibility and effectiveness of the methods for addressing a variety of target behaviors and functions. Additional examples and discussion are provided in the sections describing each method. The remainder of this chapter provides an in-depth treatment of the intervention method that is appropriate when the student cannot perform the replacement behavior.

METHOD 1: TEACH THE REPLACEMENT BEHAVIOR
Description

Method 1 is the proper method to use when a student lacks the skills needed to successfully function in the environment, and in particular, when the student lacks the skills needed to perform the replacement behavior. The replacement behavior may be as simple as asking for help, or it may be more complex, such as engaging in reciprocal social interactions. Chapter 2 describes criteria for choosing an appropriate replacement behavior.

In Method 1, the antecedent conditions are adjusted so new behavior can be learned and aversive conditions avoided; consequences are adjusted so the student is positively reinforced for the newly learned skill, and the consequence that previously reinforced the target behavior is withheld (see Table 6.2).

How do you know whether the individual can perform the replacement behavior? The answer depends on the task or activity associated with the target behavior and the complexity of the antecedents. However, it is likely that the individual cannot perform the replacement behavior if it has seldom, or never, been observed in the environment. Often, the functional assessment interviews and observations will provide enough information to answer this question. For example,

- The target behavior consistently occurs during oral reading. The student's test scores show that he reads three grade levels below his current placement, and both the teacher and the student interview indicate that he stumbles over words and reads very slowly.

- The target behavior occurs during gym class. The student indicates that she cannot play volleyball and that the other girls make fun of her.

- The target behavior occurs while the individual is at work or at a job training site. Observations indicate the individual has limited verbal communication skills and does not interact socially with coworkers.

TABLE 6.2
Method 1: Teach the Replacement Behavior

Key elements	• Adjust antecedent conditions so new behaviors are learned and aversive conditions avoided.
	• Provide appropriate reinforcement for the replacement behavior.
	• Withhold the consequence that previously reinforced the target behavior.

In a few cases, additional observations or interviews focused on specific questions will be necessary. Some examples that identify observation techniques and questions are provided in the next section. In addition, Example 2, presented at the end of the chapter, describes a situation in which the interview with the student provides additional information that pinpoints a deficit in communication skills.

Adjusting the Antecedent Conditions

Research focused on teaching replacement behaviors commonly teaches acceptable ways to communicate, engage in (or avoid) social interactions, manage one's own behavior, or successfully complete school or work activities. The specific forms of the replacement behavior depend on the function identified in the FBA. The forms may include

- Communication responses such as requesting a break, asking for assistance with a task, or requesting additional instruction
- Social skills such as joining a group, giving and receiving compliments, making appropriate responses to aggression, or listening and asking questions
- Academic skills that provide instruction in prerequisite or component skills
- Self-management techniques such as learning to record and evaluate one's own behavior

More complex and structured social, communicative, or instructional behaviors may also be included as part of the current or long-term intervention plan.

Communication Skills Deficit. Interventions that teach an individual to communicate wants and needs in a more acceptable manner have been used across various populations, including students with developmental disabilities, students with emotional/behavioral disorders, students at risk, and students without an identified disability (cf. Carr et al., 1999; Lane, Umbreit, & Beebe-Frankenberger, 1999). Communication strategies use a signifier (verbal or sign) to provide an individual with an alternative means to achieve the purpose served by the target behavior. The logic is as follows: If you want something, ask for it; if you want to escape something, ask to do so.

Communication deficits are not only limited to individuals with a language or speech disability, but may also include those who cannot communicate because they speak a language different from the general population and those who have not learned the needed behavior in their family, culture, or at school. In other cases, the problematic behavior may have been so effective in producing the desired result that the individual has simply not learned the needed skill. The point is, do not assume that an individual knows an acceptable way to communicate his or her needs. If you are not sure about the individual's communication skills, you can complete additional interviews and observations. Ask the individual exhibiting problem behavior, "How do you think you communicate with others?" You may also identify additional environments in which the target behavior does not occur (e.g., with parents or in another classroom). Observe and interview people in these other environments to identify differences that make communication more likely. Example 2 at the end of this section is an example of an antecedent manipulation that teaches the individual a different way to communicate.

Social Skills Deficit. Many schools include social skills instruction as part of a schoolwide plan that addresses behaviors such as bullying, fighting, and harassment. Lessons may be scheduled on a daily basis, often occurring as part of the first period of the day when students also listen to announcements. Implementation of the curriculum varies from teacher to teacher, based on differences in the amount of effort and "buy-in" they convey to students. Although many students display social skills deficits and can benefit from consistent implementation of a research-based social skills curriculum, this is not the kind of social skills instruction identified for use in Method 1.

When social skills instruction is included as part of an intervention plan, it should focus on the particular skill deficit connected to the target behavior (Lane et al., 2003). Does the preschool child who grabs toys from other children need instruction in sharing (positive reinforcement—tangible)? Can we teach the boy who pushes his way into a basketball game to wait to be chosen (positive reinforcement—activity)? Does the young woman who screams at coworkers need to learn strategies for controlling her anger (negative reinforcement—attention)? This type of social skills instruction may include both group and individual activities, but it should occur more frequently and with many more opportunities for practice than the group instruction described previously. Individual instruction provides intense and focused training. Practicing with a group of peers or the whole class allows the individual to receive the needed information without stigma, provides all students with a common experience, and enables students to practice social skills with their peers.

The interviews and observations conducted during the FBA are always a primary source of information about skill deficits. However, there are many social skills assessments and rating forms that can be used when more information is needed (e.g., Gresham, 2001). In addition, you can purchase research-based social skills curricula and programs from numerous resources (e.g., Committee for Children, National Educational Service, Pro-Ed, Research Press, Sopris West). Finally, you will find information about social skills and ideas for instruction in textbooks and other educational literature (e.g., Mercer & Mercer, 2001; Walker, Ramsey, & Gresham, 2004). Walker and his colleagues also provide a list of rules for conducting social skills training that will help ensure you are using the most effective curriculum and instructional practice. Example 1 at the end of this section provides an illustration in which social skills instruction is an appropriate strategy.

Academic Skill Deficit. Problem behavior can occur if the student does not know how to execute the task or has not previously demonstrated the skill in question. This "skill" deficit signifies that the student cannot do the task; it should not be confused with a "performance" deficit in which the student is able to perform the skill but finds it more effective to not do so (Gresham, 2002). Performance deficits are addressed with Method 3.

If the student does not have the necessary prerequisite skills or prior knowledge, you may need to conduct assessments and observations in addition to the FBA that will help identify the specific deficit. A simple strategy is to ask the teacher, student, or parent additional questions about the task or conduct additional observations while the student completes the task. An example of this strategy is provided by Jolivette, Wehby, and Hirsch (1999). They identified errors in the procedures students used to solve math problems (e.g., failure to regroup) by observing them as they worked the problem.

A more formal strategy is to complete a curriculum-based assessment that identifies the appropriate difficulty level or prerequisite skill. Roberts, Marshall, Nelson, and Albers (2001) demonstrated a procedure that included the curriculum-based assessment as part of the FBA.

The individual who knows how to execute a task but cannot perform at an acceptable level (is not fluent) also displays an academic skill deficit. The following case provides an example of the difference between a knowledge deficit and a fluency deficit. Inger exhibited off-task behavior during reading. The results of the FBA demonstrated that the behavior was maintained by negative reinforcement (i.e., Inger's behavior allowed her to escape the activity). The teacher determined that Inger could read and understand at grade level. That is, she had the knowledge to complete the task. However, during a one-on-one assessment, although Inger remained focused on the task the entire time, she needed 15 min to read a single page. It was determined that Inger had a fluency problem, and fluency can be taught. In this example, the intervention strategy was to have Inger practice reading a story and reinforce the rate at which she read (i.e., reinforce the number of words read in the time allotted, gradually increasing the number required for reinforcement). In addition, the teacher made tapes of herself reading the story at different rates. Inger listened to a tape that was just a little faster than her current reading rate and read along. After only a few stories practiced in this manner, Inger was able to read new stories at a rate that was comparable to the other children in the class.

Other Skill Deficits. The preceding discussion by no means exhausts the behaviors that may need to be taught as part of the intervention strategy. For example, disorganization and "messiness" may interfere with on-task behavior in the school or work environment. Gross and fine motor skill deficits can lead to avoidance or escape behavior during gym class, on the playground (or other social events in which gross motor activities are required), or during written assignments. When problem behavior is related to any task that the individual cannot perform because it is too difficult, Method 1 calls for you to eliminate the antecedent (the original difficult task) by teaching prerequisite skills, breaking the task into smaller units, or breaking it into component parts and teaching each component.

Self-Management Strategies. Self-management strategies include self-recording (counting and recording your own behavior), self-evaluation (making a judgment about how well you are doing), and self-reinforcement (determining whether the reinforcement has been earned and taking it). These strategies provide the student with visual and auditory cues that indicate he or she is performing the alternative behavior correctly and completely and is not engaging in the target behavior. The advantages of self-management strategies include

- Their efficacy has been demonstrated across a number of behaviors and a variety of students (Nelson, Smith, Young, & Dodd, 1991).
- Independence is inherent within the strategy and, therefore, increases the opportunity for the student to develop independent control of the behavior (e.g., Mithaug & Mithaug, 2003).
- Generalization and maintenance are enhanced because the student can implement the intervention in other environments and for longer periods of time without relying on others.

Although much of the self-management research was conducted without the benefits of an FBA, Kern, Ringdahl, Hilt, and Sterling-Turner (2001) incorporated self-management techniques within a function-based intervention. They successfully taught students to self-manage both the replacement behavior and requests for reinforcement that were functionally related to their target behaviors (i.e., in the case of positive reinforcement—attention, the student requested attention; in the case of negative reinforcement—activity, the student requested a break).

Self-management strategies are appropriate for even very young children when instruction includes modifications that simplify recording, such as the use of happy and sad faces to signify occurrence or nonoccurrence of the replacement behavior. Example 2 includes self-management as part of the intervention.

Adjusting the Consequences

Method 1 strategies change the consequences so reinforcement is provided for the replacement behavior and an extinction procedure is implemented whenever the target behavior occurs. When the replacement behavior provides an alternative to the target behavior, the consequence is functionally equivalent to that which originally reinforced the target behavior. For example, if the target behavior originally resulted in escaping a task, asking for a break provides a short escape; if the target behavior originally resulted in attention, smiling and saying "hello" provides access to attention.

However, in some cases in which the behavior is maintained by negative reinforcement, the antecedent strategies provide escape from the task or activity and the replacement behavior should be positively reinforced. In these cases, you must have correctly identified all the antecedent elements that produced the target behavior (e.g., the student does not have the prerequisite knowledge needed to complete the task) and changed the antecedent task or activity so those elements no longer exist. For example, if the target behavior originally resulted in escaping a geometry worksheet, the new task avoids the worksheet and teaches prerequisite skills, and the replacement behavior (completing the assignment) is positively reinforced. In another example, if the target behavior originally resulted in attention and/or access to the ball in a basketball game, the new activity eliminates the game, provides skill instruction in small groups, and provides positive reinforcement for both group interaction and following game rules.

Teaching the replacement behavior changes the conditions so the target behavior should no longer occur. However, it is important that you remember to identify and implement an extinction procedure as a strategy to be used when the target behavior is exhibited.

METHOD 1 EXAMPLES

This section includes three examples that link functional assessment information to an intervention using Method 1: Teach the Replacement Behavior: (a) when the function of the behavior is positive reinforcement, (b) when the function of the behavior is negative reinforcement and the intervention also provides negative reinforcement for the replacement behavior, and (c) when the function of the behavior is negative reinforcement and the intervention provides positive reinforcement for the replacement behavior. Each example includes a short discussion of issues raised by the choice of intervention strategies and how they are linked to the assessment.

Method 1: Example 1—Positive Reinforcement
Summary: Record Review, Interview, and Observation
Ronald is a sixth-grade student who exhibits behaviors that include demanding to join groups and loud talking, which sometimes escalate to pushing, yelling, and attempts to leave the area. During interviews, you are told that Ronald primarily exhibits these behaviors during gym class. In fact, no one has ever seen him behave in this manner in another class. However, Ronald indicates that he also has problems on the playground with peers who will not let him join their games.

You observe Ronald during gym class and during recess on two occasions each. During the two gym class observations, Ronald talks in a very loud voice (identified as yelling by the coach); he criticizes the coach and other players 20 times, pushes 4 times, and, on one occasion, walks to the gym door where he says he is going to leave. Ronald was sent to sit on the bench for each incident of pushing and for three of the incidents of yelling. Seventeen incidents of yelling were ignored. When Ronald said he was leaving, the coach went to get him and spent 5 min telling him that his behavior was going to get him in trouble. In all cases prior to exhibiting the target behavior, Ronald had asked for the basketball, but the other students had refused to give it to him. Ronald says he likes to play basketball, but the other kids do not like him and he gets tired of waiting.

Although Ronald also exhibited the target behavior at recess, it was less severe, other students exhibited similar behaviors, and neither the students nor the monitor responded in the same manner as the coach and players in gym class. This was the reason that Ronald's teachers were unaware that the behavior also occurred during recess. In fact, Ronald yelled at other students 15 times and pushed another student twice. Antecedents included two attempts to join the group playing basketball and 15 requests for the ball, all of which were initially refused. The consequence for 15 incidents of yelling was that Ronald got the ball or was allowed to join the group. The consequence for pushing was that Ronald was placed next to the playground monitor who talked to him for a few minutes and then sent him back to the group.

Statement of Function

Based on the interview and observations, you identify the function of the behavior as follows: When peers refuse to allow Ronald to join a game and/or take control of the ball, he pushes, yells, and threatens to leave the area until he is allowed to join, is given the ball, or receives one-on-one attention from the adult supervising the area. Ronald's target behaviors are maintained by positive reinforcement—attention and positive reinforcement—tangible/activity.

Behavior Definitions

The target behavior is disruptive and aggressive behavior that includes pushing, yelling, and attempts to leave the area.

In consultation with Ronald's teachers and parents, you define the replacement behavior as socially acceptable requests to join and play in a group that include asking politely to join the group or to get the ball while playing, waiting for a reply, and following game rules.

Function-Based Intervention

Ask the key questions:

1. *Can Ronald perform the replacement behavior?*

In this situation, you determine that Ronald does not have the prerequisite skills needed for appropriate social interaction in the two environments in which the athletic games are a component. He cannot perform the replacement behavior.

2. *Do the antecedent conditions represent effective practice?*

In this situation, you determine that antecedent conditions do represent effective practice. There are rules posted on the playground and in the gym. Students are given reminders before the class begins and the playground

TABLE 6.3
Intervention Elements for Example 1—Positive Reinforcement

Method Elements	Resulting Intervention Elements
Adjust antecedent conditions so new behaviors are learned and aversive conditions avoided.	Provide social skills instruction for Ronald (new behavior).
	Adjust the antecedent condition so Ronald briefly rehearses appropriate social skills at the beginning of class (new behavior).
	Adjust the antecedent condition so social interactions are easier, such as breaking the class into smaller groups for games (aversive conditions avoided).
Provide appropriate reinforcement for the replacement behavior.	Provide positive reinforcement for appropriate interaction (e.g., asking permission to join, complimenting other students).
Withhold the consequence that previously reinforced the target behavior.	The antecedent adjustment (i.e., making social skills easier and teaching them to Ronald) removes the conditions that occasioned the target behavior so it should no longer occur. If it does, ignore it.

monitor provides reminders when the students enter the playground. In both gym class and on the playground, students are praised and receive "good behavior" tickets (positive reinforcement) for following rules. In gym class, students are taught to play the games and are reinforced for playing correctly.

Use Method 1: Teach the Replacement Behavior. First, provide social skills instruction for Ronald and the other students in his class (see Table 6.3). At minimum, the instructions include following the rules and strategies for joining groups or activities. This provides three benefits: (a) the whole group receives instruction, which they needed based on the playground observation; (b) it allows instruction for Ronald without singling him out and further emphasizing his social skill deficits; and (c) it allows Ronald to practice the new skills with students he also sees in gym class and on the playground.

Second, adjust the antecedent condition so Ronald briefly rehearses appropriate social skills at the beginning of the class. In this example, the coach spends the first few minutes practicing class rules and game rules with the class. These practice sessions provide more information than the coach's previous reminders but take only a few additional minutes to complete.

Third, adjust the antecedent condition so social interactions are easier, such as breaking the class into smaller groups for games. This strategy allows Ronald more frequent opportunities to participate in game play, demonstrate his social skills (the replacement behavior), and receive reinforcement.

Fourth, provide positive reinforcement for appropriate interaction (e.g., asking permission to join, complimenting other students). The most powerful reinforcement for Ronald would be to allow him to enter the group as soon as he asks (positive reinforcement—activity). In the beginning, this may mean that the situation is contrived to allow Ronald to enter the game and play more often than the other students. It may not always be possible for him to enter immediately, but if he is left out of the game too long or too often, he will likely revert to the target behavior. Once the replacement behavior is established in Ronald's repertoire, consequences can return to a more natural schedule. Social reinforcement should also be used because the FBA identified positive reinforcement—attention as one of the functions of Ronald's behavior. Examples of natural reinforcement include praise from other students and the teacher, "high fives," or other indications of approval typically used in Ronald's environment and in discussions about the game.

The final strategy is to withhold reinforcement if Ronald exhibits the target behavior. This means that Ronald does not have access to the consequences that previously reinforced his behavior. He is not allowed to join the game and the teacher does not interact with Ronald, such as explaining why he cannot join the game or leave the area.

Discussion

In this example, the environmental changes are such that the student can be successful, appropriate social behavior is more likely, and the target behaviors are less likely to occur. The intervention ensures the consequence for the replacement behavior is functionally equivalent to the consequence originally provided. That is, Ronald receives both positive reinforcement—attention and positive reinforcement—activity for appropriately asking to join a game, appropriate game interactions, and waiting when necessary. To strengthen and maintain the newly learned skills most effectively, it is essential that you provide a greater magnitude of reinforcement than Ronald receives when he exhibits the target behavior.

The intervention is also designed so it does not stigmatize Ronald. The recess observation demonstrated that all students had some problems with games, and all could benefit from intervention.

Method 1: Example 2—Negative Reinforcement

Summary: Record Review, Interview, and Observation

Tara is a third-grade student who exhibits behaviors that include ripping her papers, throwing her papers on the floor or in the garbage can, making loud comments such as "This is stupid," and wandering around the classroom. Interviews with Tara's teacher reveal that the behavior occurs during math instruction and, occasionally, in the last few minutes of reading, which immediately precedes math. Two observations during reading and math include three incidents of the target behavior. Two incidents occur during math when Tara is given a worksheet of long division problems. The consequence consists of a cycle of reprimand and redirection. On one occasion, Tara is sent to the office. On both occasions, she avoids the math assignment. Another incident occurs during reading when the teacher reminds the students to turn in their math homework from the previous night. The consequence is a reprimand, after which Tara returns to her reading without turning in the assignment, again avoiding the math assignment.

Tara tells you that she loves reading and would like to do it all day long. She also likes math, but it takes too long to do the worksheets and she is tired of sitting. This information stimulates you to review the interview and observation data from a different perspective, through which you discover that reading and math together require 1 h of seatwork. Tara generally does not exhibit the target behavior until about 10 min into the math instruction.

Statement of Function

Based on the interview and observations, you identify the function of the behavior as follows: When presented with a math worksheet that immediately follows at least 30 min of seatwork in another academic task, Tara destroys her papers, throws her papers away, makes loud comments, and/or wanders around the classroom. The function of Tara's behavior is negative reinforcement—activity.

Behavior Definitions

The target behavior is defined as disruptive behavior that includes ripping papers, throwing the papers on the floor, speaking about nontask-related things in a loud voice, and leaving her seat. The replacement behavior is defined as on-task behaviors that include remaining in her seat and completing problems on the math worksheet.

Function-Based Intervention

Ask the key questions:

1. *Can Tara perform the replacement behavior?*

Think about the skills required for Tara to perform the replacement behavior. In addition to knowing how to complete the math problems, she must also be able to sit in her seat for the length of time the teacher has designated or to request a break from seatwork.

Tara's math skills have been tested, and she is able to complete the math problems on her assignments. However, she appears unable to sit in her seat for an hour and does not know how to request a break. Therefore, she cannot perform the replacement behavior. However, Tara can learn to request a break from working on math after a prescribed period of time and to monitor her own behavior (the amount of time she spends doing in-class assignments).

2. *Do the antecedent conditions represent effective practice?*

Determining the answer to this question requires additional classroom observation. The observations indicate that, yes, the antecedent conditions represent effective practices. In some cases, an hour might be too long for a student to work on in-class assignments. However, the observations reveal that the teacher varies the assignments, allows students some choices as to how the assignments will be completed, and provides opportunities for stu-

TABLE 6.4
Intervention Elements for Example 2—Negative Reinforcement

Method Elements	Resulting Intervention Elements
Adjust antecedent conditions so new behaviors are learned and aversive conditions avoided.	Teach Tara to request a break after a specified period of time (10 min in this example) (new behavior leading to avoidance of aversive condition).
	Teach Tara to self-monitor and self-record.
Provide appropriate reinforcement for the replacement behavior.	Provide positive reinforcement for working on math problems and self-monitoring (reinforcement).
	Provide negative reinforcement in the form of a break for working on math problems and requesting a break after a specified period of time (reinforcement).
Withhold the consequence that previously reinforced the target behavior.	The antecedent adjustment (i.e., teaching Tara a different way to communicate that she needs a break) removes the conditions that occasioned the target behavior so it should no longer occur. If the behavior recurs, do not allow her to escape or avoid the situation.

dents to move to different areas of the class between reading and math. She tells you that she always considered this movement to be a break. During your observation, you also noted that some students took advantage of this time, but Tara continued to read.

Use Method 1: Teach the Replacement Behavior. First, teach Tara to request a break after she has worked on her math assignment for 10 min (see Table 6.4). You identified this length of time as an appropriate interval because your observations indicated that Tara usually worked on her math assignment for about 10 min before she began exhibiting the target behavior.

Second, teach Tara to self-monitor and self-record. Tara is taught to set a timer for 10 min and to ask for a break if she has worked on and completed math problems (the replacement behavior) during this time (self-monitoring). She records her behavior by checking "yes" on a list (e.g., I was on-task, or I worked on my math assignment) she keeps at her desk.

Third, provide negative reinforcement for the replacement behavior. In this example, the function of the original behavior is provided for the replacement behavior. Tara gets to escape math (take a break) for appropriate behavior (working on her math assignment for a specified period of time). Fourth, provide positive reinforcement for self-monitoring and appropriate requests for a break. The interview forms ask the student and other interviewees about positive reinforcers. Reinforcers for Tara may consist of simply telling her that she has correctly monitored herself and taken a break. In some cases, displaying correct implementation of the replacement behavior in a graph effectively reinforces and maintains the behavior. Other preferred reinforcers may also be provided as choices within a schoolwide system that includes incentives such as points, tickets for tangibles or activities, and "caught-you-being-respectful" cards.

The final strategy is to withhold reinforcement if Tara exhibits the target behavior. This means that Tara must complete and turn in her math assignment even when she is disruptive. This must happen every time, without fail. If Tara is allowed to escape the math assignment when she is disruptive, the intervention will not be successful.

Discussion

This example demonstrates the importance of ensuring the new antecedent condition teaches appropriate skills. The intervention must be instructive in nature. One could simply adjust the antecedent (e.g., eliminate the task demand) so target behaviors are not likely to occur. However, if the task demands were appropriate in the first place, this adjustment merely avoids triggering problematic behavior and does not teach the math or self-management skills Tara needs to be successful. The adjustment would be inappropriate. The teacher might be negatively reinforced for reducing demands (i.e., the student no longer causes a problem in the classroom), but Tara would not learn appropriate behaviors that she both needs and deserves. The discussion of social validity in Chapter 12 should be reviewed in relation to this issue.

The inclusion of self-monitoring increases Tara's responsibility for the intervention, provides her with additional control over her environment, and teaches her a skill she can use in other classes. It also provides an example of student participation in the intervention process that increases the likelihood of maintenance and generalization of the replacement behavior.

In this example, Tara was able to master self-management techniques after some instruction, but other students may find this too complicated. In those cases, the teacher can signal time for a break.

This example also illustrates an intervention in which the consequence for the replacement behavior is functionally equivalent to the consequence for the target behavior. Tara received a break from math by working on her assignment for 10 minutes. Attempts to escape math by exhibiting the target behavior were extinguished.

Tara's interview and the additional observations included information that was key to developing a successful intervention.

Method 1: Example 3—Negative Reinforcement

Tara's reinforcement for the replacement behavior was functionally equivalent to that of the target behavior (i.e., she was able to avoid the task by requesting a break). In other instances of negative reinforcement, the original consequence is not provided for the replacement behavior because the antecedent is changed so it no longer evokes the target behavior. Although the original consequence is not provided, the specific changes made in the antecedent are still determined based on the function of the behavior. Example 3 illustrates this issue using a situation similar to that described in Example 2.

Summary: Record Review, Interview, and Observation

Daphne exhibited disruptive behavior in her fifth-grade classroom that included talking and laughing loudly, engaging other students in conversations, and leaving her seat. According to the teacher, the behavior occurred primarily when she asked Daphne to complete math seatwork, usually a sheet of practice problems on the lesson she had just taught. Observation confirmed the target behavior and that it occurred during math. No instances of the target behavior were observed during other classroom activities. When Daphne exhibited the behavior, the teacher (a) redirected her to her assignment, (b) warned her that she would not be allowed to go to recess if she continued, and (c) sent Daphne to the office.

Records from the previous year showed that Daphne had passed math but "had difficulty with subtraction." During the student interview, Daphne said that she hated math and that the problems were too hard. She also indicated that her mother helped her with her homework assignments.

Statement of Function

Based on the interview and observations, you identify the function of the behavior as follows: When presented with a math worksheet, Daphne talks with other students, laughs loudly, and leaves her seat without permission. The function of Daphne's behavior is negative reinforcement—activity.

Behavior Definitions

The target behavior is defined as off-task behavior that includes speaking in a loud voice, engaging other students in nontask-related conversations, and leaving her seat without permission. The replacement behavior is on-task behavior that includes remaining in her seat, completing problems on the math worksheet, and requesting help, when needed.

Function-Based Intervention

Ask the two key questions:

1. *Can Daphne perform the replacement behavior?*

The replacement behavior requires the same skills that Tara's did. Daphne must know how to complete the math problems, and she must be able to remain in her seat. We know from observation that Daphne can stay in her seat and work on assignments because she has done so in other academic areas, often for longer periods than required for math. Based on the record review and Daphne's interview, we suspect that she may not know how to complete the math problems. A short one-on-one tutoring session indicates that Daphne cannot subtract when the problem includes borrowing. The conclusion must be that Daphne cannot perform the replacement behavior because she cannot complete the math assignment.

2. *Do the antecedent conditions represent effective practice?*

Daphne's environment also represents effective practice. The teacher varies the modality in which assignments are presented, allows choices, monitors, and provides frequent feedback. However, Daphne's behavior allowed her to escape math assignments and effectively masked her academic

TABLE 6.5
Intervention Elements for Example 3—Negative Reinforcement

Method Elements	Resulting Intervention Elements
Adjust the antecedent conditions so new behaviors are learned and aversive conditions avoided.	Teach Daphne prerequisite math skills (in this case, borrowing). Change her math assignment so it addresses her deficit. This eliminates the original task demand (avoid aversive condition).
Provide appropriate reinforcement for the replacement behavior.	Provide positive reinforcement for the replacement behavior (completing math problems and correct responses).
Withhold the consequence that previously reinforced the target behavior.	Ensure the assignment is completed if the target behavior is exhibited.

skill deficit. Classroom rules, organization, and routines are also in place but proved ineffective for this particular situation.

Use Method 1. Adjust the assignment to teach Daphne the prerequisite skills, provide positive reinforcement for correct responses, and withhold reinforcement if Daphne exhibits the target behavior (see Table 6.5). In this example, you

1. Change the environment by adjusting the assignment (the antecedent) so it addresses Daphne's deficit (borrowing).

2. Teach Daphne a new skill (borrowing during subtraction).

3. Provide positive reinforcement (e.g., praise or other preferred reinforcer) for the replacement behavior (sitting in her seat while working on her math assignment).

4. Ensure Daphne completes the assignment, even if she exhibits the target behavior (by not allowing her to escape, you put the target behavior on extinction).

This plan allows the student to avoid the original set of math problems that evoked the target behavior. Because the new task is one in which the student can be successful, appropriate (on-task) behavior is more likely to occur than escape-motivated problematic behaviors.

Naturally occurring reinforcement would include praising Daphne for completed math problems and allowing her to go to the next activity, which is recess. However, this reinforcement may not be potent enough to strengthen and maintain Daphne's new behavior. The interviews you completed with her and her teacher provide information about Daphne's preferences, which will be the most powerful reinforcers you can use. These can be added to items or activities that are part of a schoolwide or classwide token system or may be provided directly to Daphne when she works on her math assignment. Reinforcement should be provided both for working on the assignment and for completing it correctly.

Discussion

When the original task is changed so completely, as it was in this case, providing the original reinforcer—escape or avoidance—is unnecessary and often inappropriate. The antecedent (the original task request) that evoked the target behavior has been removed.

One goal of adjusting antecedent conditions is to eliminate the need for the student to engage in escape-motivated behavior. The other goal is to teach the student skills that should make escape unnecessary in the future. When a student has the necessary skills to be successful, it should be possible to reintroduce the original assignment without difficulty.

SUMMARY

The term "function-based intervention" refers to the development of behavior change strategies that are directly linked to information and data gathered during the FBA. Strategies selected based on the FBA are successful because they address the antecedents and consequences that influence and maintain behavior. However, the process of linking interventions to assessment results has been complicated and difficult.

The Function-Based Intervention Decision Model described in this chapter provides a specific, straightforward technique for linking assessment results with interventions. This technique sends practitioners back to the assessment information through a series of questions that identify which of three intervention methods will most directly address the behavioral function.

The three intervention methods described in the model are

- Method 1: Teach the replacement behavior
- Method 2: Improve the environment
- Method 3: Adjust the contingencies

Each method is effective and appropriate to use whether the behavior's function is positive or negative reinforcement. Interventions designed using the three methods are multicomponent, addressing both antecedents and consequences. Methods may be combined to provide a more comprehensive intervention, when appropriate.

Two simple questions help determine which method will facilitate identification of the most appropriate function-based intervention. The first question asks whether the student can perform the replacement behavior. The second asks whether the antecedent conditions represent effective practices that evoke the replacement behavior and decrease or eliminate the target behavior. If either or both questions are answered "No," the practitioner follows the strategic guidelines in the applicable method to design a function-based intervention. If both questions are answered "Yes," contingency manipulations are recommended.

Method 1: Teach the replacement behavior was also described in this chapter. It is the appropriate method to use when the student lacks the skills necessary to successfully function in the environment and, in particular, when the student lacks the skills needed to perform the replacement behavior. In Method 1, (a) the antecedent conditions are adjusted so new behavior can be learned while aversive conditions are avoided, (b) consequences are adjusted so the student is reinforced for the newly learned skill, and (c) the consequence that originally reinforced the target behavior is withheld.

Replacement behaviors should be taught if the individual needs a more appropriate way to communicate, engage in (or avoid) social interactions, and successfully complete instructional activities. The specific forms of the replacement behavior depend on the function identified in the FBA.

Steps in Selecting an Intervention Method and Developing an Intervention Using Method 1: Teach the Replacement Behavior

The following list summarizes the steps and activities involved when using the Function-Based Intervention Decision Model to select an intervention method, and when developing an intervention for a student who cannot perform the replacement behavior.

When Selecting an Intervention Method:

1. Review FBA results.
2. Ask two questions to identify the intervention method or methods appropriate for use with the behaviors and antecedents identified in the FBA.
   - Can the student perform the replacement behavior?
     - If the answer is "No," use Method 1: Teach the replacement behavior, and
     - Ask the next question.
   - Do the antecedent conditions represent effective educational practice?
     - If the answer is "No," use Method 2: Improve the environment
     - If the answer to both questions is "Yes," use Method 3: Adjust the contingencies
     - If the answer to both questions is "No," use Methods 1 and 2.

When Method 1 has been selected:

1. Adjust the antecedent conditions so new behavior can be learned and the aversive condition avoided.
2. Provide appropriate reinforcement for the replacement behavior.
3. Withhold the consequence that previously reinforced the target behavior if it recurs.

EXERCISES

1. Betty exhibits behavior identified as disruptive tapping, which is defined as making noise by tapping on the table or book with her hands or a pencil. Tapping occurred 12 times during your observation when (a) she was given instructions for an assignment that required independent work, (b) she was listening to other students read, and (c) she waited for the teacher to transition to the next activity. The consequences for her disruptive tapping behaviors were inconsistent verbal prompts to "stop" or redirection to "get to work," as well as frequent visual attention from the teacher as he "monitored" her activities. She also received peer attention in the form of snickers and requests for her to "be quiet." Interviews and A-B-C data indicated that Betty's tapping behaviors were maintained by positive reinforcement—attention from both the teacher and her peers.

    The replacement behavior is to seek the teacher's attention by raising her hand when she requires assistance during instructional time and to seek peer attention appropriately during free time.

    a. Do you need additional information to identify whether Betty can perform the replacement behavior? If yes, describe the additional information you want to collect and how you would collect it.

    b. Assume that Betty cannot perform the replacement behavior. What is your next step?

    c. Identify the appropriate method to use and the components of an intervention based on that method.

2. Apply the model to an FBA you have previously completed or are completing. Summarize the results of interviews and observations, and identify replacement behaviors. Indicate which method to use, and use the two key questions from the model to justify your decision.

REFERENCES

Carr, E. G., Horner, R. H., Turnbull, A. P., Marquis, J., Magito-McLaughlin, D., McAtee, M. L., et al. (1999). *Positive behavior support for people with developmental disabilities: A research synthesis.* Washington, DC: American Association on Mental Retardation.

Dunlap, G., & Kern, L. (1996). Modifying instructional activities to promote desirable behaviors: A conceptual and practical framework. *School Psychology Quarterly, 11*(4), 297–312.

Gresham, F. M. (2001). Assessment of social skills in students with emotional and behavioral disorders. *Assessment for Effective Intervention, 26*(1), 51–58.

Gresham, F. M. (2002). Social skills assessment and instruction for students with emotional and behavioral disorders. In K. L. Lane, F. M. Gresham, and T. E. O'Shaughnessy (Eds.), *Interventions for children with or at risk for emotional and behavioral disorders* (pp. 242–258). Boston: Allyn & Bacon.

Horner, R. H., & Day, M. (1991). The effects of response efficiency on functionally equivalent, competing behaviors. *Journal of Applied Behavior Analysis, 24,* 719–732.

Iwata, B. A., Pace, G. M., Cowdery, G. E., & Miltenberger, R. G. (1994). What makes extinction work: An analysis of procedural form and function. *Journal of Applied Behavior Analysis, 27,* 131–144.

Jolivette, K., Wehby, J. H., & Hirsch, L. (1999). Academic strategy identification for students exhibiting inappropriate classroom behaviors. *Behavioral Disorders, 24*(3), 10–21.

Kern, L., Ringdahl, J. E., Hilt, A., & Sterling-Turner, H. E. (2001). Linking self-management procedures to functional analysis results. *Behavioral Disorders, 26*(3), 214–226.

Lane, K. L., Wehby, J., Menzies, H. M., Doukas, G. L., Munton, S. M., & Gregg, R. M. (2003). Social skills instruction for students at risk for antisocial behavior: The effects of small-group instruction. *Behavioral Disorders, 28,* 229–248.

Lane, K. L., Umbreit, J., & Beebe-Frankenberger, M. E. (1999). Functional assessment research on students with or at-risk for EBD: 1990 to the present. *Journal of Positive Behavior Interventions, 1*, 101–111.

Mercer, C. D., & Mercer, A. R. (2001). *Teaching students with learning problems*. Upper Saddle River, NJ: Merrill/Prentice Hall.

Mithaug, D. K., & Mithaug, D. E. (2003). Effects of teacher-directed versus student-directed instruction on self-management of young children with disabilities. *Journal of Applied Behavior Analysis, 36*, 133–136.

Nelson, J. R., Smith, D. J., Young, R. K., & Dodd, J. M. (1991). A review of self-management outcome research conducted with students who exhibit behavioral disorders. *Behavioral Disorders, 16*(3), 169–179.

Roberts, M. L., Marshall, J., Nelson, J. R., & Albers, C. A. (2001). Curriculum-based assessment procedures embedded within functional behavioral assessments. *School Psychology Review, 30*(2), 264–277.

Sugai, G., Horner, R., Dunlap, G., Hieneman, M., Lewis, T., Nelson, C. M., et al. (2000). Applying positive behavior support and functional behavior assessment in schools. *Journal of Positive Behavior Interventions, 2*(3), 131–143.

Walker, H. M., Ramsey, E., & Gresham, F. M. (2004). *Antisocial behavior in school: Evidence-based practices*. Belmont, CA: Thomson/Wadsworth.

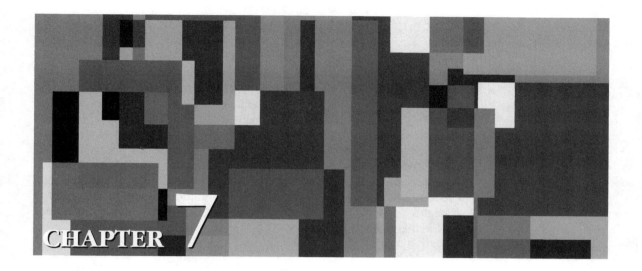

CHAPTER 7

Intervention Method 2
Improve the Environment

OUTCOMES

After reading this chapter, you will be able to

- Describe the role of antecedent manipulations in reducing problem behavior and increasing replacement behaviors.
- Identify research-based antecedent manipulations that have been successfully used to decrease problem behavior and/or increase task engagement.
- Link the results of the FBA to Method 2 of the Function-Based Intervention Decision Model.
- Develop interventions when the FBA results indicate antecedents represent ineffective classroom practices.

Chapter 6 introduced the Function-Based Intervention Decision Model and described Method 1, the appropriate method when the person is unable to perform the replacement behavior. The next step is to ask, "Do the antecedent conditions represent effective strategies in the environment in which the behavior occurs?" If the answer is "No," Method 2 should be used.

This question is appropriate, even if the student cannot perform the replacement behavior, because it focuses your attention on other antecedent conditions that may make it more difficult for the individual to acquire and maintain skills needed to perform the replacement behavior. Adjustments to antecedent conditions provide alternatives that enable you to develop an intervention that most effectively and efficiently decreases problem behavior, prevents it from recurring, and generates and maintains the replacement behavior.

This chapter describes Method 2 of the Function-Based Intervention Decision Model. Specifically, it introduces and describes a framework in which to understand antecedent strategies, provides examples of effective antecedent conditions, and provides examples and discussion of intervention strategies when the assessment indicates that antecedent conditions do not represent effective practice.

ANTECEDENT VARIABLES

This section begins with a discussion of research that addresses antecedent conditions that elicit problem behavior. The type of antecedent and the strategies used to address them will form the basis for an understanding of the role of antecedent manipulations in function-based interventions. Readings related to effective instruction provide further strategies for changing antecedents. Finally, the section considers possible limitations and additional recommendations for effective practices.

Evidence from FBA Research

We know that we can reduce problem behavior by changing antecedent conditions when the changes are based on the results of an FBA. In a number of studies, students with disabilities exhibited fewer problem behaviors and increased replacement behaviors when antecedent conditions were manipulated. Two recent reviews provide some indication of the scope of antecedent variables, intervention strategies, and the populations involved in these studies. Kern, Choutka, and Sokol (2002) reviewed 24 studies involving 42 participants that ranged in age from 1 year old to adult. Conroy and Stichter (2003) identified 17 studies involving 42 participants in the same age range as Kern et al.'s (2002) study. Only four studies were common to both reviews. Examination of the reviews and current publications provided the following information.

The range of diagnoses and behaviors that were addressed by these studies suggests that antecedent interventions are effective and appropriate for children and adults with an assortment of challenges. Participants' diagnoses included mental retardation, autism, emotional and behavioral disorders, ADHD, mental illness, severe disability, developmental disabilities, hearing and vision impairment, and at risk. Some individuals without disabilities were also included. Problem behaviors were aggression, disruption, off-task, noncompliance, self-injury, inappropriate social behavior, and elopement (running away).

TABLE 7.1
Research-Based Antecedent Variables

Antecedent Variables	Examples
Academic task	Too difficult
	Lengthy completion time required
	Student not interested in material
	No choices
Environmental factors	Wait time with no activity
	Change in scheduled activities with no warning
	Length of time spent on bus
	Far from teacher
	Talking to peers in close proximity
	Lack of materials
	Level of praise
Social factors	Group discussion or activities
Physiological factors	Sleep deprivation
	Hunger

Most important, the studies provide an inventory of antecedent conditions that have been shown to set the occasion for problem behavior to occur. These conditions included task materials and presentation, environmental arrangements in and outside the classroom, and physiological states (see Table 7.1).

By far, the largest number of problem behaviors was related to academic tasks. Antecedents included tasks that were too long or were not at the correct difficulty level for the student, tasks and instruction that were not varied, an absence of student choice, or tasks and materials that were not matched to the student's interest or preference (e.g., tasks were not immediately useful and practical, student was not interested in reading material).

The second largest category of antecedent conditions addressed environmental arrangements and routines. These included distracting classroom arrangements, noisy peer activity, routine procedures that were not in place or well managed, seating assignments, transitions that were not well planned, and changes in routine or transitions effected without a warning.

Social and physiological antecedents represented a small portion of studies. Social antecedents primarily addressed group discussion or activities. Physiological antecedents addressed lack of sleep and hunger.

In each study, antecedents were altered so they no longer included the event or condition that set the occasion for the behavior targeted for intervention. The revised conditions prevented the problem behavior from occurring and increased the occurrence of the replacement behavior.

Literature on Effective Instruction

There is a general consensus that certain antecedent conditions can prevent or minimize the occurrence of problem behavior and increase time engaged in learning or related task behaviors. The phenomenon of behavioral allocation provides an explanation of the mechanism by which prevention can occur. **Behavioral allocation** suggests that there is a limited amount of time in which behavior can occur such that increased time exhibiting one behavior decreases the amount of time available for exhibiting another behavior. You can probably think of many cases in which behavioral allocation is evident in your own life.

For example, if you spend 3 h reading for class, you have less time in which to surf the net, or vice versa. For the purposes of this discussion, if a student increases the amount of time engaged in an academic task, for example, completing math problems, there will be less time available for engaging in shoving the student standing next to him or her, playing with random objects on his or her desk, or arguing about the assignment. The catch is that you must provide the most effective conditions in which to present the math problem, which brings us to effective practices.

The conditions that decrease problem behavior and increase task engagement include a range of effective organizational, management, and instructional practices. They have been prescribed for preschool children (e.g., McGee & Daly, 1999) and students exhibiting antisocial behavior (e.g., Walker, Ramsey, & Gresham, 2004), and as part of schoolwide positive intervention systems (e.g., Horner & Sugai, 2000). These conditions are included within the broad range of effective instruction research and are some of the most commonly manipulated antecedent variables described in the FBA research discussed earlier (e.g., Conroy & Stichter, 2003; Kern et al., 2002).

Antecedent variables identified for preventing problem behavior can be divided into three categories. One group of strategies provides suggestions for designing an **optimal structure and organization** for the environment. They address room arrangement, seating assignments, posted schedules, established and independent routines, and activities that ease transitions and reduce wait or dead time. A second group describes **effective management practices.** These include a clearly identified incentive plan, a clearly stated behavior management plan, a small number of positively stated rules, teaching expected behaviors, and planned reminders of expectations. The third group identifies effective practices for delivering instruction. These include establishing instructional objectives, planned variation of instruction, using a variety of preferred or high-interest materials, relevant practice (both independent and guided), mastery learning, high teacher expectations, assurance that students have prerequisite skills, instructional match, and flexibility that allows some student choice (see Table 7.2).

In addition to preventing problem behavior, effective instruction research specifies a number of antecedent variables that result in increased attention to task and improved correct responding (Algozzine, Ysseldyke, & Elliott, 1997; Mastropieri & Scruggs, 2002; Ysseldyke & Christenson, 1993). Ysseldyke

TABLE 7.2
Examples of Preventive Antecedent Conditions

Instructional Delivery	Structure and Organization of Environment	Behavior Management
Establish instructional objectives	Arrange the room for success	Clearly state the incentive plan
Provide instructional variation	Well planned seat assignments	Clearly state behavior management plan
Vary preferred materials	Post schedules	Establish a small number of positively stated rules
Provide high-interest material	Establish independent routines	Teach expected behaviors
Vary student response modes	Provide activities to ease transitions	Prompt expected behavior
Use relevant practice	Reduce wait/dead time	
Ensure students have prerequisite skills	Warn students before transitions	
Include student choice		

and Christenson developed a comprehensive system of 12 checklists that can be used to assess the instructional environment and effective practices in school settings. The Instructional Environment System-II (TIES-II) includes 190 items in the areas of instructional presentation, classroom environment, teacher expectations, cognitive emphasis, motivational strategies, relevant practice, academic engaged time, informed feedback, adaptive instruction, progress evaluation, instructional planning, and student understanding. Five additional checklists can be used to identify effective practices in the home.

Other Considerations

First, the strategies identified previously have been successfully applied in various settings and with many different students, including those with disabilities. However, most of the original research was conducted with general education students and used correlations to assess the relationship between the instructional strategy and basic skills achievement. A few included special education or low-achieving students and another smaller group of studies assessed the impact of instructional practices using only special education students. This means that these strategies may not define the most effective antecedents for a specific student. For example, a young child with autism may be unable to sit in a large group, even for very short periods of time, despite reports that indicate 10 min of large-group instruction is an effective strategy with children his or her age. Students diagnosed with ADHD may need shorter practice periods or other modifications (e.g., using a computer instead of a pencil) to complete their work. Some students with disabilities may need clearer information about rules, additional reminders, or a picture schedule. Students with emotional and behavioral disorders may need more choices of when and how they will complete an assignment.

Second, although this discussion has centered on effective practices in school settings, there are similar descriptions of effective practices in other environments. For example, Bredekamp and Copple (1997) summarized developmentally appropriate practices (DAPs) in preschool settings, whereas Knowles, Holton, and Swanson (2005) summarized effective practices in adult education settings.

Third, although it is important to design an environment in which the antecedents provide the best support for students, function-based interventions always derive from the FBA, not the correlational literature on effective instructional practices. Even the most effective environment will not remediate a problem behavior if it does not address the function of the behavior.

METHOD 2: IMPROVE THE ENVIRONMENT
Description

This method is appropriate when (a) antecedent conditions do not conform to effective practice, and (b) the target behavior has more efficiently and reliably resulted in the consequence that maintains it. Let us consider this statement.

First, when antecedent practices do not conform to effective practice, the conditions that prevent problem behavior and increase appropriate responding are not present. Although some students exhibit appropriate behavior under less than optimal conditions, the FBA informs us that the student we have assessed does not. Of equal importance, we know that it may be difficult to generate and maintain a replacement behavior, especially one that is not currently in the student's repertoire (see Chapter 6), in classrooms in which instruction and management practices are less than effective.

The second part of the statement means that the problem behavior occurs because the student gets what he or she wants more quickly (e.g., immediately) and more consistently (e.g., every time) than anything else he's done. For example, John kicks, screams, and bites to escape circle time (negative reinforcement—activity). The teacher's aide immediately removes him from the circle every time he exhibits this behavior. When John raises his hand to ask for a break (replacement behavior), the teacher rarely or never allows him to take a break and sometimes does not even acknowledge that he is raising his hand.

At any given moment during circle time, John can choose to raise his hand or he can choose the alternative of kicking, screaming, and biting (target behavior). The Matching Law helps us understand why he chooses the target behavior (Herrnstein, 1961). The **Matching Law** provides a way to predict

TABLE 7.3
Method 2: Improve the Environment

Key elements	• Adjust antecedent variables so the conditions that set the occasion for the target behavior are eliminated and new conditions are established in which the replacement behavior is more likely to occur. • Provide appropriate positive reinforcement for replacement behavior. • Withhold the consequence that previously reinforced the target behavior.

choices based on rate of reinforcement for competing behaviors, quality and immediacy of reinforcement, and the effort each behavior requires (see Billington & DiTommaso, 2003, for an overview of basic choice research and the Matching Law). For the purposes of this discussion, the Matching Law predicts that John will only raise his hand if that behavior secures reinforcement as easily, quickly, and reliably as the target behavior did. Because it does not, John is likely to continue to kick, scream, and bite when he wants out of circle.

The components of Method 2 are as follows:

• Adjust the antecedent variables so the reason the individual exhibited the target behavior is eliminated and the new conditions make it very likely that the replacement behavior will occur.

• Provide appropriate positive reinforcement when the replacement behavior occurs.

• Withhold reinforcement if the target behavior occurs (see Table 7.3).

Linking the FBA to an Antecedent Intervention

What is the best way to determine the answer to Question 2? In most cases, interviews and observations conducted as part of the FBA provide the information you need. Remember, the "antecedent" refers not only to the specific stimulus (or event) that immediately precedes a behavior, but also to the entire context or situation in which the behavior occurs.

First, review the interview and observation information to identify antecedents that occur prior to the target behavior (see Table 7.4). An FBA conducted for Tak will provide an example as we work through the steps in the process. Tak leaves his seat without permission, talks to other students during instructional time, and slides off his chair onto the floor, refusing to rise.

Review the Interviews. Tak's teacher tells you that his problem behaviors occur intermittently during all instructional activities and she does not know what starts them. She estimates that the behaviors occur about 50% of the time.

TABLE 7.4
Procedures to Identify the Changes Needed to Improve the Environment

Step	Procedures
1	Conduct FBA.
2	Identify the function of the problem behavior.
3	Determine if the student can perform the replacement behavior.
4	Determine if the antecedent conditions represent effective practice.
5	Review interview and observation data to pinpoint the relevant antecedent conditions.
6	Compare the antecedent conditions you observed to those considered effective practice.
7	Adjust antecedent conditions so they represent effective practice.
8	Complete the intervention with the consequence components of Method 2.

Comment: This information provides only a little help. The teacher has not specified any particular curriculum area or time of day.

Further questioning reveals that Tak works at his grade level and completes most of his assignments.

Comment: This information suggests that the problem is not the task but some other environmental condition. You definitely need to observe during various activities and should have no trouble observing the behavior because of its high rate.

Tak tells you he likes all subjects and does not have a problem completing assignments. He also says that everyone in the class does what he does, and he does not understand why you and the teacher are picking on him.

Comment: Again, not much help. However, Tak's interview provides more evidence that the problematic antecedent is something other than the task.

Review the Observation.   Your observation reveals that Tak leaves his seat to sharpen his pencil, drop the completed assignment into the designated bin, and go to the bathroom. He talks to other students when he is out of his seat and during transitions between activities. You observe other students leave their seats and talk to each other during class, but Tak's voice is louder and he leaves his seat a little more frequently. During the observation, Tak leaves his seat and talks with other students 17 times and slides onto the floor 4 times. When he leaves his seat, the antecedents are (a) he finishes his assignment before the other students (11 times), or (b) there is a lag between activities (6 times). When Tak slides onto the floor (4 times), the antecedent is that the teacher reprimands him for leaving his seat and talking to other students.

> **Comment:** Tak exhibits the target behaviors when he has
> nothing to do, during transitions or wait/dead time, and when
> he has been reprimanded. In addition, he is louder than the
> other students, which may indicate he does not understand the
> teacher's requirements about the volume she expects when
> students interact in the classroom.

Next, identify the function of the behavior. In each instance, Tak gained attention from the teacher and other students. The function of his behavior is positive reinforcement—attention.

Finally, compare the antecedent conditions you observed with those considered to be effective practices.

> **Comment:** For this FBA, you want to know about routines,
> what strategies to use during wait time and transitions, and how
> to help Tak identify and follow the teacher's expectations.

Effective practices include establishing independent routines, providing high-interest activities when assignments are completed, providing activities during transitions, clearly defining expectations, reminding students about expected behaviors in advance of an activity, continuously monitoring compliance with expected behaviors, and handling disruptive behavior immediately.

> **Comment:** The teacher has established independent routines,
> and materials are located in appropriate areas of the classroom.
> However, effective practice research suggests that Tak will be
> less likely to exhibit the target behavior if the teacher also
> (a) provides high-interest activities that he can access independ-
> ently during wait time, (b) reviews expected behaviors with all
> students prior to beginning a task, (c) posts expected behaviors,
> and (d) provides more frequent reminders about expected
> behaviors. Changing antecedents to conform to effective practice
> forms the beginning of the intervention plan. Consequence ma-
> nipulations complete the intervention. Both are based on the
> function of the behavior.

In most cases, the initial interview and observation will include the information you need to identify relevant antecedents. In some cases, questions raised during the observation require additional information from the teacher or the student. Sometimes these questions lead to more observations that continue for longer periods of time, for additional days, at different times, or in areas other than the one in which the target behavior generally occurs. For example, two observations may indicate that Stephen talks to Jason when he stands in line or walks in close proximity to him. Three observations or one extending over a longer period of time may reveal that expected line behaviors are not discussed, rules are not posted, and the students often line up 3 to 5 min before they are to leave an area. Similarly, one observation indicates that Christine slides to the floor and rocks her desk when presented with a math task. Additional observations confirm that procedures for completing the task are not clearly specified, math activities frequently address skills already learned and/or are not important for learning current material, and there is a lack of variety in the materials and modes of presentation.

In a small number of cases, you may have to do more extensive assessment. An example will help clarify what this means when applied to the classroom. Taylor throws tantrums when presented with a reading worksheet. The FBA indicates that the function of the tantrum behavior is negative reinforcement—activity. Our observation indicates that reading worksheets evoke the target behavior. The question we must ask ourselves is why this is so. Is it because the reading is too difficult? Or too easy? Is the length of the activity too long? Does it follow a similar activity so there is no variety in the presentation? Does it require too much writing? Further observation and testing will provide the answers to these questions and will help pinpoint the specific antecedent adjustments that will have the greatest potential for success.

Structural analysis is another method you can use to identify specific information about the source of the target behavior. Structural analysis of antecedents, completed as part of the FBA, systematically manipulates antecedent events, while holding the consequence constant to establish functional relationships between the antecedent and the behavior (e.g., Peck, Sasso, & Jolivette, 1997; Umbreit & Blair, 1997).

A structural analysis completed as part of Taylor's FBA could manipulate the number of items by comparing Taylor's behavior when the reading worksheet contains 25 items (as it currently does) versus when it contains 12 items. If the target behavior occurs in both cases, we know that the number of items on the worksheet is not the relevant antecedent. A second manipulation could be to change the order in which reading instruction occurs. An example would be to compare Taylor's behavior when reading instruction follows science (the current order) versus when it precedes science. If the target behavior occurs under both conditions, we know we have not yet identified the relevant antecedent.

A third example is to assess Taylor's reading skills to determine whether the worksheets are too easy or too difficult. This can be done by embedding curriculum-based assessment within the FBA (as described in Chapter 6). The point is, you must continue the process of interview, observation, and, if needed, more formal assessment as long as there are questions about the relationship between the antecedent, the behavior, and the consequence.

METHOD 2 EXAMPLES

This section includes three examples. The first two link functional assessment information to an intervention when only Method 2: Improve the environment is used. The first example demonstrates the method when the function of the behavior is positive reinforcement. The second example demonstrates the method when the function of the behavior is negative reinforcement. The third example describes a situation that calls for using Methods 1 and 2. Remember, you always need to ask both key questions, and the answer to each question could be "No." If the student cannot perform the replacement behavior and the antecedents do not represent effective practice, both methods will be needed. Each example in this section includes a short discussion of issues raised by the choice of intervention strategies and how the strategies are linked to the assessment.

Method 2: Example 1—Positive Reinforcement

Summary: Record Review, Interview, and Observation

Carl, a fourth-grade student, has been referred for talking to other children, making faces, and telling jokes during class. The teacher's interview indicates that this behavior occurs frequently throughout the day, regardless of the lesson assigned. When he is redirected to the assignment, Carl is often noncompliant, continuing the off-task conversation until the teacher finally sends him to the office. She also tells you that Carl can complete his assignments, but his behavior interferes to such an extent that he is failing three subjects, and she is considering referring him for special services. According to her estimate, Carl exhibits the target behavior during 60% of his class time.

Carl insists that there is nothing wrong with his behavior and that his teacher is "out to get him." He does not find the assignments difficult; he simply wants to talk to his friends. The review of Carl's records shows only one mention of similar disruptive behaviors when Carl was in second grade. Carl's mother tells you he is a very social child who enjoys playing with friends after school and on weekends. She is worried about him failing but does not know what to do about his behavior.

You observe Carl on 2 consecutive days for 30 min in the morning and 30 min after lunch. During these observations, the target behavior occurs 31, 36, 15, and 29 times, respectively. In every case, the students laughed at and/or spoke to Carl, or the teacher reprimanded him and redirected him to his assignment. The third observation, in which the target behavior occurred only 15 times, was particularly important because it pointed to differences in the antecedents between those times when Carl did and did not exhibit the behavior. When Carl was working on individual assignments at his desk, antecedents included (a) another student soliciting Carl's attention (15% of incidents), and (b) students walking past his desk (85% of incidents). You observed an almost steady stream of students walking past Carl's desk to get to the pencil sharpener, which is directly behind him, and the tray for completed assignments, which is directly across from him. However, when the teacher taught a lesson, students (including Carl) stayed in their seats and focused their attention on the teacher.

The observations also provided an indication of how long Carl works on assigned tasks. During the third observation, he attended to the teacher for 20 min before exhibiting the target behavior. In the remaining observations, he worked on tasks an average of 10 min before exhibiting the target behavior.

Statement of Function

Based on the interview and observations, you identify the function of the behavior as follows: When peers are in close proximity to Carl and not engaged in an academic task, Carl engages in conversations that are not task related and fails to complete assignments. Carl's problem behaviors are maintained by positive reinforcement from the other children and the teacher (positive reinforcement—attention).

Behavior Definitions

In consultation with the teacher, you define Carl's target behavior as off-task, which includes talking to other students, making faces, and telling jokes during class. You define the replacement behavior as on-task (i.e., working on and completing his assignment, and raising his hand when he needs assistance).

Function-Based Intervention

Ask the key questions:

   1. *Can Carl perform the replacement behavior?*

   In this instance, all indications are that Carl can perform the replacement behavior. The record review and your observation confirmed the information the teacher provided during the interview. First, Carl's test scores show that he is functioning above grade level in reading and math. Second, he sat quietly, listened to the teacher's instruction, and raised his hand to be called on during a large part of the observation in which the teacher presented a lesson to the class.

   2. *Do the antecedent conditions represent effective educational practice?*

   As an education professional, you know that effective practices are those that arrange the environment and routines so all functions necessary for effective instruction can be accomplished without distracting students. You believe Carl will refrain from talking to other students if the teacher rearranges the room so high traffic areas, such as the pencil sharpener and bins containing class material, are positioned where Carl has less contact with others trying to access those items.

   Use Method 2: Improve the Environment. First, eliminate the antecedent conditions that set the occasion for the target behavior by moving Carl to a quieter, less congested area of the room (see Table 7.5). Discussions with the teacher and your observation will identify an appropriate location. Another option is to leave Carl where he is but move the pencil sharpener and bins so Carl's classmates no longer walk past him when they want to use either of these items. This is an appropriate strategy if the location of these items results in problem behavior for other students as well.

   Second, establish new conditions in which the replacement behavior is more likely to occur by providing Carl with additional reminders of the expected classroom behavior. These are those behaviors you identified

TABLE 7.5
Intervention Elements for Example 1—Positive Reinforcement

Method Elements	Resulting Intervention Elements
Adjust the antecedent conditions so the conditions that set the occasion for the target behavior are eliminated and the replacement behavior is more likely to occur.	Move Carl to a quieter, less congested area of the room, or move the pencil sharpener and bins.
	Provide Carl with additional reminders of the expected classroom behavior (replacement behavior).
Provide appropriate reinforcement for the replacement behavior.	Set a reinforcement schedule that includes positive social reinforcement from teachers and opportunities for Carl to interact with his peers based on task completion, raising his hand, and attending.
Withhold the consequence that previously reinforced the target behavior when it occurs.	The antecedent adjustment (i.e., moving Carl) removes the conditions that occasioned the target behavior so it should no longer occur. If it does, ignore the behavior.

earlier as the replacement behaviors. An effective management strategy is to provide all students with reminders about expected behavior in advance of an activity. However, Carl may need additional, tangible reminders as you begin the intervention. One method would be for the teacher to verbally remind Carl before each class. Another would be to have Carl recite expected behaviors. A third would be to provide Carl with a list of expected behaviors. You may also teach him to use the list as part of a self-monitoring strategy. As noted in Chapter 6, when appropriately taught and applied, self-monitoring allows the student to participate in the implementation of the intervention, as well as assists with generalization and maintenance.

Third, provide Carl with increased positive reinforcement for quietly working on and completing his in-class assignment and raising his hand if he needs assistance (replacement behavior). The results of Carl's FBA showed that his preferred reinforcement is attention from the teacher and his peers. The teacher should provide attention and praise when Carl exhibits the replacement behavior. Use the observation information to help you set a reinforcement schedule. Carl was able to attend to task 20 min when no one walked past him and an average of 10 min when they did. A safe schedule would be to begin by reinforcing Carl approximately every 15 min. You can then gradually increase the amount of on-task time required for reinforcement.

Because peer attention was the principal reinforcer of Carl's target behavior, it will be a powerful reinforcer for the replacement behavior if you provide Carl additional opportunities to interact with his peers. Except at lunch and recess, peer interactions can be a difficult reinforcer to orchestrate because of its potential to disrupt the learning environment. A possible solution is to use a token system that includes peer interactions as one of the exchanges. Tokens offer several advantages—they can be delivered frequently, peer interaction can be scheduled when it will not disrupt learning, and tokens are easy to fade when use of the replacement behavior is well established (see Chapter 12).

The final strategy is to withhold attention when the target behavior occurs. The intervention adjusts the antecedent conditions so the target behavior should not occur. However, if it does, you need to be prepared with the proper response. The teacher and other students should ignore Carl if he exhibits the target behavior. Remember the discussion about extinction in Chapter 6? The teacher should only respond to questions when Carl raises his hand. Ensure the whole class understands the expectations. Other students can be instructed to ignore anyone who speaks to them during the time they are working on assignments. In this manner, the instructions do not call attention to the fact that Carl has a BIP, but they make it less likely that his peers will reinforce him.

Discussion

For Carl, the antecedent conditions that set the occasion for the target behavior are removed. Instead, he is reinforced for exhibiting the replacement behavior. Under the new antecedent conditions, the target behavior is unlikely to occur. If it does occur, the intervention ensures that Carl will not receive attention.

The consequence for the replacement behavior is functionally equivalent to the consequence originally provided for the target behavior. That is, Carl receives positive reinforcement—attention from both the teacher and his peers. The use of self-monitoring and tokens increases control over fading the reinforcement schedule during the maintenance phase of the intervention. Chapter 12 provides information about maintenance and generalization in function-based interventions.

Method 2: Example 2—Negative Reinforcement

Summary: Record Review, Interview, and Observation

Dina, a 4-year-old girl in an early childhood education setting, leaves "morning circle" on a daily basis. During morning circle, the teacher and assistant gather all 20 children in the classroom into a circle on the floor, while the teacher presents instructional information such as months of the year, days of the week, and numbers. The circle is scheduled for 35 min, but Dina usually stays for approximately 10 min before running to the dramatic play area to dress and feed the dolls. When the assistant attempts to get her back to the circle, she resists by throwing a tantrum (target behavior). Specifically, she screams very loudly, kicks anyone who tries to get near her, and lies on the floor.

The teacher tells you that morning circle is important and Dina must participate. If she leaves Dina alone, other children begin watching her instead of the teacher. If the assistant tries to get Dina to come back to the circle, Dina throws a tantrum and no one can hear the teacher.

During your observations, you notice that Dina readily comes to morning circle and stays in the circle for 12 to 15 min. After that time, she leaves the circle, goes to the dramatic play area, and ignores the teacher. You also confirm that the children watch Dina instead of the teacher and that Dina resists returning to the circle by screaming, kicking, and lying on the floor. In all cases, the consequence of Dina's behavior is that she does not sit in the circle. When you try to interview Dina, she tells you that her mother told her not to talk to strangers. An interview with her mother indicates that Dina only sits for short periods of time at home and prefers imaginative play to all other activities.

Statement of Function

Based on the interview and observations, you identify the function of the behavior as follows: After sitting in a large group activity for 12 to 15 min, Dina leaves the activity and resists returning by throwing a tantrum. Dina's problem behaviors are maintained by negative reinforcement—activity.

Behavior Definitions

In consultation with the teacher, you define Dina's target behavior as tantrums, which include kicking, screaming, and lying on the floor. You define the replacement behavior as on-task behavior, which includes sitting in the circle, looking at the teacher, and responding to questions for the length of the activity.

Function-Based Intervention

Ask the key questions:

1. *Can Dina perform the replacement behavior?*

Dina has demonstrated that she can participate in morning circle for 12 to 15 min, but not for the 30 min the circle is scheduled. Remember the example of Tara in Chapter 6? Tara also could not sit for the length of time designated for the activity. However, the differences between Dina and Tara are apparent when you ask the second question.

2. *Do the antecedent conditions represent effective educational practice?*

The answer to this question is that the antecedent conditions do not represent effective practice. First, all 20 children are in the circle at the same time. Good practice suggests the groups should be smaller (maybe two groups with no more than 10 students in each). Second, group instruction for children Dina's age should be time limited. Dina cannot sit for 30 min, nor should she have to. You believe that Dina will stay in the group and

TABLE 7.6
Intervention Elements for Example 2—Negative Reinforcement

Method Elements	Resulting Intervention Elements
Adjust the antecedent conditions so the conditions that set the occasion for the target behavior are eliminated and the replacement behavior is more likely to occur.	Reduce the number of children in the circle. Reduce the time that children have to sit in morning circle to 15 min.
Provide appropriate reinforcement for the replacement behavior.	Provide positive reinforcement for sitting in the circle and participating in the activities (replacement behavior).
Withhold the consequence that previously reinforced the target behavior when it occurs.	The antecedent adjustment (i.e., reducing the time in the circle) removes the conditions that occasioned the target behavior so it should no longer occur. If it does, Dina should not be allowed to play in other areas of the room and should be returned to the circle.

participate (replacement behavior) if the size of the group is reduced and if the activity is limited to 15 min.

Use Method 2: Improve the Environment. Eliminate the antecedent conditions that set the occasion for the target behavior, and establish new conditions in which the replacement behavior is more likely to occur by eliminating the large group. Place children in two smaller groups of 10 children each and provide morning circle for each group separately. Smaller groups will allow more individual attention and more frequent participation by each child (see Table 7.6). The second antecedent strategy is to limit morning circle to 15 min, following DAP guidelines.

The antecedent strategies have permanently changed the activity so the conditions that caused Dina to exhibit the target behavior no longer exist. She can permanently avoid the activity.

Third, provide Dina and the other children with increased positive reinforcement for participating in the circle. Dina's mother and teacher also indicated that she liked "being the center of attention" and that she was very happy to be recognized for her accomplishments. When they were questioned further, it appeared that Dina liked acknowledgment in the form of praise and that she liked to talk. The teacher will focus on these two areas for positive reinforcement, both of which provide attention for the replacement behavior. Teachers will praise Dina for being in the circle, listening, and responding to questions. They will also give Dina more frequent opportunities for attention by calling on her to respond to questions and ideas presented during group. As the intervention proves successful, attention can be gradually reduced to a more natural rate. Although Dina is the focus of the intervention, the other children should also be reinforced at a slightly higher rate for paying attention during circle time.

If the target behavior recurs, the final strategy is to withhold the consequence that previously reinforced it. If Dina should leave the circle, prevent her from playing in other areas and always return her to the circle once the tantrum is over. Reinforce the other children for continuing to participate in the circle rather than watching Dina.

Discussion

In this example, Dina's behavior demonstrated that she could not sit for the length of time required to participate in morning circle activities. Asking whether the antecedents represent effective practice in an early childhood setting correctly identified an intervention that adjusted teacher expectations rather than teaching Dina to sit longer.

One might also argue that decreasing the number of children in the group was not a necessary component for changing Dina's behavior because she demonstrated that she could sit in a large group. This strategy was included because the teachers were interested in implementing developmentally appropriate practice (DAP) more fully in the preschool. In other situations, you may find it difficult to implement all the intervention strategies because of staff or time limitations. When this occurs, you can test each component of the intervention to see which is necessary for behavior change to occur (see Chapter 10).

The intervention included positive reinforcement for sitting in the circle. This is essential to ensure Dina consistently exhibits the replacement behavior. Happily, the need to reinforce Dina coincided with the staff's desire to increase their use of DAP. Dina's preferred reinforcers were activities that were interesting and fun, as well as interactions with the teacher. Because DAP also calls for using varied activities and materials and making learning fun, the staff were able to implement Dina's reinforcement naturally within the context of their new daily routine.

When the intervention changes the antecedent so the aversive conditions that elicited the target behavior are no longer present, as they did in this case, it is inappropriate to provide escape as a reinforcer. The goal of adjusting antecedent conditions (also discussed in Example 3 in Chapter 6) is to eliminate the need for escape-motivated behavior and to teach the student a skill (i.e., on-task behavior in this example) that is maintained long term by positive consequences available in the environment. The most efficient way to get to this point is if appropriate behavior comes under the control of positive reinforcers.

Methods 1 and 2: Example 3—Positive and Negative Reinforcement

Remember the example of Charlie in Chapter 5. The function of his behavior was identified as both positive reinforcement—attention and negative reinforcement—tangible/activities. This example uses the data gathered in Charlie's FBA to develop an intervention that addresses both Method 1 and Method 2 elements.

Summary: Record Review, Interview, and Observation

Charlie is a 9-year-old boy in the third grade. His classroom teacher referred him for special education services because he has problems with handwriting. He has not yet been found eligible for services. She identified Charlie's problem as off-task behavior that includes talking with peers, walking around the room, repeatedly restarting assignments, and rooting around in his desk or backpack. The behavior interferes with his ability to learn and complete his work.

During the interview she explained that the behavior occurs under two conditions: (a) shortly after he is presented with a task that calls for extended writing, such as developing three or more complete sentences around a single theme; and (b) when he is seated next to certain classroom peers, who the teacher reports are Charlie's friends. The consequence of condition one is that Charlie fails to complete his work. The consequence of condition two is his friends attend to him with the result that they are all off-task.

Your interview with Charlie confirms the teacher's perceptions and adds other details. Charlie reports that gym class and being with his friends are probably his favorite activities in school. He most dislikes the morning writing tasks and does not really understand how to write paragraphs. Charlie recognizes his off-task behavior as a problem only in that he "gets in trouble" more than other students.

Three observations are conducted during morning classroom routines, when much of the off-task behavior occurs. You witness several occurrences of off-task behavior during each observation. The antecedents of Charlie's off-task behavior include (a) the presentation of handwriting tasks that involve developing paragraphs and (b) proximity to specific peers. You also discern that the consequences do indeed include failure to complete work and social responses from peers around him.

Statement of Function

Review of the Function Matrix produces two function statements:

1. When seated in the proximity of certain peers, Charlie engages in off-task behavior (e.g., talking with peers, walking around the room, repeatedly restarting assignments, rooting around in his desk or backpack) to gain peer attention (positive reinforcement—attention).

2. When asked to complete tasks that require writing paragraphs, Charlie engages in off-task behavior (e.g., talking with peers, walking around the room, repeatedly restarting assignments, rooting around in his desk or backpack) to escape the activity (negative reinforcement—activity).

Behavior Definitions

In consultation with the teacher, you define Charlie's target behavior as off-task, which includes talking with peers, walking around the room, repeatedly restarting assignments, and rooting around in his desk or backpack. His replacement behavior is on-task, which includes working on and completing assignments, attending/listening to the teacher's instruction, and remaining in his seat.

Function-Based Intervention
Ask the key questions:

1. *Can Charlie perform the replacement behavior?*
This question must be asked for all replacement behaviors defined previously. Can Charlie attend to the teacher and remain in his seat. The answer to this question is "Yes." When he sits with other students and is not given a writing assignment, he focuses on and completes his work.

Can Charlie work on and complete writing assignments? When the question refers to Charlie's writing assignment, the answer is "No," he does not have the necessary prerequisite skills to complete the extended writing assignment.

2. *Do the antecedent conditions represent effective educational practice?*
The answer is "No," the antecedent conditions do not represent effective practice. Charlie's teacher has posted classroom rules but does not remind students about expected behavior prior to an activity and does not consistently enforce expectations. The teacher has also not addressed Charlie's seating arrangement and has allowed him to remain seated with friends who disrupt his learning.

Begin by identifying the antecedent strategies for both Methods 1 and 2. First, using Method 1, you provide the prerequisite instruction and practice needed for Charlie to compose sentences around a theme (e.g., paragraph construction) (see Table 7.7). This strategy changes the conditions that led to the target behavior and allows him to avoid the writing assignment until he has the knowledge to complete it correctly.

The remaining antecedent strategies address Method 2. The second strategy is to move Charlie's seat so he is not in proximity to his friends and, third, reassign instructional groupings that include Charlie and his friends. This strategy should eliminate the conditions that produced off-task behavior when Charlie was near his friends.

Fourth, remind the class of the behavior the teacher expects in the classroom (rules). This may include reteaching the expected behavior using examples and nonexamples. However, if the class follows the rules most of the time, a discussion that refreshes their understanding of expected behavior may be an acceptable alternative.

Fifth, provide Charlie with additional reminders of expected classroom behaviors. Because Charlie has had difficulty following rules and exhibiting expected behavior, he will need additional reminders. The tactics you use are similar to those that were suggested for Carl (Method 2, Example 1). They may include verbal and/or written reminders, or you may ask Charlie to sign a contract in which he agrees to exhibit the expected behavior.

TABLE 7.7
Intervention Elements for Example 3—Positive and Negative Reinforcement

Method Elements	Resulting Intervention Elements
Adjust the antecedent conditions so new behaviors are learned and aversive conditions avoided (Method 1).	Provide the prerequisite instruction and practice needed for Charlie to compose sentences around a theme (e.g., paragraph construction).
Adjust the antecedent conditions so the conditions that set the occasion for the target behavior are eliminated and the replacement behavior is more likely to occur (Method 2).	Move Charlie's seat so he is not in proximity to his friends. Reassign instructional groupings so Charlie is not with his friends. Remind the class of expected behavior by reteaching and/or discussing the rules. Provide Charlie with additional reminders of expected classroom behaviors.
Provide positive reinforcement for the replacement behavior (Methods 1 and 2).	Provide frequent praise and acknowledge expected behaviors. Examples include • Allow Charlie to earn free time that he can spend at the end of the day interacting with his friends who have also earned free time. Stickers, stamps, and tokens provide an easy method to exchange for free time. • Send good reports home to his parents. • Publicly acknowledge Charlie for improvement during regularly scheduled ceremonies in the school and classroom.
Withhold the consequence that previously reinforced the target behavior when it occurs (Methods 1 and 2).	The antecedent adjustment removes both conditions that occasioned the target behavior so it should no longer occur. If it does, redirect Charlie to his seat to finish his assignment or seat him away from his friends so he cannot receive attention from them.

As you design strategies that address consequences, you will find that both Methods 1 and 2 require you to provide positive reinforcement for the replacement behavior. Therefore, the sixth strategy is to provide Charlie with increased positive reinforcement for exhibiting on-task behavior (i.e., working on and completing his assignments, attending to the teacher's instructions, and remaining in his seat). You must remember that positive reinforcement is to be provided whenever Charlie is on-task, but it should be increased during writing assignments. Because his off-task behavior begins immediately upon receiving the writing assignment, reinforcing him on average of every 3 to 5 min will be a good place to begin. The frequency can be faded to a more natural level as Charlie's behavior improves.

What sort of reinforcement seems appropriate for Charlie? He does not need to escape the writing task because the changes you made will allow him to avoid the aversive condition. You have also eliminated the second condition in which he exhibited off-task behavior by seating him in an area away from his friends. However, by doing so, you have removed a potent reinforcer. Attention from his friends would seem to be the most effective reinforcer you can provide under all conditions when Charlie exhibits on-task behavior. One idea is to allow him to earn free time that he can spend at the end of the day interacting with his friends who have also earned free time. Stickers, stamps, and tokens provide an easy method to exchange for free time.

In addition, the teacher should provide frequent praise and acknowledgment of expected behaviors, send good reports home to his parents, and publicly acknowledge Charlie for improvement during regularly scheduled ceremonies in the school and classroom. Although these forms of acknowledgment do not include Charlie's friends, their use provides him with attention, and they are naturally occurring in the school setting, which means they will be more readily available in the future.

The final strategy is to withhold the consequence that previously reinforced the target behavior. If Charlie exhibits off-task behavior during the writing assignment, he must be redirected to his seat to finish his assignment. If Charlie is off-task because he is interacting with his friends, the students should be separated so he cannot receive attention from them. Remind all students of expected behavior, and redirect them when they fail to exhibit expected behavior.

Discussion

This example illustrates a situation in which the target behavior is the same but serves different functions under two different conditions. The function of off-task behavior was positive reinforcement—attention when Charlie was seated near his friends and negative reinforcement—activity when he was presented with an extended writing task. When behavior serves different functions, the key questions must be asked for each function. The answers provide the information you need to address multiple conditions.

This example also demonstrates the ease with which the function-based intervention methods can be integrated. One intervention was designed that addressed both conditions in which Charlie exhibited the behavior. The difference was in the addition of antecedent manipulations.

SUMMARY

This chapter described Method 2 of the Function-Based Intervention Decision Model. This method is appropriate when antecedent conditions do not conform to effective practice, and the problem behavior has more efficiently and reliably resulted in reinforcement than the replacement behavior.

Antecedent manipulations, when supported by completion of an FBA, represent an alternative method for addressing problem behavior. A growing research base demonstrates the effectiveness of this approach with behavior maintained by either positive or negative reinforcement. Method 2: Improve the Environment works by changing the antecedent conditions so they no longer set the occasion for the problem behavior to occur. The new behavior (replacement behavior) that occurs as a result of the changes must be reinforced immediately and consistently. In fact, an important component of this method is that the student must be able to gain a preferred reinforcer that is more powerful and efficient than the reinforcer previously supplied by the target behavior. In addition, reinforcement of the target behavior is eliminated in the event the target behavior does occur.

Research has shown that antecedent interventions can successfully reduce problem behaviors and increase replacement behaviors when those interventions are developed from information learned through an FBA. This was true for individuals who varied in age from preschool to adult, represented a range of mild to severe disabilities, and exhibited a wide range of problem and replacement behaviors. Antecedent conditions that were shown to set the occasion for problem behavior to occur included task-related materials and instructional presentation, environmental conditions, and physiological conditions. The majority of the studies addressed escape-motivated behaviors, with the largest number being related to academic tasks that did not meet the criterion for effective practices.

Additional antecedent conditions representing effective practice were also described in this chapter. These practices have been correlated with increased time engaged in learning. They are also prescribed to prevent or minimize the occurrence of problem behavior.

Steps in Developing an Intervention When Using Method 2: Improve the Environment

The following list summarizes the steps and activities involved in developing an intervention when the environment does not represent effective practice:

1. Compare the antecedent conditions you observed to those considered effective practice in the environment in which the behavior occurs.
2. Eliminate the antecedent conditions that set the occasion for the target behavior to occur.
3. Estiblish new antecedent conditions in which the replacement behavior is more likely to occur.
4. Provide appropriate positive reinforcement for the replacement behavior.
5. Withhold the consequence that previously reinforced the target behavior should it occur.

EXERCISES

1. Levon is a 6-year-old kindergarten student. He exhibits off-task behavior, which is defined as frequently getting out of his seat for nontask-related purposes, such as sharpening his pencil and calling to the teacher to ask for help. If the teacher ignores him, he will attempt to leave the classroom or will throw himself on the floor. The teacher has moved his desk next to hers, but it is turned so he is not facing the blackboard on which the teacher writes assignments. The teacher reports that she often sends Levon to the office because she finds it too difficult to cope with him in class. Antecedents to the problem behavior were (a) the teacher gave instructions on how to complete an assignment, (b) the teacher began teaching a lesson, (c) other students approached the teacher's desk to ask for assistance, and (d) students walked past Levon's desk. In each case, the consequence of the problem behavior was the student avoided the assignment and received attention from the teacher and other students. Interviews and A-B-C data indicate that Levon's problem behaviors are maintained by negative reinforcement—activity and positive reinforcement—attention.

   The target behavior is off-task, defined as Levon frequently getting out of his seat for nontask-related purposes, such as sharpening his pencil, calling to the teacher to ask for help, attempting to leave the classroom, and falling on the floor. The replacement behavior is on-task, which is defined as remaining in his seat, raising his hand if he needs assistance, and focusing on the teacher's instruction or assignment.

   a. Assume that Levon can perform the replacement behavior. Identify the antecedent variables you would review and the method you would use to assess whether they represented effective instructional practice.

   b. Assume that the classroom does not provide effective instructional practices. Identify the components of an intervention for Levon that would address his problem behavior.

2. Apply the model to an FBA. Summarize the results of interviews and observations, and identify replacement behaviors. Identify the appropriate method to use, and justify your decision.

REFERENCES

Algozzine, R., Ysseldyke, J., & Elliott, J. (1997). *Strategies and tactics for effective instruction*. Longmont, CO: Sopris West.

Billington, E., & DiTommaso, N. M. (2003). Demonstrations and applications of the matching law in education. *Journal of Behavioral Education, 12*(2), 91–104.

Bredekamp, S., & Copple, C. (Eds.). (1997). *Developmentally appropriate practice in early childhood programs* (Rev. ed.). Washington, DC: National Association for the Education of Young Children.

Conroy, M. A., & Stichter, J. P. (2003). The application of antecedents in the functional assessment process. *Journal of Special Education, 37*(1), 15–25.

Herrnstein, R. J. (1961). Relative and absolute strength of response as a function of frequency of reinforcement. *Journal of the Experimental Analysis of Behavior, 4*, 267–272.

Horner, R. H., & Sugai, G. (2000). School-wide behavior support: An emerging initiative (special issue). *Journal of Positive Behavioral Interventions, 2*, 231–233.

Kern, L., Choutka, C. M., & Sokol, N. G. (2002). Assessment-based antecedent interventions used in natural settings to reduce challenging behavior: An analysis of the literature. *Education and Treatment of Children, 25*(1), 113–130.

Knowles, M. S., Holton, E., & Swanson, R. A. (2005). *The adult learner: The definitive classic in adult education and human resource development.* Boston: Elsevier.

Mastropieri, M., & Scruggs, T. (2002). *Effective instruction for special education* (3rd ed.). Austin, TX: Pro-Ed.

McGee, G. G., & Daly, T (1999). Assessment-based interventions for children with emotional and behavioral disorders. In A. Repp & R. Horner (Eds.), *Functional analysis of problem behavior: From effective assessment to effective support* (pp. 197–214). Belmont, CA: Wadsworth.

Peck, J., Sasso, G. M., & Jolivette, K. (1997). Use of structural analysis hypothesis testing model to improve social interactions via peer-mediated interventions. *Focus on Autism and Other Developmental Disabilities, 12,* 219–230.

Umbreit, J., & Blair, K. (1997). Using structural analysis to facilitate treatment of aggression and non-compliance in a young child at-risk for behavioral disorders. *Behavioral Disorders, 20,* 75–86.

Walker, H. M., Ramsey, E., & Gresham, F. M. (2004). *Antisocial behavior in school: Evidenced-based practices.* Belmont, CA: Thomson/Wadsworth.

Ysseldyke, J., & Christenson, S. (1993). *The Instructional Environment System-II: A system to identify a student's instructional needs.* Longmont, CO: Sopris West.

CHAPTER 8

Intervention Method 3
Adjust the Contingencies

OUTCOMES

After reading this chapter, you will be able to

- Link the results of the FBA to Method 3 of the Function-Based Intervention Decision Model.

- Develop interventions that focus on contingency manipulations.

This chapter describes Method 3. It focuses primarily on manipulating consequences so the target behavior decreases and the replacement behavior is more likely to occur. Antecedents are also addressed, but tend to be narrowly focused when compared with antecedent manipulations described in Methods 1 and 2. When you use Method 3, you have already determined that the student can perform the replacement behavior, and existing antecedent conditions represent the most effective practices and context in which the replacement behavior is to occur.

This chapter also completes the discussion of strategies that use the Function-Based Intervention Decision Model to provide a technique for successfully linking assessment information to an intervention that directly addresses the function of the behavior. In the decision model, two questions focus your attention on assessment information about the student's behavior and the environment in which it occurs. The answers to the questions identify the strategies that are most likely to decrease the target behavior and increase the replacement behavior.

Specifically, this chapter describes the conditions under which Method 3 should be used, provides examples and discussion of intervention strategies, and reviews important considerations about designing interventions across all three methods.

METHOD 3: ADJUST THE CONTINGENCIES

This method is appropriate when (a) the individual can perform the replacement behavior and (b) antecedent conditions conform to effective practice, but (c) the target behavior has more efficiently and reliably resulted in reinforcement than the replacement behavior. Method 3 has three components (see Table 8.1). First, the consequence that previously reinforced the target behavior is provided for the replacement behavior. This component requires the consequence for the replacement behavior to be functionally equivalent to the consequence that maintained the target behavior. That is, it must provide the same type of reinforcement as the target behavior to be effective.

Second, the reinforcer is withheld when the target behavior occurs (extinction). In some cases, it will not be possible to completely withhold the reinforcer. For example, potentially dangerous behaviors (e.g., an individual is aggressive toward another person) that result in gaining attention will require immediate action that includes at least some attention from others. This will not sabotage our approach to intervention. The approach should still be successful as long as students receive only minimal attention for the target behaviors and much more attention for appropriate behavior. Because appropriate behavior is reinforced often, its rate should increase dramatically. Simultaneously, because the target behavior is not reinforced, or results in very low levels of attention, the rate of this behavior should drop dramatically or extinguish completely.

The third component is to adjust the antecedent conditions to increase the likelihood that the replacement behavior will occur. Although Method 3 focuses on consequence (C) manipulations, all three terms of the contingency statement (A, B, and C) are included in the intervention. Antecedent (A) conditions are also adjusted to make it easier to strengthen the replacement behavior (B).

TABLE 8.1
Method 3: Adjust the Contingencies

Key elements	• Provide the consequence that previously reinforced the target behavior, but only for the replacement behavior.
	• Withhold the consequence when the target behavior occurs (extinction).
	• Adjust the antecedent conditions to make it more likely that the replacement behavior will occur.

Often, the antecedent adjustment is a minor variation of standard classroom procedure, such as reminding a student that the contingencies have changed. Terry provides an example. She yells out answers to questions rather than raising her hand, and yelling has been reinforced with teacher attention. One strategy for adjusting contingencies would be for the teacher to provide Terry with attention when she raises her hand and ignore her when she yells answers. To increase the likelihood that Terry will raise her hand, the teacher might remind her at the beginning of each new class period that she must raise her hand to be recognized (antecedent adjustment).

METHOD 3 EXAMPLES

This section includes two examples that link FBA information to an intervention using Method 3: Adjust the contingencies. The first example demonstrates the method when the function of the behavior is positive reinforcement, whereas the second example demonstrates the method when the function of the behavior is negative reinforcement. Each example includes a short discussion of issues raised by the choice of intervention strategies and the manner in which strategies are linked to the assessment.

Method 3: Example 1—Positive Reinforcement

Summary: Record Review, Interview, and Observation

Fisher is a second-grade student who has a diagnosed learning disability. He is fully included in the second grade with some modifications provided by the resource teacher. Fisher has received multiple office referrals for disruptions in the cafeteria. His records indicate that he exhibited similar behavior in first grade that resulted in him spending lunch recess in the "responsibility room" for the majority of the year. Fisher's mother complained that he is upset that he does not get to go to recess, and she wants something done.

The lunch monitor says that Fisher's problem behaviors begin when he enters the cafeteria, even though the teacher and classroom assistant escort the class. Fisher jostles the other students and moves from the back to the middle to the front of the line. The lunch monitor believes the teacher is in charge while the students are in line and does not respond to the behavior until Fisher sits at a table. He describes Fisher's behavior as "horseplay" and "disruptive." Fisher yells at the other students; spits water at them; tosses food, napkins, and utensils across and down the table; blows milk or other drinks out of his nose; and crawls under the table and pulls on their clothes. Sometimes the other students participate, and all four or five of them are sent to the responsibility room. Fisher tells you that he likes to play with his friends and that the teacher will not let them even talk in class. He knows Mr. Jackson, the lunch monitor, gets mad at him, but says that sometimes he cannot help himself. Fisher identifies recess and playing games with his friends as preferred activities. He also likes receiving the cards the teacher passes out for being good because he gets to redeem them for extra free time.

The teacher tells you that Fisher is sometimes disruptive in class, but not often, and that he returns to his normal good behavior when reminded of the rules. He also tells you that Fisher is very social and that his interactions are as appropriate as the rest of the students in the class. The first grade receives social skills instruction as part of a schoolwide program, and he does not think Fisher needs any additional instruction in this area. The teacher leaves the cafeteria once the students get in the lunch line, and he does not believe Fisher exhibits problem behavior on the way to the cafeteria.

You observe Fisher on 3 consecutive days for 30 min. Because the lunch monitor indicated that the problem begins immediately when Fisher enters the cafeteria, you begin the observation in the classroom. Before the students leave the room, Fisher's teacher has them repeat the rules for the hall and cafeteria.

On all 3 days, Fisher walked to the cafeteria with only minor disruptions (talking to other students and jostling the person behind him on one occasion). The teacher praised students who were following the rules and ignored the minor disruptions.

In the cafeteria line, Fisher bumped into other students, laughed, and teased them during all three observations. The consequence of these behaviors was that other students responded by bumping Fisher, laughing at him, or telling him to leave them alone. On one occasion, Fisher moved from the end of the line to the front. As a consequence, other students yelled at him.

At the lunch table, Fisher exhibited the target behavior on all 3 days—three, seven, and four times, respectively. The consequence of this behavior was an escalating series of reprimands by the lunch monitor and loss of points. After each reprimand, Fisher ate quietly for a short period before resuming the target behavior. Many of the other students at Fisher's table and the adjacent table laughed at him and talked to him. On the second day (seven incidents), Fisher was sent to the office. On the third day, he was moved to an empty table after the fourth incident.

During the observation, you review the environment and find that there are three rules posted conspicuously. In addition, you observe that most of the students follow the rules and that the cafeteria monitor praises students for doing so. When you ask Fisher about the rules, he readily repeats them.

Statement of Function

Based on the interview and observations, you identify the function of the behavior as follows: In the cafeteria, Fisher engages in disruptive behaviors to gain the attention of his peers. Fisher's target behaviors are maintained by positive reinforcement—attention.

Behavior Definitions

Fisher's target behavior is disruptive behavior that includes bumping, touching, and pushing other students; throwing food and other items; spitting and playing with his food; getting out of his seat before he is finished eating; and speaking in a loud voice.

The replacement behavior is sitting in his designated seat, eating his food, keeping hands and feet to himself, and speaking in a quiet voice.

Function-Based Intervention

Ask the key questions:

1. *Can Fisher perform the replacement behavior?*

In this instance, all indications are that Fisher can perform the replacement behavior. The record review and your observation confirm that Fisher knows the rules and can follow them in other areas of the school (e.g., hall, classroom). He is also able to appropriately access peer attention.

2. *Do the antecedent conditions represent effective educational practice?*

The answer to this question is also "Yes," the antecedent conditions represent effective practice. Rules are posted, the teacher reminds the students of the rules before leaving the classroom, and reinforcement is available for following the rules.

Method 3 is the correct method to use. First, increase the attention Fisher receives for exhibiting the replacement behavior (see Table 8.2). The lunch monitor and the teacher will praise Fisher for correctly entering the cafeteria, standing in line, and speaking quietly. The monitor will walk with Fisher to the table and engage him in pleasant conversation, including praise for following the rules and being responsible. Praise will continue throughout the time Fisher is in the cafeteria, initially delivered an average of once every 3 min. A "caught you being responsible" card (used by the teacher in the classroom) will be given to Fisher if he maintains the replacement behavior throughout the lunch period, which lasts 15 min. The card can be exchanged at the end of the week for increased time playing games with his friends or for other preferred items and activities. Other students will be reminded to attend only to those students who are following the rules and will be praised for doing so. Fisher's mother also receives a progress report daily so she can reinforce any increase in the replacement behavior.

The FBA indicates that peer attention is the most powerful reinforcer for Fisher. The intervention includes peer attention as one option when he exchanges his "caught you being responsible" card. Peer attention has also been redirected so his peers are more likely to attend when he exhibits the replacement behavior.

Second, adjust the antecedent conditions by having the lunch monitor greet Fisher at the door. This provides a cue that the supervision is about to change and also enables the lunch monitor to provide attention for the replacement behavior.

Third, adjust the antecedent conditions by reminding the students in Fisher's class of appropriate behavior in the cafeteria. Have them role-play correct and incorrect behavior. Fourth, use the opportunity to tell them to ignore any student who does not follow the rules and to talk instead to those students who are. Both the teacher and the lunch monitor should participate in this activity.

Fifth, enlist Fisher in designing the plan and have him list the behaviors he will exhibit in the cafeteria and identify ways he can avoid the target

TABLE 8.2
Intervention Elements for Example 1—Positive Reinforcement

Method Elements	Resulting Intervention Elements
Provide positive reinforcement for the replacement behavior.	Use the following intervention methods to increase attention for exhibiting replacement behaviors: • Monitor and teacher provide attention and social interaction when Fisher enters the cafeteria. • Monitor and teacher praise Fisher for standing in line and speaking quietly. • Monitor walks Fisher to the table and engages him in pleasant conversation, including praise for following rules and being responsible. • Continue praise while in the cafeteria, on average, once every 3 min. • Give the "caught you being responsible" card if he maintains the replacement behavior throughout the lunch period. • Exchange the card at the end of the week for preferred items and activities. • Redirect attention from his peers so it is provided when he exhibits the replacement behavior. • Send daily progress report to Fisher's mother so she can reinforce increased replacement behavior.
Adjust the antecedent conditions to make it more likely that the replacement behavior will occur.	Monitor greets Fisher when he enters the cafeteria. Remind all students of cafeteria rules. Tell other students to ignore anyone who does not follow the rules. Have Fisher go over the rules and how he will behave. Give Fisher a more specific and additional reminder before he leaves the classroom. Seat Fisher next to students who are more likely to ignore the target behavior.
Withhold the consequence that previously reinforced the target behavior when it occurs.	Instruct students to ignore rule infractions. Speak only minimally when directing Fisher to the appropriate replacement behavior.

behavior. Negotiate reinforcement preferences with him. Sixth, Fisher's teacher should continue to remind all students about appropriate cafeteria behavior before they leave the room and will give Fisher an additional reminder that includes a list of behaviors to exhibit and methods for avoiding problems.

Seventh, in the lunchroom, ensure Fisher sits near students who are least likely to engage in disruptive behavior with him. (Fisher himself suggested this when he identified methods for avoiding the target behavior.)

If Fisher should exhibit any disruptive behavior, eliminate the attention he has been receiving. Fisher's disruptive behavior is being reinforced by attention from his peers and from the lunch monitor. The eighth strategy addresses peer reinforcement by instructing other students to ignore rule infractions. Remind all students during the role-play exercise suggested previously, and reinforce them for ignoring Fisher's disruptive behavior in the cafeteria.

Ninth, the monitor will minimize conversation with Fisher when directing him to the appropriate replacement behavior (e.g., speak in an inside voice, keep your feet on the floor) and will praise a student who is exhibiting the behavior. As noted earlier in this chapter, it is sometimes difficult to implement a plan in which the target behavior is completely ignored, especially by peers. However, this plan eliminates most of the attention Fisher was receiving.

Discussion

In this example, positive reinforcement was increased not only when Fisher was at the table, when he was most likely to exhibit the target behavior, but also when he entered the cafeteria and stood in line. Catching Fisher early carries forward the momentum of the appropriate behavior he exhibits in the classroom and hall. Research identifies behavioral momentum as an effective strategy to use to increase replacement behaviors (Lee, Belfiore, & Scheeler, 2004; Mace, Hock, & Lalley, 1988; Nevin, 1996).

The lunch monitor greets Fisher at the door both to provide reinforcement and to establish himself as a positive reinforcer. In addition, the teacher and the monitor demonstrate the interconnection between the classroom and the cafeteria environments when both conduct the retraining session, provide feedback and reinforcement while the students are in line, and use the "caught you being responsible" card in the cafeteria and in the classroom.

When the teacher and the lunch monitor remind all students about the cafeteria rules, they address those few students who occasionally exhibited problem behaviors with Fisher and remind all students not to interact when Fisher exhibits the target behavior, although they do not specifically identify him as a problem.

Students have also been instructed to talk only to those who are following the rules. This should enhance peer attention for Fisher when he exhibits the replacement behaviors. Peer interaction follows naturally from the appropriate behavior. Fisher is included in the plan as a prelude to self-monitoring and also to ensure the reinforcement is preferred.

Method 3: Example 2—Negative Reinforcement

Summary: Record Review, Interview, and Observation

Annie, an eighth-grade student diagnosed with an emotional and behavioral disorder, has been referred for disruptions in her math class that include cussing, tearing or breaking her materials, reading unrelated material, talking to students sitting next to her, and making loud noises. Annie's teacher says that these behaviors occur most frequently when she asks Annie to solve a problem in front of the class, when she presents new material to the class, and occasionally when she has the class practice new material, even though she provides a lot of assistance, feedback, and support.

The teacher attempted to intervene first by ignoring Annie's behavior and later by increasing consequences for both appropriate and problem behavior. She also discussed this behavior with Annie to get her input as to why the behavior occurs, but she did not get a clear answer. The teacher uses a token system that is tied to the classroom rules. Students can exchange tokens for preferred items and activities at the end of the week. The teacher believes that Annie has the necessary skills and knowledge to complete the tasks and cites her high math scores on standardized tests. However, Annie is failing math because she is sent to the office an average of twice per week.

Annie tells you that she can do the math but thinks it is "really stupid," she does not think she will use it in real life, and she hates talking in front of the other students. She likes the teacher but does not care whether she earns the tokens because she cannot ever earn enough to get what she wants. She prefers time on the computer, favorite reading material (consisting primarily of comics), and time to draw.

During 3 h of observation occurring on Monday, Wednesday, and Friday of one week, the antecedents and consequences relating to 15 instances of target behavior were recorded. Annie's behavior occurred (a) when she was asked to solve a problem in front of the class (6 instances), (b) when the teacher presented a new lesson (2 instances), and (c) when she was given a practice assignment to complete with a peer or group (7 instances). In every case, the consequence of her behavior was that she avoided completing the assigned task.

Statement of Function

Based on the interview and observations, you identify the function of the behavior as follows: When presented with a math assignment that requires her to present in front of others or work in a group with others, Annie engages in disruptive behavior to escape the activity. Annie's behaviors are maintained by negative reinforcement—activity.

Behavior Definitions

The target behavior is disruptions, which include cussing, tearing or breaking her materials, reading unrelated material, talking to students sitting next to her, and making loud noises.

The replacement behavior is on-task, defined as sitting in her seat, working on practice material either in a group or individually, looking at the teacher when she presents new material, and complying with requests to complete a problem in front of the class.

Function-Based Intervention

Ask the key questions:

1. *Can Annie perform the replacement behavior?*

Annie has demonstrated she can complete the math assignments as homework and on curriculum-based and standardized tests. She has also worked with a group, presented in front of the class, and focused on the teacher when learning new material without exhibiting the target behavior. The answer to this question is "Yes," Annie can perform the replacement behavior.

2. *Do the antecedent conditions represent effective practice?*

The answer to this question would also appear to be "Yes." The material is at the appropriate level for the student, teacher expectations are clearly conveyed, the lesson is well designed with functional and interesting materials and activities, and the classroom environment is designed to maximize productive use of time.

Method 3 is the correct method to use. Begin by providing negative reinforcement for completing academic activities with other students. First, after Annie works on a group activity for 10 min, she can leave the group and complete the activity on her own (see Table 8.3). Annie is allowed to escape (take a break from) the group once she has participated for a fixed period of time. She keeps track of the time she spends in group and asks the teacher to allow her to return to her seat at the end of the 10 min. She also continues to receive positive reinforcement in the form of tokens and praise for completing her assignments in class. Second, award Annie an escape card each time she completes a problem in front of the class. She can use this card to escape one presentation of her choosing.

TABLE 8.3

Intervention Elements for Example 2—Negative Reinforcement

Method Elements	Resulting Intervention Elements
Provide negative reinforcement for the replacement behavior.	After Annie works on a group activity for 10 min, she can leave the group and complete the activity on her own.
	Award an escape card each time Annie completes a problem in front of the class.
Withhold the consequence that previously reinforced the target behavior when it occurs.	Annie stays in the group even if she exhibits the target behavior.
	Continue to choose Annie to complete a problem in front of the class.
Adjust the antecedent conditions to make it more likely that the replacement behavior will occur.	Complete a behavior contract itemizing the expected replacement behavior.
	Signal Annie to remind her of the contract and the expected behavior before class begins.

The teacher must also withhold the consequence that previously reinforced the target behavior. This means that Annie must not be allowed to escape working in groups or completing problems in front of the class. The third strategy is to ensure Annie stays in the group if she exhibits the target behavior. The teacher continues to assign her to groups, and students in her group continue to interact with her.

Fourth, the teacher must continue to call on Annie to complete a problem in front of the class. If Annie refuses to participate, the teacher may go on to another student for that problem but must continue to ask Annie to complete each problem until the end of the activity. The only way Annie can avoid attention is to complete the task.

Antecedent adjustments that make it more likely Annie will participate complete the intervention. In this case, the teacher and consultant presented the intervention components to Annie, asked for her input, and made minor adjustments that included adding an escape card for class presentations. The fifth strategy was for Annie to sign a behavior contract that listed the expected replacement behaviors. The sixth strategy was for the teacher and Annie to devise a subtle way for the teacher to remind her of the contract and the expected behavior before class began.

Discussion

This intervention maintains the group and presentation activities, which the teacher believes are important parts of learning. It also provides reinforcement for the replacement behavior that is functionally equivalent to the reinforcer previously produced by the target behavior. It allows Annie to escape the group if she works on her math assignment for 10 min while participating within the group. The "escape" cards allow her to avoid making presentations in front of the class. Continuing positive reinforcement for completing activities provides additional incentive for Annie to participate.

Annie is not allowed to escape if she exhibits the target behavior (i.e., she must continue to work in groups, complete her assignments, and present in front of the class). As noted earlier, extinction of the target behavior is also necessary to ensure the intervention is successful.

Because the student's input was solicited for the intervention, she felt more invested. The behavior contract provides clear and specific guides for Annie and the teacher to follow. Both developed and agreed to the six intervention strategies. The escape card was Annie's choice of intervention; it had the added benefit of providing her with ongoing choices of when and how she would participate.

IMPORTANT CONCEPTS AND COMMON ERRORS

Chapters 6 to 8 provide the strategies and tactics needed to design an intervention that is based on the information gathered during the FBA. Each contains basic concepts and other important elements to consider during this phase of developing a function-based intervention. These concepts include

1. Ask both questions on the Function-Based Intervention Decision Model. A common mistake is to ask the first question, decide that the student cannot perform the replacement behavior, and proceed to design the intervention. In some cases, the environment will not support the new behavior because antecedents do not represent the most effective practices. Both deficits must be addressed to provide the most successful behavior change. Example 3 in Chapter 7 provides an example of an intervention that includes both Method 1 and Method 2 strategies.

2. Include both consequence and antecedent manipulations in the intervention strategies. Although Methods 1 and 2 focus on antecedent conditions, the consequence is always changed so the replacement behavior is reinforced and the target behavior is not. Method 3, which emphasizes adjusting the consequence, also includes antecedent changes designed to encourage and support the replacement behavior.

3. Identify a replacement behavior that is a skill. The replacement behavior should not simply identify the absence of problem behavior. It should be active, requiring the student to, for example, complete an activity or task, raise his or her hand, or interact.

4. Ask whether the student can perform every replacement behavior identified in the intervention. The third example in Chapter 7 requires Charlie to remain in his seat, listen attentively to the teacher, and work on the writing assignment. Although he could sit and listen, Charlie could not complete the writing assignment. If the interventionist had not asked whether Charlie could perform each behavior, an important part of the intervention would have been missed.

5. Design reinforcement for the replacement behavior so it is more effective, efficient, and robust than it was for the target behavior. Refer to the Matching Law discussed in Chapter 7 where the student chooses the problem behavior because he gets what he wants faster (e.g., immediately) and more consistently (e.g., every time) than with any other behavior. If you want him to exhibit the replacement behavior, you must arrange the conditions so it secures reinforcement more easily, quickly, or reliably than the target behavior did.

6. Allow the student to escape if he or she exhibits the replacement behavior and if the target behavior was maintained by escape. Sometimes a teacher or other professional may balk at allowing an individual to escape an important activity, such as a math lesson, as described in Example 2 in this chapter. However, in most cases, the intervention describes a break, not a complete escape. Remember, too, that the examples we present in this section are the initial change plans and do not include maintenance strategies that would decrease breaks over time.

7. Provide peer attention as reinforcement if indicated in the FBA. When the target behavior is maintained by peer attention, the attention increases the disruptive nature of the behavior, especially in school settings.

Peer attention can be a difficult reinforcer to provide, and staff may resist reinforcing the replacement behavior in this manner. However, the student is telling you with his behavior that this is his preferred reinforcer. With the help of the teacher, interventions can be designed that provide peer attention while maintaining the classroom environment. Example 1 in Chapter 7 and Example 1 in this chapter provide instances in which peer attention is used as one of the reinforcers for the replacement behavior.

8. Withhold reinforcement for the target behavior. A common error is failure to withhold the consequence that previously reinforced the target behavior. The term for withholding reinforcement is **extinction.** If the target behavior was maintained by positive reinforcement, you must ensure the student no longer obtains the attention, tangible, activity, or sensory stimulation that was provided in the past. If the target behavior was maintained by negative reinforcement, you must ensure the student does not avoid or escape the attention, tangible, activity, or sensory stimulation that he or she escaped in the past. This can be difficult if the individual exhibits dangerous behavior such as running into traffic or hitting another person. As previously discussed, you must provide as little of the reinforcer as possible (e.g., provide minimal attention and identify an appropriate time and place for the individual to complete an activity that he or she was trying to escape). The key is to make the consequence for the replacement behavior more reinforcing than the consequence for the target behavior (see item 3).

9. Change the task so it provides escape. When a target behavior is maintained by negative reinforcement, changing the task allows the student to avoid the conditions that originally produced the target behavior. Under these circumstances, the replacement behavior should be positively reinforced. To make this work, you must eliminate all antecedent elements that produced the target behavior. You must also ensure the target behavior no longer allows the individual to escape or avoid the situation. Example 3 in Chapter 6 provides an example of this strategy.

10. Use the student interview. The student interview often provides information that is critical to the intervention's success. In all examples across the three methods, the student's input made the plan more effective. In Examples 1 and 2 in this chapter, the student provided information that led to an intervention strategy. Sometimes the student will refuse to provide information (e.g., Example 2 in Chapter 7) or will be unable to provide relevant information (e.g., Tak in Chapter 7). In those cases, consider completing additional interviews with parents or others who interact with the student in environments in which the behavior does not occur.

11. Do not assume the student can perform the replacement behavior. If no one has seen the individual perform the replacement behavior, it may be because they cannot do so. Additional assessment, interviews, and

observations may be necessary to ensure you have the correct information you need to determine a performance deficit.

12. Teach to eliminate specific deficits. Provide training that specifically addresses the skill deficit exhibited by the student. You can also teach broad categories of, for example, social or communication skills, but unless the intervention addresses the specific deficit that produced the target behavior, the intervention will not be successful.

13. Catch the student before he or she exhibits the target behavior. Provide reinforcement before the student exhibits the target behavior, that is, while he or she is being appropriate. Example 1 in this chapter demonstrates this concept. The lunch monitor greeted Fisher at the door and praised him for entering the cafeteria, waiting in line, and speaking quietly. By the time Fisher sat at the table, where he previously exhibited the target behavior, he had received a lot of positive reinforcement and was more likely to continue demonstrating appropriate behavior.

SUMMARY

This chapter described Method 3 of the Function-Based Intervention Decision Model. In Method 3, you provide the consequence (reinforcer) only when the individual exhibits the replacement behavior, and adjust the antecedent conditions so the replacement behavior is likely to occur. If (a) the student can perform the replacement behavior and (b) the antecedent conditions represent effective practice, this method should be used.

The chapter also listed important concepts and common errors that affect all three intervention methods. The next step is to identify an appropriate measurement system.

Steps in Developing an Intervention When Using Method 3: Adjust the Contingencies

The following list summarizes the steps and activities involved in developing an intervention when the student can perform the replacement behavior and the environment represents effective practice:

---

1. Adjust the antecedent conditions to make it more likely that the replacement behavior will occur.

2. Provide the consequence that previously reinforced the target behavior when the student exhibits the replacement behavior.

3. Withhold the consequence that previously reinforced the target behavior if the student exhibits the target behavior.

EXERCISES

1. Ali is a 16-year-old 11th-grade student. She is identified as having an emotional and behavioral disorder and has been referred because she is noncompliant in gym class. Noncompliance is defined as refusing to change

into her gym clothes and to participate in class activities (e.g., running, lifting weights, playing volleyball). She also cries and asks to go to the nurse's office an average of once per week. The teacher explains that Ali is not disruptive, but she is failing gym because she refuses to participate, preferring to sit on the sidelines or go to the nurse's office.

The behavior begins when it is time for gym class. If she goes to class, she immediately refuses to don the required shorts and shirt. You observe three classes and find that she refuses to enter the locker room and spends the entire class sitting on the bench. She does not ask to go to the nurse's office during your observation. You note that she is significantly overweight. During your interview with Ali, she tells you that the gym clothes do not fit her correctly and that she will not get undressed in front of the other girls who are "skinny witches." The FBA information indicates that Ali's target behaviors are maintained by negative reinforcement—activity and negative reinforcement—attention. The gym teacher agrees to modify the activities so Ali can participate, but cannot work with her if she does not suit up.

The target behavior is refusing to dress appropriately for gym. The replacement behavior is changing into the appropriate shorts and shirt so she can participate in gym.

a. Ali can perform the replacement behavior. She knows how to change her own clothes.

b. Assume that the gym class provides effective instructional practices. With the adjustments the gym teacher is willing to make for Ali to succeed, antecedent changes have already been implemented that tailor class procedures to meet Ali's needs.

c. Design an intervention for Ali using Method 3.

2. Apply the model to an existing FBA. Summarize the results of interviews and observations, and identify replacement behaviors. Identify the appropriate method to use, and justify your decision.

REFERENCES

Lee, D. L., Belfiore, P. J., & Scheeler, M. C. (2004). Behavioral momentum in academics: Using embedded high-p sequences to increase academic productivity. *Journal of Applied Behavior Analysis, 41*(7), 789–801.

Mace, F. C., Hock, M. L., & Lalley, J. S. (1988). Behavioral momentum in the treatment of non-compliance. *Journal of Applied Behavior Analysis, 21*(2), 128–141.

Nevin, J. A. (1996). The momentum of compliance. *Journal of Applied Behavior Analysis, 29*(4), 535–547.

CHAPTER 9

Identifying an Appropriate Measurement System

OUTCOMES

After reading this chapter, you will be able to

- Select an appropriate measurement system.
- Select an appropriate time to collect data.
- Record useful data.
- Assess interobserver agreement (IOA).
- Avoid problems that can compromise data.

At this point, you have completed the FBA and systematically identified the components of a function-based intervention that is very likely to be effective. Now, you will need to identify an appropriate measurement system so you can test whether the intervention is effective (discussed in Chapter 10) and monitor its effectiveness when it is implemented (discussed in Chapters 11 to 13). This chapter addresses how to identify an appropriate behavioral measurement method.

All reputable textbooks about applied behavior analysis cover the basics of behavioral measurement. Some good examples include books by Zirpoli (2005); Alberto and Troutman (2006); Martin and Pear (2003); Miller (2006); Sulzer-Azaroff and Mayer (1991); Cooper, Heron, and Heward (1987); and Cooper (1981). These texts provide solid overviews of the types and methods of behavioral measurement as they might be used in any positive behavioral support program in the school, home, workplace, or community. Our goal is to cover this topic specifically as it pertains to conducting FBAs and to testing and monitoring function-based interventions. Although our focus is on using these methods appropriately in school settings, the same methods and considerations apply equally to FBAs and function-based interventions in other settings.

The task of selecting an appropriate measurement system becomes easier if you have a clear understanding of why we measure behavior.

WHY MEASURE BEHAVIOR?

To many school staff, the idea of collecting data is about as welcome as root canal surgery. Data collection is an activity school staff had to do when they were in college or graduate school but would never do in the "real world." There are several reasons for this predicament. First, school staff have many demands on their time. The addition of another potentially time-consuming task is not met with enthusiasm. Second, many school staff question the value of the collected data. Their doubts often stem from personal experiences in which they spent significant time generating data that either was not used or was of little value. Given the demands on their time, not to mention the ever-increasing amount of time and effort staff must devote to various types of paperwork, their reluctance is not surprising.

Applied behavior analysts did not help the situation when, during the 1960s and 1970s, they developed and promoted many elegant data collection systems that benefited research but held little practical value for practitioners. This period in our history has been referred to by some (e.g., Wetzel & Hoschouer, 1984) as the "documentation mania" phase of our field. The term is apt because the methods used often produced mounds of data, much of which was not useful. This led Wetzel and Hoschouer to recommend that practitioners should always try to collect the least amount of data that will tell them what they need to know. This guideline is a good one because, in fact, data collection is undertaken for a specific purpose, which is to learn something in particular about a person's behavior.

Given this state of affairs, one could ask, "Why bother collecting data at all?" The answer is simple: Data provide the only objective way to know whether an intervention is effective. Because we have no better way to evaluate our efforts to improve behavior, it is helpful to understand how to identify appropriate methods for measuring behavior and how to use them efficiently.

Because we must collect data to evaluate an intervention's effectiveness, it is helpful to rethink the nature of data collection. Bijou and colleagues (e.g., Bijou, 1970; Lund, Schnaps, & Bijou, 1983) suggested long ago that data collection is nothing more than record keeping. People who run businesses keep "data" of all sorts (e.g., inventories of stock, sales receipts, salaries paid). Banks keep a record of every customer's deposits, transfers, and expenditures. Schools keep records of every course a student takes, every grade that is given, and every diploma that is awarded. In fact, schools also keep track of every day and every class session that a student attends or misses. Although people rarely think of this information as data, it is.

In the same vein, school personnel who attempt to improve behavior also keep data that pertain to what students do. In essence, the data collected on an intervention's effectiveness are nothing more than a form of record keeping about the impact of an intervention designed to improve behavior. If a child's behavior is so problematic that it warrants an FBA and a function-based intervention, then the effectiveness of that intervention must be evaluated. Without objective evaluation measures (via data on the student's behavior), there is no way to justify the time spent conducting the FBA or the time invested in implementing a function-based intervention.

School staff often believe it is not necessary to document a student's behavior to see that it has improved. Although there is some merit in this belief, there is also considerable risk because people often see things differently than they actually are. Consider the following example. For the past few years, we have worked with schools interested in developing schoolwide positive behavioral support systems (cf. Lewis & Sugai, 1999; Liaupsin, Jolivette, & Scott, 2004; Sugai & Horner, 2002). This approach requires school staff to identify the behaviors they expect from students and to directly teach and reinforce these behaviors. A key element of the approach is that the schools also keep data on office disciplinary referrals as a way to evaluate and improve the effectiveness of their efforts. Office disciplinary data include not only the problem behavior that occurred, but also the student who was involved, the time of day the incident occurred, and its location. Regular review of these data has helped many schools isolate their areas of greatest need.

One of our most outstanding elementary schools initially rebelled at the idea of systematically collecting office disciplinary data because they "already knew" their problems. In fact, they immediately volunteered that their primary problems were with the children's behavior on the playground and in the hallways. Fortunately, we persisted, and they reluctantly agreed to collect the data just to prove their point. As it turned out, their data showed that they were wrong. The problems were not most prevalent on the playground but, rather, on the way back to class once recess ended. Similarly, problems rarely occurred in the hallways. However, there were substantial problems in three of their classrooms in which the teachers needed additional training on effective academic instruction.

Collecting data accomplished two goals: (a) it enabled the school's staff to accurately identify where attention was most needed, and (b) it convinced the staff of the value that effective data collection can provide. Since then, this school's staff have ardently supported the need to collect objective data. In fact, this school's top administrators now mentor staff at other schools that are attempting to develop a schoolwide positive behavioral support system. They always stress the need to make decisions based on objective data and routinely "take to task" any school administrator who attempts to make decisions without the data they need.

Data collection is not a luxury; it is a necessity. With that said, it is important that you know how to collect meaningful behavioral measures and how to collect them efficiently. We now take up that task by addressing the different dimensions of behavior that can be measured.

DIMENSIONS OF BEHAVIOR

As mentioned in Chapter 2, behavior has several different dimensions. It is important to understand these dimensions before you attempt to select an appropriate method of behavioral measurement. Just as objects are not one dimensional, neither is behavior. For example, a car could be "measured" with regard to its physical properties (e.g., height, length, width) or with regard to its performance (e.g., maximum speed, time going from 0 to 60 mph, fuel efficiency in average miles per gallon). Similarly, it can be "measured" with regard to its value (e.g., initial cost, resale value).

In this respect, behavior is no different because it is also multidimensional. In fact, most experts agree that behavior has at least six dimensions. These dimensions are

- Frequency/rate
- Duration
- Latency
- Topography
- Locus
- Force

Frequency refers to how often a behavior occurs. **Rate** refers to how often a behavior occurs within a certain time frame. For example, does a child hit others once per minute, once per hour, or once per day?

Duration, the second possible dimension of behavior, pertains to how long the behavior lasts. For example, is the child "off-task" for 5 min/h or 55 min/h?

Latency, the third possible dimension of behavior, refers to the length of time between when a behavior is requested and when it actually begins. For example, if a parent tells a child it is time to get ready for bed, how long does it take until the child actually starts to get ready for bed? Immediately, after 5 min, or a full 15 min after the fifth reminder?

Topography, the fourth possible dimension of behavior, refers to the shape or form of the behavior (i.e., what it looks like). For example, does a child hold a pencil with an immature or mature grip? Does a student type using the two-finger hunt-and-peck method, or does he or she use all 10 fingers while looking away from the keyboard?

Locus, the fifth possible dimension of behavior, addresses where the behavior occurs. For example, does the child eat in the cafeteria, on the playground, in the hallways, or in the classroom?

Force, the final dimension of behavior, addresses the strength or intensity of the behavior. For example, does the child scream or speak softly? More specifically, does the child speak loudly enough to be heard from 5 ft away, from 20 ft away, or from across the playground?

Any behavior can be measured with regard to all six dimensions. For example, 7-year-old Jimmy often uses a profane gesture. Assume we know certain facts about his use of this gesture. For example, we know that Jimmy uses the gesture, on average, three times per hour and that each occurrence lasts for less than 5 s. The gesture occurs immediately after someone else makes a disparaging comment to him, and within 5 min after his teacher tells him to read or do math. Furthermore, he uses the same gesture repeatedly (i.e., it always has the same shape), uses it in all school environments (e.g., classroom, hallways, playground, cafeteria), and is always dramatic in presenting it (i.e., waves and shakes his arms at the same time). With this information, we can describe several relevant dimensions of Jimmy's gesture: its rate (three times per hour), its duration (5 s or less), its latency (immediately in response to comments or within 5 min of receiving an academic assignment), its topography (each arm raised with middle finger extended), its locus (all school environments), and its force (arms and fingers waving rapidly).

Fortunately, we rarely, if ever, need to address all six possible dimensions of behavior. In fact, only one or two dimensions are addressed in most cases. At this point, your task is to determine which dimensions of the target behavior are most relevant. Are you most concerned about how often the behavior occurs? If so, you will concentrate on the behavior's rate. Perhaps you are not particularly concerned with the behavior's rate, but rather with how long it lasts or how long before it begins. If so, you would focus on the behavior's duration or latency. Perhaps the behavior is acceptable in some environments (e.g., the playground) but not in others (e.g., the classroom). If so, you would be concerned with the behavior's locus. Similar questions apply to the other dimensions of behavior. Before going further, you should ask yourself which dimension is of primary concern. The answer will help you identify the dimensions of behavior that will be most relevant in selecting an appropriate measurement system.

MEASURING BEHAVIOR

Several different methods can be used to measure behavior. Miller (2006) suggested it is possible to group these methods as "event based" or "time based" by first considering a behavior's uniformity. **Uniform** behaviors are those in which every performance takes about the same length of time as every other. For example, each swear word a child utters will last roughly the same length of time as any other swear word, or each hit of another child also lasts approximately the same length of time as all other hits. Whenever each performance of a behavior lasts about the same length of time, we can describe it as a uniform behavior. In contrast, many behaviors are **nonuniform** in length. A child may be off-task for 30 s on one occasion and for 10 min on the next occasion. Others, behaviors such as crying, reading, and talking are similar in that each occurrence can last for different lengths of time. Behaviors that can vary in length can be described as nonuniform behaviors.

This basic categorization helps in identifying an appropriate measurement system because, in most cases, uniform behaviors are likely to be best measured by **event-based** methods, and nonuniform behaviors are likely to be best measured by **time-based** methods. In the following sections, you learn about several event-based and time-based methods for measuring behavior. For each, we cover the specifics of the method, the manner in which data are recorded, and the requirements the method places on an observer.

Event-Based Methods

This section presents four event-based methods for measuring behavior. Specifically, we cover the methods used to measure permanent products, frequency of behavior, rate of behavior, and the intensity/magnitude of behavior.

Permanent Products. The first event-based method you could use, permanent product recording, actually does not measure behavior directly. Rather, it measures the products of behavior that last long after the behavior's occurrence. Many examples can be found in the school setting. For example, when a student takes a spelling or math test, he or she often writes answers on a sheet of paper. These written answers are products of the student's actual behavior (solving the problem and writing). When students write graffiti on bathroom walls or carve their initials into a school desk, the products of their behavior (the graffiti and the initials) can be observed and recorded long after the behavior that produced them. Anytime a behavior generates products that last, you can use the permanent product recording method.

The procedure for measuring these products is fairly simple. For example, with the spelling or math test, the teacher would record, at a later time, the number or percentage of words spelled correctly or math problems calculated correctly. Permanent product recording places few demands on the observer because the behavior's product can be measured at a convenient time long after the behavior occurs. The drawback of the method is related to its convenience: One is not measuring behavior directly. Unfortunately, most concerns about behavior that lead to an FBA and a function-based intervention revolve around the behavior itself, rather than its products. Therefore, although this method is useful, easy, and convenient, it is not likely to be the method of choice in most situations.

Frequency. The measurement of the frequency of behavior (i.e., how often it occurs) is perhaps the most basic unit of measurement in the field of applied behavior analysis. Frequency recording is appropriate for measuring uniform behaviors that have a clear beginning *if* the observation periods are

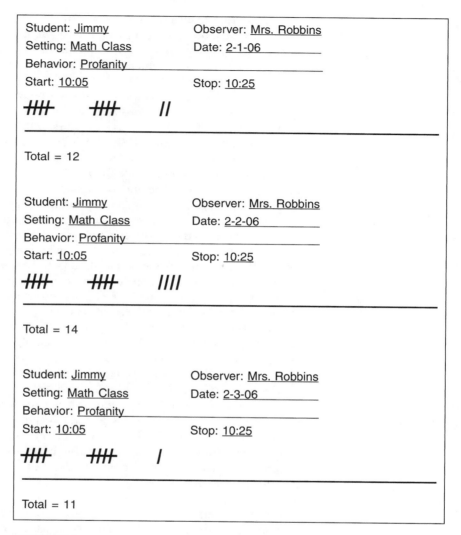

FIGURE 9.1
Example of frequency recording.

equal in length (e.g., always 10 min or always 15 min long) (Zirpoli, 2005).
If observation periods vary in length (e.g., if some are 10 min long and others are 15 or 20 min long), you will need to convert the frequencies into rate
data, as described here.

Frequency recording is fairly simple. You must attend during the entire
length of the observation and record, usually with a tally mark, each time the
behavior occurs (see Figure 9.1). At the end of the observation period, simply
count the number of tallies to identify the frequency of the behavior during
that session. For example, Figure 9.1 shows the number of times Jimmy used

profanity during math class on 3 consecutive days. Frequency recording is fairly demanding because the observer must attend throughout the entire observation period. After multiple observation sessions of equal length, one can compare the behavior's frequency across sessions.

Rate. Rate recording is identical to frequency recording, except that the data come from observation sessions that vary in length. Specifically, rate identifies the number of times a behavior occurs within a specified time frame. Nonbehavioral rate measures (e.g., mph) are common in our society. Behavioral measures of rate are essentially the same.

To calculate rate, simply divide the number of occurrences of the behavior (i.e., its frequency) by the number of minutes the student was observed. The result is usually expressed as number per minute or number per hour. Rate data often produce odd numbers, such as a rate of 0.2 swear words per minute. This is somewhat akin to the report that the average American couple has 1.96 children. Of course, no one has 1.96 children, and no one emits 0.2 responses per minute. Nevertheless, the method enables us to compare the relative strength of behavior when observation sessions vary in length. For convenience and communication, you may find it helpful to convert rate per minute to rate per hour or rate per day. For example, a rate of 0.2 responses per minute, when multiplied by 60 (i.e., the number of minutes in an hour), results in a rate of 12 times per hour. If the school day is 6 h long, multiplying the hourly rate (12) by 6 (i.e., the number of hours in the school day) produces a daily rate of 72. Many school staff find these converted rates to be easier to manage.

When collecting rate data, the demands on the observer's time are the same as those in collecting frequency data, except that the observer must also carefully track and record the length of each observation. Despite these demands, rate measures provide very useful information for assessing a behavior's strength. The fact that observation periods can vary in length offers a degree of convenience to the observer and may make the rate recording method an attractive option.

Intensity/Magnitude. The measurement of the intensity or magnitude of a behavior addresses its force. These measures usually require judgment by the observer, which makes them less attractive than other options in most cases. Measures of intensity or magnitude are usually estimates based on a predetermined qualitative scale. They often require an observer to rate a behavior's force (e.g., as "very strong, strong, weak, or very weak" or as "very loud, loud, quiet, or very quiet"). Ratings of this sort are often problematic because they are subjective. In some cases, it may be possible to use more objective criteria (e.g., loud enough to be heard from 5 ft away, 10 ft away, or 20 ft away). Nevertheless, the measurement of a behavior's intensity/magnitude is inevitably far less precise than frequency or rate measures of uniform behaviors. Fortunately, the intensity or magnitude of a behavior is usually not a school staff's primary concern. Frequency and rate measures are typically much more useful when the need to measure uniform behaviors arises.

As with frequency and rate recording, the measurement of intensity/magnitude places considerable demands on the observer. Careful attention throughout the observation period is essential. This requirement, combined with the difficulties inherent in subjectively rating a behavior's force, make the use of the intensity/magnitude recording method relatively unattractive to school staff when they are selecting an appropriate method to measure uniform behaviors.

Time-Based Methods

This section covers five time-based methods that can be used to measure behavior. Specifically, we cover the methods used to measure a behavior's duration and latency, two methods of interval recording (partial interval and whole interval), and time sampling.

Duration. The recording of a behavior's duration is fairly straightforward. To do this, simply keep track of how long each occurrence of the behavior lasts. This can be done by using any clock that has a seconds hand, including a stopwatch, a wristwatch, or a clock on the classroom wall. You may simply record the duration of each occurrence of the behavior (called **response duration**), or you may start and stop the timer every time the behavior occurs, which results in a total duration for the session.

Duration measures provide precise information about how long a behavior occurs. However, the method is very demanding. The observer must watch carefully throughout the entire observation period and also start and stop a timer, possibly on multiple occasions. These demands make duration recording much less attractive than the interval recording methods described later. Nevertheless, duration recording does have some uses. For example, in a middle school or high school, a student may have difficulty with transitions from one class to another. Specifically, some students leave one class on time but rarely show up at the next class promptly. In these cases, school staff often find it useful to measure the duration of the student's transition from one class to another. For example, if the passing periods are 5 min long, but the student typically takes 15 min to arrive at the next class, the staff might develop an intervention to correct the problem. By tracking when the student leaves one class and arrives at another, you can calculate the average duration of transitions for a student and measure improvements in transition times (i.e., duration) as the intervention is implemented.

Latency. The measurement of latency is identical to the measurement of duration, except the observer is not measuring how long the behavior lasts. Rather, the observer measures the length of time that elapses between when an instruction is given and when the behavior begins. The advantages and disadvantages of latency recording are the same as those associated with duration recording.

Interval Recording (Partial Interval and Whole Interval). The interval recording methods are used quite often in research and in practice because they are flexible and provide useful data. Their common feature is that an observation period is divided into blocks of time, or **intervals,** and observations are recorded separately for each interval. Typically, a period of time is divided into equal intervals. For example, a 15-min observation period may be divided into 30 intervals, each of which is 30 s long. The observer then makes recordings based on what occurs during each interval. The recordings are usually fairly simple, such as a "+" or "−" for each interval, to indicate occurrence or nonoccurrence of the behavior. The observer does not record the frequency of the behavior during the interval, but rather its presence or absence.

The observer may choose to use either the partial interval or whole interval recording method. With the **partial interval** method, the observer records whether the behavior occurred at all during the interval. If the behavior occurs even once, the observer would record a "+" for that interval (see Figure 9.2). It does not matter whether the behavior occurs once or 10 times during the interval because the observer scores only its presence ("+") or its absence ("−"). This process continues interval by interval throughout the entire recording session. When the session is finished, the observer calculates the percentage of intervals in which the behavior occurred. In Figure 9.2, the observer determined that the behavior occurred during 45% of the intervals. This was determined by dividing the number of intervals in which the behavior occurred (9) by the total number of intervals (20), and then multiplying the result by 100%. This percentage provides a useful estimate of the overall strength of the behavior.

If the **whole interval** method is used, the procedures are identical with one exception: A "+" is scored only if the behavior lasts throughout the entire

**FIGURE 9.2
Partial interval
recording.**

Student: Jimmy	Observer: Ms. Smith
Setting: Math Class	Date: 2-1-06
Behavior: Profanity	
Start: 10:05	Stop: 10:15

10 min: 30-s intervals

1	2	3	4	5	6	7	8	9	10	11	12	13	14	15	16	17	18	19	20
+	+	+	−	−	−	−	−	−	+	−	+	−	−	+	+	−	+	−	+

\+ = occurrence
− = nonoccurrence

Summary
Profanity occurred during 9/20 = 45% of the intervals

interval. The whole interval method is most appropriate when observing behaviors that are nonuniform, such as on-task behavior. Conversely, the partial interval method is most appropriate when observing brief, uniform behaviors that have distinct beginnings and endings. Common examples include profanity, hitting, or making noises. Both interval methods place considerable demands on the observer because they typically require constant attention throughout the observation period. Nevertheless, many school staff find the interval methods attractive because they are easy to do and usually result in a useful estimate of a behavior's strength. By comparing the data from one observation session to another over time, school staff can easily determine whether an intervention is effective.

Time Sampling. The final time-based method, time sampling, is also very popular because of its simplicity and usefulness. Time sampling, sometimes called **momentary time sampling,** is identical to the interval methods with one important exception: A behavior is scored as occurring ("+") or not occurring ("−"), based solely on whether it is occurring *at the end* of the interval. Therefore, the observer only needs to observe directly at the end of the interval. The method of recording and calculating the percentage of intervals in which the behavior occurred is the same as with the interval methods.

Time sampling is an appropriate method for measuring nonuniform behaviors such as on-task behavior; it is not an appropriate method for measuring brief, uniform behaviors that might occur frequently but never exactly at the end of the interval. For these behaviors, frequency, rate, or the partial interval recording method are more appropriate.

In addition to requiring less of an observer's time, time sampling may offer another advantage. Although most observations use fixed intervals, or intervals that are the same length, it is possible to use intervals that vary in length but have a common average duration. With this method, called **variable interval time sampling,** you might record after 30 s, then after 1 min, then after 20 s more, and so on. Using this method, if a total of 30 observations were made during a 15-min period, the average interval length would be 30 s. Because this method is very flexible, it is particularly useful if the observer suspects a student is aware that his or her behavior is being recorded (a problem called reactivity, which is discussed later in this chapter).

Now that you know the basic methods of measuring behavior and their relative advantages and disadvantages, we discuss the pragmatics of how to collect data, how to manage an observation session, and how to avoid common problems that can compromise the data you collect.

HOW TO COLLECT DATA: METHODS AND CONSIDERATIONS

This section covers several practical tasks and considerations that will influence the quality and usefulness of the data you collect. Specifically, we address the problem of determining the "right" measurement method. We also review the identifying information that needs to be included on data collection forms, and the topics of when and how often to observe. This is followed by information on how to determine appropriate observation lengths when using both event-based and time-based measurement methods. Finally, we cover the topic of interobserver agreement (IOA), identify factors that can compromise the validity of data, and identify common mistakes that can nullify your data collection efforts.

Picking an Appropriate Measurement Method

It would be ideal if there was a simple formula or set of questions that would identify exactly the "right" measurement method for every occasion. Unfortunately, no such formula or set of questions exists. Therefore, you will need to use your knowledge of the different measurement methods, and of the student and situation, to identify the appropriate method. However, sometimes more than one method may be appropriate. The ultimate choice among appropriate methods will rest on the ease of data collection, the demands made on the observer, and personal preference.

Fortunately, common sense and reason can help you identify which methods are potentially appropriate and inappropriate for a given situation. Earlier, we stated that your first task is to identify the dimension of the student's target behavior that concerns you the most. Assume a student's target behavior is off-task and the replacement behavior is on-task. In this instance, your greatest concern is most likely how long each type of behavior lasts (i.e., its duration). Knowing this, you can eliminate the event-based methods. You can also eliminate the partial interval recording method because it is most appropriate for measuring brief, uniform behaviors. This leaves three options: duration recording, whole interval recording, and time sampling. Each method would give you useful information about the strength of the student's on- and off-task behaviors. Now, consider which method is the easiest to implement, makes the fewest demands on your time, and provides the most useful information. In this situation, many people would select time sampling because it is easy to perform and makes relatively few demands on their time. However, others might choose the whole interval method, especially if their goal is for the student to be on-task all or most of the time. Although the whole interval method makes greater demands on the observer's time, it provides the most conservative possible estimate of on-task behavior because credit is given for being on-task only if the behavior occurs throughout the entire interval.

With a different student, the target behavior might be profanity. Once again, begin by identifying the dimension of behavior that is of greatest concern. Most staff would focus on the frequency of the behavior. Each use of profanity is brief and the behavior is uniform, so you can automatically eliminate most of the time-based methods as being inappropriate. Once again, this leaves you with three options: frequency, rate, or partial interval recording. Each could provide useful information. Some school staff may count frequencies because they want precise data and are able to observe at the same time and for the same length of time. Others may choose the rate method because they are not always able to observe at the same time or for the same length of time. Still others may select the partial interval method because it provides a useful estimate of the behavior's strength and is easier to implement.

Given that there is often not a single "right" method for every situation, how do you proceed? First, identify which methods are potentially appropriate for measuring the dimension of behavior about which you are most concerned (see Figure 9.3). Second, ensure the method chosen provides useful information. Finally, weigh the relative demands of each potentially appropriate method, and select the one that is easiest to perform given your knowledge of the student, his or her behavior, and the setting and situation in which data must be collected. This process of decision making, combined with judgment and experience, should enable you to identify at least one measurement method that is appropriate for your needs.

Identifying Information

Because data collection is a form of record keeping, you will need to make sure your data collection sheet or form contains certain identifying information. Zirpoli (2005) recommended that every data collection form should include the following information: the student's name, the target behavior

FIGURE 9.3
Process for selecting a measurement method.

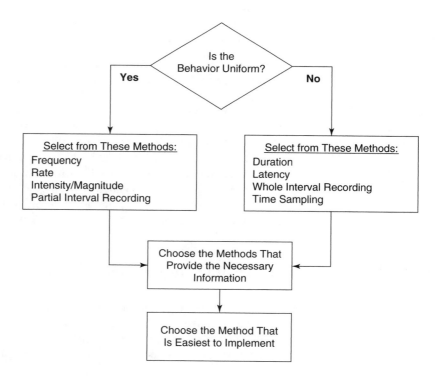

(and replacement behavior if both are being recorded), the environment or situation in which the student is being observed, the observer's name, and the date of the observation. We suggest also noting the time at which the observation begins and ends. Figures 9.1 and 9.2 are good examples of data collection forms that include this information. Store receipts include similar information (e.g., date, time of day, item purchased, cost). You should be no different. Proper record keeping requires that you include the identifying information listed previously. Without it, you may have potentially useful data that you cannot use.

When to Observe

In Chapter 4, we suggested collecting A-B-C data when the target behavior is most likely to occur. Use the same approach when collecting data designed to test an intervention or evaluate its long-term effects. Information gathered as part of the FBA will be very helpful in identifying the best times to collect data. It will also help you avoid needlessly wasting time. Many school staff have complained that they made time for an observation, identified an appropriate measurement system, and prepared appropriate data collection forms only to find that the behavior rarely occurred during observation. Although their presence may have influenced the child's behavior, it is equally likely that they simply picked a poor time to observe. By using already available information from the FBA, you can avoid this problem and use your time productively.

How Often to Observe

During the early stages of an intervention, you should observe frequently, preferably every day. Once a function-based intervention has produced consistently positive results, you can reduce the frequency of formal data collection to once or twice per week. If an intervention is ineffective, this approach will prevent its unnecessary long-term implementation and provide an important cue that a better function-based intervention is needed. In the same respect, the approach will help you verify when a function-based intervention is, in fact, effective. This information is very important, especially to parents and staff who are attempting to implement the intervention. The approach will also provide the information needed to identify when you can begin fading the function-based intervention, a topic that is addressed in Chapters 12 and 13.

Determining Observation Length (Event-Based Methods)

Once again, there are no hard and fast rules to help you determine the length of each observation session. As before, the decision is a judgment you will make based on your knowledge of the student, his or her behavior, and the setting or situation in which the target behavior occurs. In many cases, natural circumstances combined with information from the FBA will help you identify an appropriate observation length. For example, assume an FBA indicates that a child uses profanity during independent seatwork assignments in reading and math, that these academic areas are addressed every day, that 40 min per day are devoted to both reading and math, and that the independent seatwork portion of each day's lesson typically occupies the last 20 min of each session. Armed with this information, you could reasonably set your observation length as the 20 min of independent seatwork in each academic area.

With a different student, the target behavior might be "aggressive" behavior (pushing, grabbing, and hitting other children). From the FBA, you determine that the behaviors are most likely to occur during recess times midmorning and after lunch. Knowing this, you could reasonably observe during these recess periods. If the morning recess lasted 15 min and the afterlunch recess lasted for 20 min, these periods would naturally define the observation length.

Determining Observation Length (Time-Based Methods)

The same basic approach can be used to determine how long to observe when using time-based methods. For example, assume that an FBA reveals that a student's target behavior involves lengthy transition times getting from one class to another, and that transitions are most problematic with certain classes, while not much of a problem with others. Given this information, you could reasonably collect data during the problematic transition times. In this case, the length of the observation would be determined by how long it takes the student to get to the next class.

With a different student, the primary concern might be with on- and off-task behavior. Consider the previous example of the student who had difficulties during independent seatwork assignments in reading and math. However, in this case, assume that our concern is not with profanity but with nonuniform behavior, namely, on- and off-task behavior. As before, it is likely the natural length of the activity (i.e., 20 min) would define the observation length. In this situation, you would likely use either whole interval recording or time sampling. On the recording sheet, you would record a "+" to indicate on-task behavior and a "−" to indicate off-task behavior. In such situations, focus on measuring the replacement behavior. The goal of a function-based intervention is to improve behavior. Therefore, it is useful to know that on-task behavior occurred during only 25% of the intervals prior to intervention and rose to 95% of the intervals with intervention. Given that, you still have some work to do. Namely, because you are using an interval recording system, you will still need to determine the length of each interval.

The need to determine an appropriate **interval length** becomes obvious if you realize that simply changing the length of the intervals you use can produce drastically different results. For example, assume a behavior occurs, on average, once every minute. With a 15-s interval, we would not expect the behavior to occur more than once every four intervals, and we would conclude that the behavior occurred during no more than 25% of the intervals. By simply increasing the length of the intervals to 30 s, the behavior would likely occur once every two intervals, indicating that it occurred during as many as 50% of the intervals. If the interval length was 1 min or longer, it might occur during as many as 100% of the intervals. These three different interval lengths would produce very different results and conclusions, even though the strength of the behavior never changed. Thus, finding an appropriate interval length is important.

So, what is the appropriate interval length? Many authors (e.g., Alberto & Troutman, 2006; Cooper et al., 1987; Kazdin, 1989) have recommended that intervals should be short, ranging from 6 s to no more than 30 s. With time sampling, these authors recommend that intervals may be somewhat longer, but should not exceed 5 min. These guidelines are usually effective with the whole interval or time sampling methods, but may not apply when using partial interval recording. In fact, the best way to determine interval length when using the partial interval system is to determine the average amount of time between occurrences of the behavior (called the **average interresponse time**). To do this, first calculate the behavior's rate (e.g., 20 times per hour). Then, calculate the average amount of time between responses (i.e., 60 min divided by 20 occurrences equals an average of 3 min between responses). Using this method, you could appropriately set the interval length at 3 min. For practical purposes, you should round the average interresponse time to a convenient, approximate length for each interval (e.g., 28 s could be rounded to 30 s, and 2:04 could be rounded to 2 min).

A related concern is the number of intervals in which you record. You must have a sufficient number of intervals so you can see changes in behavior as they occur. For most practical purposes, 20 to 30 intervals will be sufficient. However, a smaller number of intervals can be problematic. For example, assume a behavior occurs, on average, once every minute, and that data are recorded for a total of 10 min. In this case, each data point counts for 10% of the total result, which creates a risk that your data can be misleading. With 20 to 30 data points per session, you are likely to avoid this risk.

Interobserver Agreement

IOA refers to the degree to which two independent observers agree. When behavioral measurement methods are used, IOA (also called **interobserver reliability** or **interrater reliability**) is the acceptable method for assessing the reliability of your data. If you were conducting research, it would be essential to regularly and systematically assess IOA. However, in all likelihood, you are not conducting research. Instead, you are attempting to use effective methods to improve a student's behavior. The question then becomes, "What importance does assessing IOA hold for you?" Kazdin (1989) offered three reasons why practitioners should consider assessing IOA, at least occasionally:

1. The data that are used to evaluate an intervention's effectiveness should reflect the student's "true" behavior. Therefore, the data must be reliable.

2. Assessing IOA minimizes **observer bias** (the possibility that beliefs or emotional feelings about individual students will influence the data recorded).

3. IOA provides independent evidence about how well a target and replacement behavior have been defined.

Therefore, even though you are not conducting research, the periodic assessment of IOA offers distinct advantages that are important, especially considering the reason we collect data is to make informed, accurate decisions about whether to implement, continue, or fade a function-based intervention.

In practice, there are no hard and fast rules about how often to assess IOA. During the initial testing of an intervention (addressed in Chapter 10), we recommend assessing IOA during every testing session. When implementing an intervention, you should check IOA at least once per week. When an intervention's effectiveness has been established, occasional IOA checks (e.g., once every 2 or 3 weeks) will help prevent the problem of observer drift (discussed later in this chapter).

When using behavioral measurement methods, always report the data of the "primary" observer. When assessing IOA, a second person (i.e., a "secondary" observer) also records data on the student's behavior. Use the secondary observer's data solely for the purpose of assessing IOA. Do not average the two observers' data to obtain a final result. The secondary observer's data tell us the degree to which we can have confidence in the data reported by the primary observer. In general, IOAs should be at least 80%, although higher percentages are preferable, especially with behaviors that are overt and easy to identify.

Calculating IOA. The method you should use to assess IOA depends on the method of behavioral measurement you are using. When using the **permanent product** method, you would derive IOA by calculating a percentage of agreement between the scores of the two observers. For example, assume that you want to calculate the IOA of two observers' scores on a 10-item math test. If the observers agreed in scoring 9 of the answers, but disagreed in scoring 1 answer, IOA would be calculated by dividing the number of agreements by the total number of items scored (i.e., number of agreements and disagreements), and then multiplying the result by 100%. In our example, the two observers had nine agreements and one disagreement, so the IOA would be 90% (i.e., 9/10 = $0.9 \times 100\% = 90\%$). Using the same formula, the IOA would be only 50% if the observers agreed on only 5 of the student's 10 answers.

With frequency and rate data, you will use a slightly different method to assess IOA. Put simply, IOA is calculated by dividing the lower reported frequency by the higher reported frequency. Assume that two observers independently recorded the number of times Jimmy made his profane gesture during a language arts lesson. If one observer counted 8 occurrences of the gesture, and the other observer counted 10 occurrences, the IOA would be 80% (i.e., 8/10 = $0.8 \times 100\% = 80\%$).

With intensity/magnitude data, calculating IOA becomes a little more complicated. First, the two observer's ratings of each occurrence of the behavior are compared independently (i.e., the two ratings for the first occurrence are compared, and then the two ratings for the second occurrence are compared, etc.). Each identical rating for a particular occurrence is considered to be an agreement, whereas any occurrence that is rated differently by the two observers is considered to be a disagreement. IOA is then calculated by dividing the number of agreements by the total number of ratings, and then multiplying the result by 100%. If two observers rated the intensity/magnitude of 12 occurrences of a behavior and agreed on 10 of the ratings, the IOA would be 83% (i.e., $10/12 = 0.83 \times 100\% = 83\%$).

With duration and latency data, the method used to calculate IOA is similar to that used with frequency and rate data: The shorter duration is divided by the longer duration, and the result is then multiplied by 100%. For example, assume that one observer recorded that it took Mario 10 min to get from one class to the next, and that a second observer recorded that it took him 11 min. In this example, the IOA would be 91% (i.e., $10/11 = 0.91 \times 100\% = 91\%$).

When you are using either interval method (partial or whole interval) or time sampling, assess IOA by using the interval-by-interval method (Kazdin, 1982). This approach is very similar to the one recommended for assessing IOA with intensity/magnitude ratings. Compare the data reported by each observer interval by interval. Look at each observer's recording (e.g., "+" or "−") for the first interval. If they are identical (i.e., if both observers scored a "+" or both scored a "−"), count that as an agreement. If the recordings are different, count it as a disagreement. Continue this process independently for every interval the two observers scored. To derive IOA, divide the number of agreements (i.e., identically scored intervals) by the total number of intervals and multiply the result by 100%. Figure 9.4 provides an example in which two observers measured Jimmy's on-task behavior for 20 min using a 1-min time sample. Comparing their recordings on each interval, we see they scored a total of 20 intervals, disagreed on 1 interval (interval 12), and agreed on the other 19. In this case, the IOA would be 95% (i.e., $19/20 = 0.95 \times 100\% = 95\%$).

When using the interval methods or time sampling, the two observers must coordinate their timing so each interval begins and ends at the same time. Timing can be synchronized by using a signal, a clock on the classroom wall, or a signal prerecorded onto a cassette tape and heard through an earphone.

Now that you know how to select an appropriate measurement method, collect the data, and assess its reliability, we consider important factors that can compromise the validity and usefulness of the data you collect.

Factors That Can Affect Measurement

Two primary problems can nullify your efforts to collect meaningful data—reactivity and observer drift.

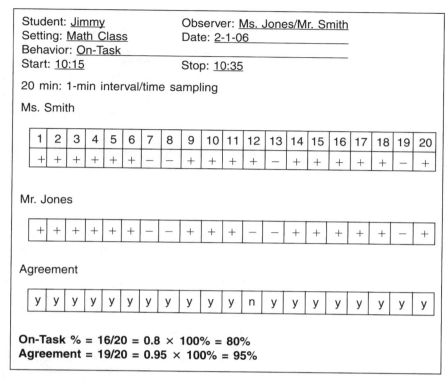

FIGURE 9.4
Assessment of interobserver agreement.

Reactivity. Sometimes people behave differently because they are being observed. This phenomenon is called **reactivity** (i.e., the student reacts to the presence of the observer by behaving differently). Sometimes the presence of an observer will increase the strength of a student's behavior; sometimes it will decrease it. If your presence decreases the strength of the behavior, do not be surprised if the teacher asks you to come every day, hoping that your mere presence might be an effective intervention. Comments such as these should be taken as an important indication that the data you have collected may not be representative of the student's usual behavior.

Kerr and Nelson (2002) offered several practical suggestions that will minimize the problem of reactivity:

1. Before the session, talk with the teacher about the purpose of your observation, what to tell the class about your presence, and the extent of your participation in the class.

2. Enter and leave the classroom "unobtrusively." This can often be accomplished by entering and leaving the class during normal breaks in the routine.

3. Avoid being "conspicuous." To do this, sit so you can see the student and monitor his or her behavior, but be out of the student's direct line of vision.

4. Do not interact with or make eye contact with any students or the teacher while observing. If a student insists on getting your attention, communicate that you are not allowed to talk, and redirect the student's attention.

5. Do not participate in any classroom activities. You are there to observe, not to participate.

6. Wait until the students have become accustomed to your presence before beginning systematic observations.

Observer Drift. Sometimes observers, without realizing it, gradually change the definition of the behavior they are observing. This phenomenon, called **observer drift,** is especially likely if observers collect data periodically, rather than regularly. If observer drift occurs, the data become meaningless because they reflect changes in the definition of the behavior, not actual changes in the student's behavior. Observer drift can be minimized if you (a) define the target and replacement behaviors carefully and precisely (as discussed in Chapter 2) at the outset of the FBA, and (b) carefully review the response definitions before each observation session.

The suggestions presented in this section help you minimize the problems of reactivity and observer drift. Remember, your goal is to collect data that will help you accurately evaluate an intervention's effectiveness. Anything that could compromise your data should be avoided at all costs.

Common Mistakes

The three most common mistakes that can compromise your data have already been identified, but they will be recapped to emphasize their importance. The first mistake is to select an inappropriate method for measuring the behavior of concern. A good example is counting the frequency of on- or off-task behavior. The frequency method is appropriate for counting brief, uniform behaviors. However, on- and off-task behaviors are nonuniform behaviors, and each occurrence may vary drastically in length. It does not help to know that a student was off-task 10 times. One occurrence may have lasted for 10 s, and the next for 10 min. What if the student is off-task only three times the next day? Is 10 more than 3? Did each occurrence last for 15 s or for 15 min? Because an inappropriate measurement method was used, we have no way of knowing. For this reason, carefully follow the guidelines presented here when selecting a method to measure behavior.

The second most common problem occurs when inadequate behavioral definitions are used. The purpose of defining behavior is to clearly identify the actions we want from students and the actions about which we are concerned. If each person who reads the definition interprets it even slightly differently, we will inevitably wind up with meaningless data and no reliable way to evaluate an intervention's effectiveness. Carefully follow the recommendations and procedures described in Chapter 2 to avoid this problem.

The third most common problem is having an inadequate amount of data to make informed decisions. This problem is most likely to emerge if you observe at the wrong time, observe for too short of a period, or do not have a sufficient number of intervals when using the interval methods or time sampling. Once again, the guidelines offered in this chapter should enable you to avoid these problems. Data collection takes time, and that time needs to be spent productively.

EXAMPLES OF BEHAVIORAL MEASUREMENT

This section presents two examples of behavioral measurement, one involving event-based methods, and the other involving time-based methods. For each, we first describe the appropriate application of the information in this chapter, and then point out errors that would have made the data unusable.

Example 1: Mary

Mary, a 9-year-old fourth grader, attended general education classes for most of the school day, but also attended a Resource Room 80 min per day to receive direct instruction in math and reading. Mary's teachers were concerned because she often "got into fights" with other students during recess in the morning and after lunch. "Fighting" occurred almost daily, had occurred regularly for 2 years, and had resulted in Mary being suspended from school several times during the past year. For this reason, an FBA was conducted and a function-based intervention was developed. School staff now needed a way to measure whether the intervention was effective.

The staff first reviewed the definitions of the target and replacement behaviors and determined they were acceptable. The target behavior, "fighting," was defined as "pushing, grabbing, hitting, or kicking another student." The replacement behavior, "appropriate interaction," was defined as "talking, playing, following instructions from staff, and following the playground rules." Next, they identified the dimension of behavior that was of primary concern. School staff wanted to eliminate all instances of fighting. They were not particularly concerned with how long a fight lasted, but with whether it occurred at all. They immediately ruled out the time-based methods, except for partial interval recording. This left three options: frequency recording, rate recording, and partial interval recording.

Each recess period was 20 min long, so the rate method was not needed. Based on their knowledge of Mary and the situation, the staff selected the frequency method to count occurrences of fighting. Because they also knew that Mary always interacted appropriately when she was not fighting, the staff concentrated on measuring the target behavior (i.e., appropriate behavior could be assumed whenever fights did not occur). Using the frequency method, observers simply recorded the number of fights that occurred during each recess period. During the testing of the intervention and the early stages of its implementation, they recorded data during every recess period. After 2 weeks, the frequency of fighting had dropped dramatically, so the staff reduced the frequency of observations to 2 days per week. The trend continued, so after another 2 weeks the staff observed only 1 day per week. IOA checks were conducted every day during intervention testing, twice per week during the next 2 weeks, and once per week after that. This approach enabled them to conclude, with confidence, that the intervention had effectively eliminated Mary's fighting.

If the recess periods had lasted different lengths of time (e.g., 15 min in the morning and 25 min after lunch), staff could have used the rate method or could have counted frequencies but treated the morning and afternoon recess sessions separately. If the staff had not carefully considered the dimension of behavior about which they were most concerned, they might have selected an inappropriate measurement method, such as duration recording, whole interval recording, or time sampling. These methods would have been inappropriate because they would not have provided the information the staff needed. Knowing how long each fight lasted would not have been helpful unless their goal had been to "shorten" the fights rather than eliminate them. Knowing whether a fight lasted through a particular 1-min interval would not have been helpful, either. Similarly, knowing whether a fight was occurring at a particular moment would have been equally unhelpful.

Example 2: Joe

Joe, an 8-year-old third grader, had been diagnosed with ADHD. He attended general education classes, and his teachers were concerned because he was frequently off-task, especially during academic instruction in math. In fact, they had discussed whether Joe might be better off going to the resource room during math so he could receive "more individual attention" and have less opportunity to compete with their ongoing math lesson.

Before selecting a measurement method, the staff first reviewed the definitions of the target behavior (off-task) and the replacement behavior (on-task). Joe was considered to be off-task if he was "engaged in any behavior that is incompatible with work completion, such as leaving his seat, doodling, talking to classmates off topic, complaining about the work, or playing with various objects." He was considered to be on-task if he was "sitting in his seat, working on his packet of assigned projects, and raising his hand when he requires assistance." These definitions were found to be adequate.

The staff then identified the dimension of Joe's behavior about which they were most concerned. Their goal was to decrease the percentage of time Joe was off-task and increase the percentage of time that he was on-task. Thus, they were concerned with how long these behaviors lasted. This decision enabled them to eliminate the event-based methods and to concentrate on the time-based methods, especially duration, whole interval, and time sampling. The staff decided to use time sampling to measure Joe's on- and off-task behavior because it was the easiest method to implement and was as likely as the other potentially appropriate methods to provide the information they needed.

Each math period lasted 25 min. The staff decided to use a 1-min interval because it would provide a sufficient number of data points per class session. During the intervention testing and the early stages of implementation, they recorded data every day. After 2 weeks, they reduced the frequency of data collection to three times per week. After another week, they reduced it to two times per week. After 2 more weeks, data were collected 1 day per week. IOA checks were conducted every day during the intervention testing, three times per week during the first 2 weeks of implementation, and once per week thereafter. Using this approach, the staff was able to verify that the intervention was highly effective (i.e., Joe's on-task behavior increased to high levels, and off-task behavior rarely occurred).

If the staff had decided to use the partial interval method, they would have generated data that would not have given them the information they needed. Partial interval data may have indicated that a high percentage of on-task behavior was occurring, even if it never lasted for an entire 1-min interval. If the staff had selected one of the event-based methods, similar problems would have occurred. For example, data on the frequency or rate of on- and off-task behavior could easily have provided misleading results. Knowing the frequency of these behaviors does not provide information about how long they last. Finally, if the staff had used a 5-min time sample, instead of a 1-min time sample, they would not have had enough data to make informed decisions about the effectiveness of the function-based intervention.

Steps in Identifying and Using an Appropriate Measurement System

The following list of steps and activities summarizes the process for identifying and using an appropriate measurement system:

1. Review the definitions of the target and replacement behaviors to ensure they are adequate.
2. Identify the dimensions of the target behavior that are of primary concern.
3. Identify the measurement methods that will provide useful information about this dimension of behavior.
4. Among potentially appropriate methods, determine which will provide the most useful information. Then, use your knowledge of the student, his or her behavior, and the setting and situation to identify the method you will use.
5. Record the necessary identifying information on the data sheet.
6. Determine when to observe.
7. Determine how often to observe.
8. Determine the length of the observation.
9. When using the interval methods or time sampling, determine the length of each interval, and ensure you have enough intervals per session.
10. Periodically assess IOA.

EXERCISES

1. Identify a permanent product of behavior from a classroom situation. Identify the measure you will take (e.g., percent of correct answers on a math worksheet). Then, measure the permanent product. Have a second person independently score the permanent product and calculate IOA.

2. Define a classroom behavior that occurs fairly often. Count the behavior's frequency for a fixed period of time (e.g., 15 or 20 min) at least twice. Have someone else record the same behavior at the same time. Report the behavior's frequency and the IOA between you and the other observer.

3. Calculate the rate for each of the following two observations. In observation 1, a child uses profanity five times in 20 min. In observation 2, the child uses profanity four times in 10 min. What is the overall rate of profanity?

4. Define a brief, uniform behavior that can be measured appropriately by the partial interval method. Include at least 20 to 30 intervals. Measure the behavior in the classroom using the partial interval recording method, then calculate the percentage of intervals in which the behavior occurred. Have someone else record the same behavior at the same time, and calculate the IOA between you and the other observer.

5. Define a nonuniform behavior that can be measured appropriately by the whole interval method. Include at least 20 to 30 intervals. Measure the behavior in the classroom using the whole interval recording method, then calculate the percentage of intervals in which the behavior occurred. Have someone else record the same behavior at the same time, and calculate the IOA between you and the other observer.

6. Define a nonuniform behavior that can be measured appropriately by time sampling. Include at least 20 to 30 intervals. Measure the behavior in the classroom using time sampling, then calculate the percentage of intervals in which the behavior occurred. Have someone else record at the same time. Calculate the IOA between you and the other observer.

REFERENCES

Alberto, P. A., & Troutman, A. C. (2006). *Applied behavior analysis to teachers* (7th ed.). Upper Saddle River, NJ: Merrill/Prentice Hall.

Bijou, S. W. (1970). What psychology has to offer education—now. *Journal of Applied Behavior Analysis, 3,* 65-71.

Cooper, J. O. (1981). *Measuring behavior* (2nd ed.). Columbus, OH: Merrill.

Cooper, J. O., Heron, T. E., & Heward, W. L. (1987). *Applied behavior analysis.* Columbus, OH: Merrill.

Kazdin, A. E. (1982). *Single-case research designs.* New York: Oxford University Press.

Kazdin, A. E. (1989). *Behavior modification in applied settings.* Pacific Grove, CA: Brooks/Cole.

Kerr, M. M., & Nelson, C. M. (2002). *Strategies for addressing behavior problems in the classroom* (4th ed.). Upper Saddle River, NJ: Merrill/Prentice Hall.

Lewis, T. J., & Sugai, G. (1999). Effective behavior support: A systems approach to proactive school-wide management. *Focus on Exceptional Children, 31,* 1-24.

Liaupsin, C., Jolivette, K., & Scott, T. M. (2004). School-wide systems of behavior support: Maximizing student success in schools. In R. B. Rutherford, M. M. Quinn, & S. R. Mathur (Eds.), *Handbook of research in behavior disorders* (pp. 487–501). New York: Guilford.

Lund, K., Schnaps, L., & Bijou, S. W. (1983). Let's take another look at record keeping. *Teaching Exceptional Children, 15,* 155–159.

Martin, G., & Pear, J. (2003). *Behavior modification: What it is and how to do it* (7th ed.). Upper Saddle River, NJ: Merrill/Prentice Hall.

Miller, L. K. (2006). *Principles of everyday behavior analysis* (4th ed.). Pacific Grove, CA: Brooks/Cole.

Sugai, G., & Horner, R. H. (2002). The evolution of discipline practices: School-wide positive behavior supports. *Child & Family Behavior Therapy, 24,* 23–50.

Sulzer-Azaroff, B., & Mayer, R. G. (1991). *Behavior analysis for lasting change.* New York: Harcourt Brace Jovanovich.

Wetzel, R. J., & Hoschouer, R. L. (1984). *Residential teaching communities: Program development and staff training for developmentally disabled persons.* Redwood City, CA: Addison Wesley.

Zirpoli, T. J. (2005). *Behavior management: Applications for teachers* (4th ed.). Upper Saddle River, NJ: Merrill/Prentice Hall.

CHAPTER 10

Testing the Intervention

OUTCOMES

After reading this chapter, you will be able to

- Arrange the conditions needed to test a function-based intervention.
- Avoid common errors that compromise the usefulness of intervention testing data.

A t this point, you have conducted the FBA, developed a function-based intervention, and identified an appropriate measurement system. Now, you will need to conduct a brief test of the intervention so you can decide whether to move to full-scale implementation. This chapter explains why it is important to test the intervention prior to implementation and addresses the methods used in intervention testing. It also presents three examples of intervention testing, including two that were done well and one in which some common mistakes were made.

WHY TEST THE INTERVENTION?

If a problematic behavior is significant enough to warrant an FBA and the development of a function-based intervention, it is important to ensure the intervention is likely to be effective before you and others invest significant amounts of time and energy into implementing it. If you skip this step in the process, you may needlessly waste the efforts of many people. Fortunately, testing the intervention is fairly easy and usually takes only a short period of time.

Sometimes function-based interventions are complex, incorporating a number of different procedures that must be implemented precisely. However, many effective function-based interventions are quite simple and straightforward. In fact, many school staff have marveled at the dramatic improvements in behavior that have resulted from simple changes that are easy to implement. The power of a function-based intervention, whether it is complex or simple, stems from the fact that it directly addresses the variables that are responsible for a student's problematic behaviors. In short, the greatest value of a function-based intervention is that it helps you identify the "right" things to do.

Regardless of whether an intervention is simple or complex, it is very helpful to know that even a brief test of the intervention produced objective data that supported its effectiveness. Armed with this information, you can then fully implement the intervention and confidently expect that it will produce positive results. Supportive data from intervention testing is very helpful to school-based teams that are responsible for developing and implementing function-based interventions. These data are also very useful with staff who harbor doubts about whether the intervention is likely to work. For these reasons, time spent testing an intervention before implementing it is time well spent.

HOW TO TEST THE INTERVENTION

The basic format used to test function-based interventions can be understood by considering the following story. Ms. Jones was a seventh-grade social studies teacher. One of her students, Sally, never turned in her homework, and homework assignments were due daily every Tuesday through Friday. Ms. Jones suspected that Sally might be motivated to turn in her homework each day if it resulted in getting to do one of her favorite activities—using the classroom computer.

To test her idea, Ms. Jones gave a homework assignment on Monday that would be due Tuesday morning. She did not mention anything to Sally about getting to use the computer if she turned in her homework. Sure enough, Sally arrived on Tuesday without her homework. After giving the homework assignment on Tuesday, Ms. Jones told Sally that she could use the classroom computer during the last 10 min of class if she turned in the homework that was due the next day. To Ms. Jones's delight, Sally arrived the next day, submitted her homework assignment, and was allowed to use the computer during the last 10 min of the class session.

To confirm that she was on to something important, Ms. Jones decided to try the old way once again. As Sally left class, Ms. Jones told her, "I'm very happy that you turned in your homework today and got to use the computer, but I don't think we will have time for the computer tomorrow." The next day, Sally arrived right on time but, as before, did not have her homework. To ensure the computer time was effective in getting Sally to do her homework, Ms. Jones decided to try that approach one more time. As Sally left class, she told her, "If you turn in your homework tomorrow, we will have time for you to use the computer again." Not surprisingly, Sally arrived on Friday and submitted her homework right on time.

Now, Ms. Jones had the information she needed. Through this simple test in which she made computer time available on certain days, but not on others, she was able to determine that computer time had a big effect on Sally's behavior. On Tuesday and Thursday, when computer time was not available, Sally did not turn in her homework. However, on Wednesday and Friday, when computer time was available, Sally turned in her homework. Knowing this, Ms. Jones had strong support for the idea that access to computer time was likely to help Sally turn in her homework consistently. Therefore, she made computer time available every day, and Sally rarely missed a chance to turn in her homework on time.

This story is useful for understanding the basic process of intervention testing. Note that Ms. Jones tested the intervention (contingent computer time) in a systematic way. First, she tried it the usual way, with no computer time available. Then, she tried the new way and got better results. To ensure computer time was doing the trick, Ms. Jones immediately reversed herself and tried it the old way again. When this was unsuccessful, as it had been the first time, she tried it the new way once again. It is important to mention that the "intervention" Ms. Jones used was not a function-based intervention developed based on the results of a systematic FBA. Rather, it was a simple example of contingent positive reinforcement that Ms. Jones tried without considering the function of Sally's behavior. Nevertheless, the same exact format is used to test a properly developed function-based intervention.

The basic format that Ms. Jones used, and that you will use to test function-based interventions, is a modified version of a research design that is known as a "reversal," "withdrawal," or A-B-A-B design. Of course, you are not conducting research; rather, you are testing the potential effectiveness of a function-based intervention. If you were conducting research, it would be necessary to conduct many more sessions at each step along the way. We refer to the approach as a "modified" reversal or withdrawal design because, in most cases, you will conduct only one session in each condition (A-B-A-B).

The first session, designated as "A," provides an opportunity to document the student's behavior under the typical classroom conditions. These conditions are also called "baseline" conditions because they reflect the circumstances that exist in the classroom before anything is done to improve the student's behavior. The first baseline session is followed by the first "intervention testing" condition, which is designated as "B." This session provides an opportunity to see how the student behaves under different conditions you believe will produce a better result. During this session, you would introduce the function-based intervention and then measure the student's behavior. If the student's behavior improves during the first intervention testing session, you would then repeat the baseline condition, which gives you the second "A" in A-B-A-B. If the student's behavior during the second baseline condition resembles what it was during the first baseline condition, you would then conduct a final session in which the function-based intervention was tested once again. By alternating between baseline (A) and intervention (B), using the A-B-A-B format, you should be able to determine whether there is good reason to move to full implementation of the function-based intervention you have developed.

Many teachers question the need to reverse to the baseline conditions if the initial intervention testing session produced positive results. They often make comments such as, "The intervention obviously worked better. Why do we have to try it the old way again?" These teachers, desperate to find something that works better, are often happy to go with whatever seems to be more effective. However, there is a problem with this approach. Without returning to baseline, we cannot be sure that the intervention is responsible for the improvement. Many interventions have produced short-term positive results that did not last. In fact, many students whose behavior warrants an FBA have been exposed to numerous interventions of this sort. Our goal is to determine whether a function-based intervention is likely to be effective. We would never want to simply try various interventions that might amount to no more than "spinning our wheels." For this reason, the return to baseline is essential.

More information about the logic and methods of the reversal design, as well as other single-subject research designs, appears in textbooks on the subject, such as those by Kazdin (1982), Kennedy (2005), and Richards, Taylor, Ramasamy, and Richards (1999). Additional descriptions of the intervention testing process we recommend for school settings can be found in journal articles, such as those by Foster-Johnson and Dunlap (1993), Dunlap and Kern (1996), and Sugai, Lewis-Palmer, and Hagan-Burke (1999–2000).

What to Do if the Test Does Not Work

Sometimes the intervention testing fails to support the effectiveness of the intervention you have developed. In most of these cases, one of two patterns emerges. The first possibility is that the student's behavior during the intervention testing conditions was hardly any better than it was during the baseline conditions. The second possibility is that the student's behavior improved during the first intervention testing condition, but failed to reverse during the second baseline condition. School staff often find these results disappointing. However, the results are actually very constructive because they point out that something about the intervention or its implementation needs to be improved before it is implemented on a larger scale. Because different problems are associated with each negative outcome, we address them separately.

What if the student's behavior during the intervention testing conditions was not better than it was during the baseline conditions? If this is the case, you will need to reconsider several aspects of the intervention and the manner in which it was implemented during the intervention testing. First, you should reconsider the data from the FBA to determine whether you may have incorrectly identified the function of the student's behavior or missed an additional function that is also affecting the student's behavior. Perhaps the student's off-task behavior is maintained not only by escape from the task at hand (negative reinforcement—activity), but also by the attention it generates from the teacher or peers (positive reinforcement—attention). If you identified one of these functions but not the other, you may then have developed a function-based intervention that was not sufficient to improve the student's behavior.

Second, even if the function you identified is correct, you will need to review the components of your function-based intervention. Perhaps you determined that the student could not perform the replacement behavior, and thus used Method 1 (Teach the replacement behavior, described in Chapter 6), but failed to consider that certain features of the classroom environment also needed to be improved. If this were the case, your intervention would need to include the components of Method 1, as well as the components required of Method 2 (Improve the environment, described in Chapter 7), before it would produce the desired results.

Third, it is possible that there were problems with the way that you tested the intervention. Even when the FBA has been conducted correctly and the function-based intervention has been developed correctly, you may have made other mistakes that generated misleading data. For instance, maybe you selected an inappropriate measurement system that failed to reveal important differences in the student's behavior. Another possibility is that the staff that implemented the testing conditions failed to deliver them correctly, a problem of treatment integrity, which is discussed in detail in Chapters 12 and 13.

All possibilities must be considered. In most cases, a careful review and reanalysis usually results in an improved function-based intervention that, in subsequent retesting, will prove to be more effective.

What if the student's behavior improved during the first intervention testing condition, but failed to reverse during the second baseline condition? This situation can easily occur if the effects of each condition (baseline and intervention) carry over from one session to the next. A common scenario is that the student's behavior begins to improve during the latter half of the first intervention testing session. Then, it continues to be better during the first half of the second baseline session, before deteriorating in the second half of that session. When this occurs, it is reasonable to suspect that the student may have begun the second baseline session still responding to the contingencies that were present in the previous intervention testing condition. As the session progresses, the student may then begin to respond to the reversal to the baseline conditions. When this pattern of behavior emerges, it is wise to conduct an additional baseline session (i.e., A-B-A-A-B) before conducting the second test of the intervention. In many cases, this modification of the intervention testing format will reveal that, with an additional baseline session, the student's behavior will better resemble that seen during the initial baseline session.

The problem of reversal failure can often be prevented if you make it clear to the student, before each session, which condition will be in effect that day. Recall that Ms. Jones did this with Sally. Our goal is to ensure a function-based intervention is likely to be effective before we plunge into full-scale implementation. During the testing of the intervention, there is no value in making the student "guess" which condition is in effect.

Whenever negative results occur during intervention testing, you will need to systematically reconsider all points raised in this section. In our own work, this process has enabled us to either improve a function-based intervention so it is effective, or to identify important errors we have made in testing the intervention. School staff with whom we have worked have had the same experience. Thus, although negative results are disappointing, they are often the key to achieving a better result. This fact provides additional credence to the importance of testing function-based interventions prior to their full-scale implementation.

EXAMPLES OF INTERVENTION TESTING

This section presents three examples of intervention testing. These examples are not hypothetical; they describe actual cases and data collected by school staff in classroom settings. Each example includes a summary of information from the FBA and details about the function-based intervention, measurement system, and intervention testing. The first and third examples are "positive" examples of intervention testing that were conducted correctly. However, the second example includes a key error in the intervention testing process.

Example 1: George

Student and Setting

George, age 11, is a fifth-grade student in a class with a student–teacher ratio of 12 to 1. He is of average height and build for his age, and is the only child in his family. George's mother is quick to contact the school if she believes he needs her support. George is above average academically and scores well on tests and project work. He is good at and likes hands-on activities and physical education. George is a very quiet and soft-spoken student. When challenged by a teacher, he becomes silent and teary-eyed, asking for his mother to be called.

George is a fast runner and likes soccer. He plays for the school team and has represented the school in athletics. Most of George's difficulties occur in health and social studies. His health teacher is also his homeroom, reading, and gym teacher. George often stares into space and/or fidgets with his pen or hair when his teacher is lecturing. When asked to participate in class discussions or answer questions, he often asks the teacher to repeat the question or says that he does not know the answer. George engages in off-topic conversation if he is sitting next to a male peer.

Behavioral Definitions

The target behavior is off-task behavior, which is defined as engaging in behavior that is incompatible with work completion, such as staring into space, playing with pencils or hair, and talking off topic to a classmate. The replacement behavior is on-task behavior, which is defined as engaging in assigned tasks, completing class assignments, following instructions, and raising his hand when he needs assistance.

Interviews

An interview was conducted with (a) Ms. Smith, George's teacher for homeroom, health, reading, and PE; and (b) George. Ms. Smith reported that George was bright and above average academically, scoring As and Bs on assessments and assignments. She believed his off-task behavior served to gain attention. She stated that George slouches in his chair or desk to get attention and that he often has to be told several times to begin his classwork. If reprimanded for talking off-topic to a peer when he should be on-task, he becomes silent and speaks in a quiet voice, which makes it difficult for the teacher to understand him. Ms. Smith said that she and other teachers decided to ignore George's off-task behavior. He does not receive any extrinsic incentives for doing well or for acting appropriately. She observed that George sometimes tries to sneak a snack, which is against class rules.

George reported that he likes most of his classes, including health and social studies. His favorite subject is PE, with football and tennis being his favorite sports. He claimed he did not like writing a lot because his hand got tired quickly. For doing well in class, George would like to be rewarded with food or by being able to play tennis. He claims to like working with others in class activities.

A-B-C Data

A-B-C data were collected in four classes—health, social studies, reading, and computer science. Each observation was 20 minutes long. The antecedents and consequences were recorded for an average of 10 instances of off-task behavior per observation. George was off-task approximately 50% of each observation. His off-task behavior occurred (a) when the teacher was lecturing and the class was expected to sit quietly and listen, and (b) during 5- to 10-min question-and-answer sessions in which the teacher reviewed course material before introducing a new concept. The consequences that followed the off-task behavior included receiving a verbal reprimand, time-out (5 min duration), a phone call home, and time-out in an alternate room (as part of in-school suspension).

Function of the Behavior

The interviews and A-B-C data indicated that George's off-task behavior enabled him to gain attention (positive reinforcement) from his teachers and to escape/avoid activities such as listening for long periods of time (negative reinforcement).

Function-Based Intervention

George was able to perform the replacement behavior, but the classroom environment needed to be improved. Therefore, Method 2 (Improve the Environment, described in Chapter 7) was used. The antecedent conditions were adjusted so (a) the conditions that set the occasion for the target behavior were eliminated and (b) the replacement behavior would be more likely to occur. In addition, positive reinforcement was provided for appropriate behavior, and attention and escape (the original maintaining consequences) were withheld when off-task behavior occurred. Specifically, the teacher

- Limited lecturing to 4 to 6 min, followed by a hands-on activity or written assignment
- Used open-ended questions to promote participation
- Provided George and peers with tokens for participating in questions and answers and for on-task behavior during hands-on or written activities
- Briefly redirected George when he was off-task, but otherwise ignored his off-task behavior

Measurement System

Data were collected using the whole interval method, with on- or off-task behavior recorded at the end of every 30 s for 15 min, for a total of 30 intervals per measurement period. IOA was calculated by having a second observer independently record data during both baseline sessions and both intervention testing sessions. Intervals scored identically by both the observers were considered agreements. IOA was 97%, with a range of 94% to 100%.

Test of the Function-Based Intervention

George's on- and off-task behavior was recorded during alternating baseline and function-based intervention sessions using the A-B-A-B format (a baseline session was followed by a function-based intervention session, another baseline session, and a final function-based intervention session). The results are presented in Figure 10.1. On-task behavior occurred during 26% of the intervals during baseline 1, rose to 83% of the intervals during the first function-based intervention session, decreased to 33% of the intervals when the baseline was reinstated, and rose again to 80% of the intervals during the

FIGURE 10.1 George's on-task behavior during intervention testing.

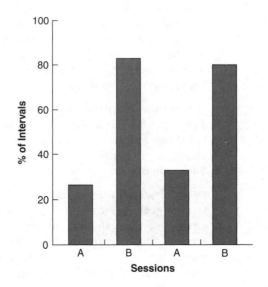

second function-based intervention session. When combined, these data reflect 29.5% on-task behavior during the baseline sessions and 81.5% on-task behavior during the function-based intervention sessions.

> **Comment.** These data provide support for the likely effectiveness of the function-based intervention. George's off-task behavior was influenced by poor instructional methods and by the attention and escape it provided. Addressing these variables, as outlined in Method 2 (Chapter 7), produced a much better result. Because the intervention was tested using the A-B-A-B format, it was clear that improvements were systematically related to the function-based intervention. If the return to baseline had not occurred in session 3, we would have had a nice result, but one that we could not attribute directly to the function-based intervention.

Example 2: Richard

Student and Setting

Richard is an 8-year-old second grader who has good verbal skills and enjoys conversing with adults. He is often affectionate toward staff. Richard is very inquisitive, has good gross motor skills, enjoys listening to stories, likes singing and music, and loves to play games on the computer. According to his teacher, he is currently functioning at grade level in all areas.

Richard has engaged in problematic behaviors since he was very young. He attended a special preschool and was retained in kindergarten through mutual agreement of his parents and the school. Richard has received psychiatric care, and his diagnoses include bipolar disorder, alcohol-related neurologic disorder, oppositional/defiant disorder, and ADHD. He takes three medications (Adderal, Risperidone, and Depakote).

In the classroom, Richard is easily frustrated, has poor fine motor skills, is disruptive (wanders around the room, yells, and interrupts students and staff), and engages in acts of verbal aggression toward staff (threatens to hit, kick, spit at, or bite them). Richard does not actually follow through and harm others, but he frequently threatens to do so.

Richard attends a regular second-grade classroom for most of the day. Because of his target behaviors, he has been assigned a 1:1 aide. Richard goes to a resource room 4 days a week for 30 min each day to work on fine motor and social skills. He is very resistant to tasks that require a handwritten product. Richard's handwriting skills are significantly delayed. His hands shake and, although he can produce legible work, all written tasks take extra time. The teacher's primary goal is to reduce Richard's acts of verbal aggression toward staff members.

Behavioral Definitions

The target behavior is verbal aggression toward staff, which is defined as any time Richard threatens to hit, kick, poke, spit at, or bite staff members. Based on the presumed function of Richard's behavior (described later), the replacement behavior is completing class assignments.

Interviews

Interviews were conducted with the teacher, the 1:1 aide, and Richard. The teacher and aide both reported that Richard does best when he is engaged in activities that require a verbal response. He enjoys working in small groups. Richard also enjoys discussions with adults and is very curious. He has a very good auditory memory. When Richard finds a task interesting, he is able to stay on-task for up to 15 min. The aide communicates with Richard's mom via a daily notebook. Both the teacher and the aide noted that Richard requires 1:1 assistance whenever he has an academic task that requires a written response. The teacher and aide both suspect that Richard engages in verbal aggressions to escape having to complete written tasks.

Richard claims that he likes all subjects but dislikes it anytime he has to do much handwriting. He said that he usually gets help when he needs it, that he would do better if he got more rewards, and that he would do the best if he "didn't have to write much." He complained that some tasks take too long because of the handwriting required.

A-B-C Data

A-B-C data were collected during three 20-min periods of instruction and assigned activity in the classroom. The antecedents and consequences related to five instances of Richard's verbal aggressions toward staff were recorded. Threats of harm occurred when he was prompted to complete an academic task and when he was asked to transition to another activity. Most cases, however, occurred when he was asked to write a response to an academic assignment. In every case, Richard's verbal aggressions resulted in being sent to "time-out" for 2 to 5 min. As a result of the time-out, Richard avoided completing the written assignment.

Function of the Behavior

The interview and A-B-C data indicated that, when assigned tasks that require a written response, Richard engages in verbal aggressions toward staff to avoid those tasks. The function of Richard's verbal aggressions was to escape from these activities (negative reinforcement—activity).

Function-Based Intervention

Richard was able to perform the replacement behavior, but the structure of class assignments, which included handwriting, made it hard for him. Therefore, Method 2 (Improve the Environment, described in Chapter 7) was used. As this method stipulates, the antecedent conditions were adjusted so (a) the conditions that set the occasion for the target behavior were eliminated and (b) the replacement behavior would be more likely to occur. In addition, positive reinforcement was provided for appropriate behavior, and escape (the original maintaining consequence) was withheld when off-task behavior occurred. Specifically, the teacher and aide

- Reduced his spelling list (a particular source of concern) from 20 to 10 words and allowed Richard to dictate his responses to reading comprehension questions

- Taught Richard to ask for a brief (1- to 3-min) break during written assignments
- Provided verbal praise when he engaged in a written assignment
- Redirected him to complete his assignment when an aggression occurred

Measurement System
Data were collected on successive days during four 20-min periods of assigned activity in the classroom. A frequency count was used to record (a) the number of acts of verbal aggression toward staff members and (b) the number of completed assignments Richard produced. IOA was calculated by having the second observer independently record data during both baseline sessions and both intervention testing sessions. The IOA was 100% for both verbal aggressions and for completing assignments.

Test of the Function-Based Intervention
The function-based intervention was tested by comparing Richard's verbal aggressions and completion of assignments during two baseline and two intervention sessions. This was done using an A-A-B-B format (two baseline sessions, followed by two intervention sessions). The results are presented in Figure 10.2. Verbal aggressions (represented by the black bars) occurred six times on day 1 and eight times on day 2. No assignments (the gray bars) were completed either day. During the two intervention sessions, verbal aggressions occurred only twice (day 3) and once (day 4). Furthermore, the assignment was completed on each of these days.

> **Comment.** In this example, a critical error was made. Although the school staff conducted the FBA properly, developed a reasonable function-based intervention, and selected an appropriate measurement system, they tested the intervention

FIGURE 10.2
Richard's verbal aggressions (black bars) and task completion (gray bars) during intervention testing.

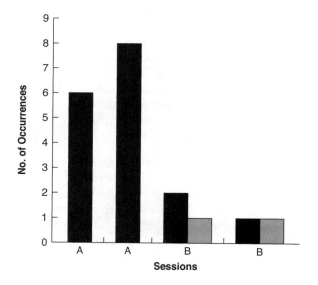

by using an A-A-B-B sequence of sessions, rather than the A-B-A-B format. If Richard had actually followed through on his threats and physically harmed others, this alternative sequence of sessions would have been reasonable (for an example, see Chapter 16). However, Richard only threatened harm; he never actually hurt others, so there was no real need to alter the usual sequence of sessions.

Because there was no return to baseline, as in the A-B-A-B design, we cannot be absolutely certain that the very positive results that occurred with Richard were produced by the intervention. It is possible that something else that occurred between days 2 and 3 was responsible for the improvement. For example, maybe Richard's mother promised him extra time with some of his favorite activities or a special treat if he did better in school. Without the return to baseline, this and other possibilities like it cannot be ruled out. A simple rearrangement of the intervention testing sessions into the A-B-A-B format could have prevented this problem.

Example 3: Donald

Student and Setting

Donald is a 5-year-old boy with mild mental retardation (IQ = 60). He is of normal height and weight for his age, has normal vision and hearing, and has excellent health. Donald attends a regular kindergarten class 3 hr each morning, 5 days per week. Among the 22 children in the class, he is the only child with special needs. The staff includes a teacher and a teacher's aide in the classroom, as well as a special education resource support teacher who is available on a consultant basis.

In the classroom, Donald frequently exhibits off-task behaviors that include closing his eyes, refusing to perform assigned tasks, sliding under his desk or table, getting up and running away, or sitting down on the floor and crying. When these behaviors occur, the teaching staff sometimes redirects him to assigned tasks and sometimes ignores these behaviors. Donald's off-task behavior has become such a problem that the teacher and aide have requested that an Individualized Education Program (IEP) meeting be held to consider placing Donald full time in a special class. The special education teacher was recently assigned to help the teaching staff with Donald's off-task behaviors in an attempt to prevent the more restrictive placement.

Behavioral Definitions

The target behavior is off-task behavior, defined as the occurrence of any of the following: closing his eyes for at least 5 s, refusing to perform assigned tasks either verbally (e.g., "No" or "I don't want to") or by sliding under the desk or table at which he is working, getting up and running away when a task is assigned, or sitting on the floor and crying. The replacement behavior is on-task behavior, which is defined as staying in his seat, engaging in the assigned task, and requesting help when needed.

Interviews

Interviews were conducted with the teacher and teacher's aide. Because of Donald's age, IQ, and limited verbal skills, he was not interviewed. Both the teacher and the aide reported that Donald's off-task behaviors had been occurring since the beginning of the school year, when he started in their class. They also stated that Donald was often cooperative. However, when his off-task behaviors occurred, it was very disruptive to the entire class. They also claimed that Donald's off-task behaviors occurred consistently under a variety of conditions, most of which involved academic task demands. They pointed out, however, that off-task behavior did not occur during all task demand situations. For this reason, they suspected that his problem behavior might be motivated by the attention it brought him from the teaching staff.

A-B-C Data

Observations were conducted in the classroom during times when Donald was given assignments that had resulted in considerable off-task behavior. A total of four 15-min observations were conducted over the course of 2 days. During these sessions, a total of 23 episodes of off-task behavior occurred. All 23 episodes occurred during task demand situations. In each case, the teaching staff responded by either ignoring the behavior or by briefly attempting to redirect Donald, and then leaving him alone when he refused to comply.

Function of the Behavior

The interviews and A-B-C data indicated that, when presented with certain academic task demands, Donald engaged in off-task behavior to avoid these activities. Specifically, he closed his eyes, refused to perform, ran away, slid to the floor, or cried because these behaviors enabled him to avoid certain academic tasks (negative reinforcement—activity).

Function-Based Intervention

Recently administered assessment data indicated that Donald was not able to perform many of the academic tasks he was being assigned. Therefore, Method 1 (Teach the Replacement Behavior, described in Chapter 6) was used. The antecedent conditions were adjusted so new behavior could be learned and aversive conditions could be avoided. In addition, the consequences were adjusted so (a) the student was positively reinforced for the newly learned skill and (b) occurrences of the target behavior were not reinforced (extinction). Specifically, the teaching staff

- Provided assignments at the proper instructional level
- Taught Donald to request help, when needed
- Praised on-task behavior, including appropriate requests for help
- Redirected him to complete the task when off-task behavior occurred

Measurement System

Data were collected using the time sampling method, with on- or off-task behavior recorded at the end of every 15 s for 15 min, for a total of 60 intervals per measurement period. IOA was calculated by having a second observer

FIGURE 10.3
Donald's on-task
behavior during
intervention testing.

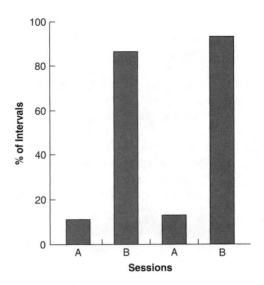

independently record data during both baseline sessions and both intervention testing sessions. Intervals scored identically by both observers were considered agreements. IOA was 97%, with a range of 93% to 100%.

Test of the Function-Based Intervention
Donald's on- and off-task behavior was recorded during alternating baseline and function-based intervention sessions using the A-B-A-B format (a baseline session was followed by a function-based intervention session, another baseline session, and a final function-based intervention session). The results are presented in Figure 10.3. On-task behavior occurred during 12% of the intervals during baseline 1, rose to 90% of the intervals during the first function-based intervention session, decreased to 13% of the intervals when the baseline was reinstated, and rose again to 97% of the intervals during the second function-based intervention session. When combined, these data reflect 12.5% on-task behavior during the baseline sessions and 93.5% on-task behavior during the function-based intervention sessions.

> **Comment.** Once again, the results provide strong support for the likely effectiveness of the function-based intervention. Donald's off-task behaviors occurred when he was given tasks that were too difficult for him. His off-task behaviors provided a way for him to escape from assignments that required skills he did not possess. Addressing these variables, as outlined in Method 1: Teach the Replacement Behavior (Chapter 6), produced a much better result. Because the intervention was tested using the A-B-A-B format, there is little doubt that the function-based intervention is responsible for the improvements.

Steps in Testing the Intervention

The following list of steps and activities summarizes the process for testing function-based interventions:

1. Identify an appropriate time and situation in which to test the intervention. The best situations are those in which the target behavior is most likely to occur. Often, the optimum intervention testing situation is the same one used to collect A-B-C data (Chapter 4).

2. Identify an appropriate measurement system that can be used to test the intervention (Chapter 9).

3. Arrange sessions so the baseline (A) and function-based intervention (B) conditions alternate in an A-B-A-B format.

4. Implement the conditions and measure the student's behavior.

5. If the results are negative (i.e., if the student's behavior does not improve, or if improvements fail to reverse), reconsider the FBA data and conclusions, the intervention components, the measurement system, and the manner in which the testing conditions were implemented. Then, make the necessary improvements, and retest.

EXERCISE

. Design the testing of a function-based intervention. Take a function-based intervention that has already been developed (preferably by you), and then identify (a) an appropriate measurement system, (b) the time, place, and length of each session, and (c) the sequence in which the baseline and function-based intervention sessions will be conducted.

REFERENCES

Dunlap, G., & Kern, L. (1996). Modifying instructional activities to promote desirable behavior: A conceptual and practical framework. *School Psychology Quarterly, 11*, 297–312.

Foster-Johnson, L., & Dunlap, G. (1993). Using functional assessment to develop effective individualized interventions for challenging behaviors. *Teaching Exceptional Children, 25*, 44–50.

Kazdin, A. E. (1982). *Single-case research designs*. New York: Oxford University Press.

Kennedy, C. H. (2005). *Single-case designs for educational research*. Boston: Allyn & Bacon.

Richards, S. B., Taylor, R. L., Ramasamy, R., & Richards, R. Y. (1999). *Single subject research: Applications in educational and clinical settings*. San Diego: Singular Publishing.

Sugai, G., Lewis-Palmer, T., & Hagan-Burke, S. (1999–2000). Overview of the functional behavioral assessment process. *Exceptionality, 8*, 149–160.

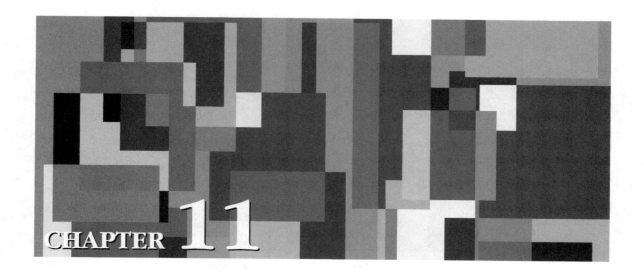

CHAPTER 11

The Behavior Intervention Plan

OUTCOMES

After completing this chapter, you will be able to

- Describe the rationale for developing a BIP.
- Name and describe the key elements of a BIP.
- Given background information and data, develop a BIP.

The process of developing a function-based intervention requires gathering information in a variety of formats. These formats include, but are not limited to, surveys to collect interview data, A-B-C forms to organize and evaluate observational data, the Function Matrix format used to identify the function(s) of the target behavior and the specific consequences that are being gained or avoided, procedures for designing a function-based intervention, and recording forms to measure the target and replacement behaviors during intervention testing. In Chapter 13, we also show you how to create a computer-based spreadsheet for summarizing the data and producing charts and graphs related to implementation of the function-based intervention. One additional format is essential in the function-based intervention process—the BIP.

All formats described thus far in this text have been used to collect, analyze, and manage data. The BIP serves a different purpose altogether. The BIP is a tool for effectively communicating the basic information necessary to implement and manage the function-based intervention. It does not need to include all information that has been collected in the course of the assessment. Instead, it should summarize the information into a strategy or proposal that

FIGURE 11.1
The elements of a behavior intervention plan.

1.	Behavioral Definitions
2.	Rationale
3.	Baseline Data
4.	Function of the Behavior
5.	Behavioral Objective
6.	Intervention Procedure
7.	Fading and Generalization
8.	Data to be Collected
9.	Program Review Date
10.	Personnel and Roles
11.	Emergency Procedures

can be easily understood. This chapter presents a guide to designing BIPs that meet this criterion.

There are many ways to organize the information in a BIP. The format we recommend (see Figure 11.1) is consistent with the function-based intervention process we have described thus far in this book. It contains the essential elements of planning that are needed to implement a function-based intervention. A corresponding BIP form that you can use appears in Figure 11.2.

This chapter presents information about each part of the BIP. Following the description of each part of the BIP, we also provide an example of the BIP that was developed for Toby, an 8-year-old second grader with ADHD whose problem behavior during academic instruction interfered with his teacher's attempts at instruction and with the learning of his classmates. As you review this information, you may find it useful to also review the completed BIPs that are included with the case study examples in Chapters 14 to 16.

FIGURE 11.2
BIP form.

Behavior Intervention Plan

Student: Toby   Class: Second Grade

Date: January 2006

Behavioral Definitions

Target Behavior:

The target behavior is off-task behavior, defined as talking with peers, walking around the room, or engaging in activities other than those that have been assigned (e.g., singing instead of reading).

Replacement Behavior:

The replacement behavior is on-task behavior, defined as sitting in his seat, working on assigned tasks, and raising his hand when he needs help.

Rationale:

Toby's off-task behavior keeps him from completing assignments and has resulted in failing grades this semester. Engaging in a higher degree of on-task behavior should allow Toby to perform more consistently in class.

Baseline Data:

During two 30-min observations in the classroom, Toby engaged in on-task behavior during 20% and 27% of observed intervals, respectively.

Function of the Behavior:

During classroom instruction and individual assignments, Toby engages in off-task behavior to gain peer attention (positive reinforcement—attention) and escape task demands (negative reinforcement—activity). That is, Toby is able to socialize with peers and avoid engaging in activities and assignments.

Behavioral Objective:

During classroom instruction and individual assignments, Toby will engage in on-task behavior during 80% of observed intervals for 7 consecutive days.

Intervention Procedures:

The intervention procedures for Toby will consist of adjusting the antecedent conditions, providing Toby with positive reinforcement for on-task behavior, and withholding reinforcement for off-task behavior.

Antecedent modifications:

1. Toby will be moved further from the group of students with whom he usually socializes during class.
2. When he enters the classroom, Toby's teacher will remind him of the consequences of staying on-task.

Positive reinforcement for on-task behavior:

1. Toby and his teacher will prepare a contingency contract specifying that Toby will earn 5 extra min to interact with peers when his on-task behavior during a class period is at or above 80% of observed intervals.
2. When Toby is on-task, Toby's teacher will provide verbal praise (quietly and unobtrusively) at least four times during each class session.

Extinction for off-task behavior:

1. When Toby is off-task, he will have no access to socializing with peers during individual assignments, and he will be redirected to complete his assignments.

A brief test of the function-based intervention revealed that, during two baseline sessions, Toby was on-task during 20% and 27% of the intervals, respectively. During two intervention sessions, Toby was on-task during 80% and 78% of the intervals.

Fading and Generalization Plan:

As soon as Toby meets the behavioral objective, the intervention team will meet to consider fading the contingency contract. Generalization is not a concern in this plan because this is the only setting in which Toby exhibits low levels of on-task behavior.

FIGURE 11.2 (*continued*)

Data to Be Collected

Target Behavior: None.

Replacement Behavior:

Data on Toby's on-task behavior will be collected daily for at least 20 min using a 1-min time sampling procedure. At the end of every minute, Toby's teacher will observe him and record whether he is on- or off-task. Data will also be collected to assess IOA (weekly).

Treatment Integrity:

Correct implementation of the intervention will be assessed weekly using a whole interval method with a 1-min interval.

Social Validity:

Assessed before and at the end of the intervention using the IRP-15 and CIRP

Generalization: None anticipated.

Program Review Date:

The BIP will be reviewed on 10/15/07.

Personnel and Roles

Toby's teacher will be responsible for discussing the function-based intervention with him, working with Toby to develop and maintain the contingency contract, and collecting data daily on Toby's on-task behavior.

The district behavior consultant will meet at least once a week with Toby's teacher. The consultant will help Toby's teacher prepare the format for the contingency contract and the data collection sheets. The consultant will also collect IOA, implementation, and social validity data, and make summary graphs of the on-task behavior data to monitor progress.

Emergency Procedures:

If Toby's behavior requires emergency procedures, his teacher will follow the standard school guidelines for dealing with such behavior. The BIP will be reviewed immediately after the second instance in which emergency procedures are implemented.

FIGURE 11.2 (*continued*)

ELEMENTS OF THE BEHAVIOR INTERVENTION PLAN

Some elements of the BIP can be taken directly from the tasks you have already performed during the process of developing the function-based intervention. However, some elements will require you to consider new issues. This chapter points out where you can use already developed material, and what you need to consider in developing the remaining portions of the BIP.

Behavioral Definitions

This section of the BIP presents the target and replacement behavior definitions that you developed when you began the FBA. These definitions identify and communicate about the behaviors of concern. The BIP starts with these behavioral definitions.

Behavioral Definitions (for Toby):
The target behavior is off-task behavior, defined as talking with peers, walking around the room, or engaging in activities other than those that have been assigned (e.g., singing instead of reading). The replacement behavior is on-task behavior, defined as sitting in his seat, working on assigned tasks, and raising his hand when he needs help.

Rationale

Developing and implementing a function-based intervention often requires a substantial investment of time and resources. This process and these activities should be undertaken whenever there is a clear reason for doing so. The Rationale section of the BIP should include a brief explanation of why the target behavior was selected for intervention and of how the replacement behavior will help the student meet the social or academic requirements of the educational environment.

Rationale:
Toby's off-task behavior keeps him from completing assignments and has resulted in failing grades this semester. Engaging in a higher degree of on-task behavior should allow Toby to perform more consistently in class.

Baseline Data

If you are a special education teacher or the parent of a child with a disability, then you may be aware that a major component of an IEP is a statement of the student's present levels of performance, which communicates the student's current educational abilities. The Baseline Data section of the BIP serves the same function but is likely to be more specific. A narrative description of the nonintervention session data collected during the testing of the intervention should be presented in this section of the BIP.

Baseline Data:
During two 30-min observations in the classroom, Toby engaged in on-task behavior during 20% and 27% of observed intervals, respectively.

Function of the Behavior

This section of the BIP is another that can be drawn directly from work that was performed in developing the function-based intervention. In this section, you should provide a statement of function in the format that was presented in Chapter 5.

> **Function of the Behavior:**
> During classroom instruction and individual assignments, Toby engages in off-task behavior to gain peer attention (positive reinforcement—attention) and escape task demands (negative reinforcement—activity). That is, Toby is able to socialize with peers and avoid engaging in activities and assignments.

Behavioral Objective

There are many formats for designing behavioral objectives (e.g., Gagné, 1977; Dick & Carey, 1996; Kemp, Morrison, & Ross, 1996). Schools and other educational agencies may also train their staffs to create behavioral objectives that meet specific criteria (e.g., aligning the behavioral objective with state or district educational "standards"). A detailed guide to writing good behavioral objectives is beyond the scope of this book. However, we provide a brief review of a common format for writing behavioral objectives and examine some common errors that people make. The format we recommend is modeled after the broadly accepted format originally described by Robert Mager in 1962. If you want to further develop your skills in this area, you should consider reading the most recent edition of Mager's classic text on creating behavioral objectives (1997).

Mager's simple format includes four basic components that are common to most versions of properly written behavioral objectives. These four components require you to identify (a) the conditions under which the behavior is expected, (b) the name of the student, (c) the behavior that is expected, and (d) the criterion for successful performance. The conditions element specifies the situation or environmental circumstances under which the student is expected to perform the behavior (i.e., the antecedent conditions). The second component, the name of the student, is self-explanatory. The third component, the behavior that is expected, is an appropriately defined replacement behavior, a topic that has been covered in detail in various chapters of this book. The final component of the behavioral objective, the criteron for performance, describes the level of proficiency with which the student must demonstrate the replacement behavior. In most cases, the criterion component of the behavioral objective should include two elements: (a) the accuracy level at which the student should perform the replacement behavior during a single session, and (b) the number of days or sessions across which the student should demonstrate this level of proficiency.

How proficient is proficient enough? To establish the appropriate level of proficiency, consider how well the student has to perform for the replacement behavior to be effective (i.e., for the behavior to be reinforced by naturally existing contingencies). In some cases, this may be obvious. In situations where an appropriate criterion is not so obvious, taking a look at the behavior of other students can provide you with the information you need. In other words, note the level of proficiency exhibited by other students.

Finally, match the measure stated in the criterion to the method you selected for collecting data on the behavior. We often see behavioral objectives in which the criterion states that a student will perform the replacement behavior "*x*% of the time." In reality, the "percentage of total time" could be determined only if you had used duration recording to measure the behavior. As you know from Chapter 9, even when duration recording is an appropriate measure, the demands it places on the observer make it an unattractive option. It is rarely the method of choice. Confusion frequently occurs when working with the interval methods of data collection. Recall that the interval method of data collection does not result in a measure of the percentage of a time period during which the behavior occurs, but a percentage of intervals during which the behavior is observed. In the criterion element of a behavioral objective, interval data should be represented as the percentage of "observed intervals" (i.e., "during 90% of observed intervals"). If you find yourself using the "*x*% of the time" in the criterion component of your behavioral objective, carefully consider whether it really matches the method you have selected to measure the replacement behavior.

Behavioral Objective:

During classroom instruction and individual assignments, Toby will engage in on-task behavior during 80% of observed intervals for 7 consecutive days.

Intervention Procedure

The description of the procedures should be brief, yet contain enough detail to allow any individual to understand the specific steps that should be taken to properly implement the intervention. You probably do not want to reference the name of the intervention procedure as described in this text (e.g., Method 2: Improve the Environment); it will not have any meaning for individuals who have not read this book. Instead, consider using the steps in the method you have selected as an outline for organizing the intervention procedures in this section of the BIP. First, list the steps of the method in a sentence or two. Then, use each step as a header. Finally, under each header, briefly describe the tasks that will be undertaken and the individual or individuals who will be primarily responsible for carrying out the task.

Intervention Procedures:

The intervention procedures for Toby will consist of adjusting the antecedent conditions, providing Toby with positive reinforcement for on-task behavior, and withholding reinforcement for off-task behavior.

Antecedent modifications:

1. Toby will be moved further from the group of students with whom he usually socializes during class.

   2. When he enters the classroom, Toby's teacher will remind him of the consequences of staying on-task.

Positive reinforcement for on-task behavior:

   1. Toby and his teacher will prepare a contingency contract specifying that Toby will earn 5 extra min to interact with peers when his on-task behavior during a class period is at or above 80% of observed intervals.

   2. When Toby is on-task, Toby's teacher will provide verbal praise (quietly and unobtrusively) at least four times during each class session.

Extinction for off-task behavior:

   1. When Toby is off-task, he will have no access to socializing with peers during individual assignments, and he will be redirected to complete his assignments.

Also, consider adding a brief paragraph describing the results of the intervention testing. Presenting these results adds relevance to the selection of the intervention method and assures the individuals involved that the intervention has been demonstrated to be successful.

> A brief test of the function-based intervention revealed that, during two baseline sessions, Toby was on-task during 20% and 27% of the intervals, respectively. During two intervention sessions, Toby was on-task during 80% and 78% of the intervals.

Fading and Generalization

Ultimately, we want to be able to fade the intervention. We also want the intervention to impact the student's behavior in a range of settings and situations. Information about fading and generalization is provided in Chapters 12 and 13. At this point, realize that concern for fading and generalization should begin when the BIP is being developed.

In this section of the BIP, you should include a brief statement about procedures for eventually fading elements of the intervention and for monitoring generalization of the replacement behavior. This statement should help focus future actions during reviews of the BIP.

> **Fading and Generalization:**
> As soon as Toby meets the behavioral objective, the intervention team will meet to consider fading the contingency contract. Generalization is not a concern in this plan because this is the only setting in which Toby exhibits low levels of on-task behavior.

Data to Be Collected

At a minimum, this section of the BIP should describe each type of data that will be collected and how frequently these measures will be taken. You will need to identify the measures you will use to monitor (a) the replacement behavior, (b) the target behavior (if necessary), and (c) IOA. You will also need to identify the measures needed for three additional concerns—the accuracy of the implementation of the intervention (treatment integrity), generalization, and social validity. Detailed information about these last three areas, and how to monitor them, appears in Chapters 12 and 13.

> **Data to Be Collected:**
> Data on Toby's on-task behavior will be collected daily for at least 20 min using a 1-min time sampling procedure. At the end of every minute, Toby's teacher will observe him and record whether he is on- or off-task. Data will also be collected to assess IOA (weekly) and implementation of the intervention (weekly using a whole interval method with a 1-min interval). Social validity will be assessed before and at the end of the intervention using the IRP-15 and CIRP. No generalization measures are anticipated.

Program Review Date

As described earlier in this chapter, function-based intervention planning is a process that does not end when the implementation of the intervention begins. Part of this formative process involves reviewing progress toward the behavioral objective and reassessing the future of the plan. Establishing a program review date ensures a definite timeframe is in place for overall evaluation of the function-based intervention plan. The program review date also gives purpose to the ongoing collection and analysis of data; the impending meeting to review the plan may drive individuals to be conscientious in implementing the plan and monitoring the target and replacement behaviors through data collection.

Keep in mind that the date selected for review of the plan is only tentative. If a situation requires it, the intervention team may meet prior to the established program review date (e.g., if the student's behavior calls for the emergency procedures, described later, to be implemented during the first few intervention sessions). Likewise, circumstances might require that the review date be postponed (e.g., if the initiation of the intervention is delayed due to the student being absent for several days). There are no "hard and fast" rules regarding the length of time an intervention should be in place before it is reviewed. However, a good initial review date would be the earliest date at which the student could conceivably meet the criterion established in the behavioral objective.

> **Program Review Date:**
> The BIP will be reviewed on 10/15/07.

Personnel and Roles

Some interventions are simple, whereas others are more complicated. Regardless of the level of complexity, most function-based interventions involve multiple tasks. The goal of the Personnel and Roles section of the BIP is to clarify who is responsible for every task necessary in carrying out the function-based intervention. In some cases, implementing the intervention will require the involvement of individuals who will contribute specific skills (e.g., a curriculum specialist, the district behavior consultant). In other cases, it will simply be more efficient or practical to "spread around" the work so that the intervention plan is easier to implement.

Personnel and Roles:

1. Toby's teacher will be responsible for discussing the function-based intervention with him, working with Toby to develop and maintain the contingency contract, and collecting data daily on Toby's on-task behavior.

2. The district behavior consultant will meet at least once a week with Toby's teacher. The consultant will help Toby's teacher prepare the format for the contingency contract and the data collection sheets. The consultant will also collect IOA, implementation, and social validity data, and make summary graphs of the on-task behavior data to monitor progress.

Emergency Procedures

Even with an effective function-based intervention, it is possible that a student may occasionally engage in the target behavior to such an extent that it is no longer possible, at the moment, to implement the intervention. In some cases, this escalation may even involve behavior that poses a physical threat to the student or to others. Colvin (1993) and Walker, Ramsey, and Gresham (2004) have described the specific stages of escalation and deescalation through which students are likely to progress when this occurs. Although this problem does not occur with most students, it could, and you need to be prepared in case it does.

Emergency procedures are planned procedures that can be implemented immediately if the need arises. They should not be confused with punishment. Emergency procedures are not intended to be punitive and should not be used for that purpose. Their sole purpose is to protect everyone from harm and to re-establish order so the function-based intervention can once again be implemented. It is essential that you develop these emergency procedures before you implement the function-based intervention.

This section of the BIP is where you should delineate these procedures. You are likely aware that most schools establish plans for dealing with a wide variety of emergency situations, such as fires, threatening weather, and unauthorized personnel on campus. In designing these plans, many schools also have procedures for handling instances of student behavior that are deemed severely disruptive or dangerous to the student or others. You should consider referencing this plan in the Emergency Procedures section if it applies to a situation that might arise while implementing the function-based intervention. However, if the school does not have such a plan in place, if the plan does not appear to apply to the circumstances you envision, or if the procedures of the plan might reinforce the target behavior, you may need to develop plans specific to the needs of your student. Keep in mind that the school administrator should be made aware of any deviation or addition to the regular school plan for dealing with these situations.

The strategies presented in this text should result in a function-based intervention plan (i.e., one that is based on the function of the student's behavior, reinforces a useful replacement behavior, withholds reinforcement of the target behavior, and promotes the replacement behavior by adjusting the environment). If it is necessary to implement the emergency procedures frequently when you begin intervention sessions, it is likely that one of the elements of the function-based intervention has been inadequately addressed or is not being implemented properly. Therefore, the Emergency Procedures section should also include language stating that the BIP will be reviewed if emergency situations become a recurring problem.

> **Emergency Procedures:**
> If Toby's behavior requires emergency procedures, his teacher will follow the standard school guidelines for dealing with such behavior. The BIP will be reviewed immediately after the second instance in which emergency procedures are implemented.

Steps and Activities for Developing a Behavior Intervention Plan

The following list summarizes the steps and activities involved in developing a BIP:

1. List the definitions of the target and replacement behaviors as developed during the FBA.
2. Provide a brief rationale for the intervention.
3. Present the baseline data on the target behavior collected as part of intervention testing.
4. Describe the function of the behavior as identified through the FBA.
5. Create behavioral objectives for each behavior that will be measured.
6. Describe the intervention procedures that were developed and tested.
7. Explain expected procedures for fading and generalization.
8. Clarify the data to be collected and the data collection methods.
9. Establish the date on which the program will be reviewed.

10. Name the relevant personnel who will take part in carrying out the function-based intervention and describe their roles.

11. Develop a set of emergency procedures for situations that may arise during the course of the intervention.

EXERCISES

Chapters 14 to 16 include three complete case studies of successful function-based intervention. Choose one of the cases and read to the point at which the student's BIP is presented. Using the background information, develop a BIP for that case. Then, compare your plan to the example in the case study. Which sections of the plan did you complete most successfully? What might you do to improve plans you will write in the future?

REFERENCES

Colvin, G. (1993). *Managing acting-out behavior.* Engene, OR: Behavior Associates.

Dick, W., & Carey, L. (1996). *The systematic design of instruction* (4th ed.). New York: Harper Collins.

Gagné, R. M. (1977). *The conditions of learning* (4th ed.). New York: Holt, Rinehart & Winston.

Kemp, J. E., Morrison, G. R., & Ross, S. M. (1996). *Designing effective instruction* (2nd ed.). Upper Saddle River, NJ: Merrill/Prentice Hall.

Mager, R. F. (1997). *Preparing instructional objectives* (3rd ed.). Atlanta: Center for Effective Performance.

Walker, H. M., Ramsey, E., & Gresham, F. M. (2004). *Antisocial behavior in school: Evidence-based practices.* Belmont, CA: Thomson/Wadsworth.

Implementing the Intervention

In Part one, you learned how to conduct an FBA. Then, in Part two, you learned how to develop and test a function-based intervention. Too often, people tend to stop at this point because they assume they have covered every necessary detail. That assumption is wrong. Even the best function-based intervention will fail if it (a) is not implemented properly or (b) does not adequately address key components that will facilitate or prevent its success.

Part three presents two chapters that give you the tools you will need to effectively monitor and manage the implementation of function-based interventions. In Chapter 12, you learn about three important components: social validity, treatment integrity, and generalization and maintenance. By including these three components, you will be able to accurately evaluate changes in student behavior, promote lasting change, and help inform future intervention efforts. In Chapter 13, you learn the answers to several commonly asked questions that will help you guide the implementation and evaluation of the intervention. This chapter addresses many of the practical aspects of intervention implementation that will make your job easier and more likely to result in successful outcomes.

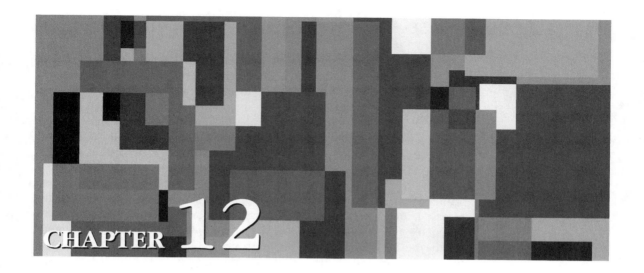

Factors That Affect Success: Social Validity, Treatment Integrity, and Generalization and Maintenance

OUTCOMES

After reading this chapter, you will be able to

- Define social validity, treatment integrity, generalization, and maintenance.
- Assess social validity from teacher and student perspectives.
- Monitor treatment integrity.
- Enhance generalization and maintenance of intervention outcomes.

At this point in the process, you have conducted the FBA and developed and tested the function-based intervention. Now, you are ready to implement the intervention. Before doing this, you need to attend to three essential components—social validity, treatment integrity, and generalization and maintenance—to ensure the best possible outcome.

As you have learned, interventions designed based on a behavior's function are far more likely to produce the desired outcomes than interventions based on the form (topography) of the behavior (Lane, Umbreit, & Beebe-Frankenberger, 1999; Mace, 1994). However, there are instances in which even function-based interventions do not yield the desired results. One possible explanation is that the correct function of the target behavior was not identified and, consequently, the intervention was not based on the correct function. A second possible explanation is that the intervention lacks key components or factors that influence intervention success. For example, it is possible that intervention goals are not viewed as important from the teacher perspective. Or, perhaps the intervention appears to be a good fit, but the actual procedures are very time consuming or involve materials not typically found in a classroom setting. Or, maybe the teacher simply does not think the intervention is likely to produce the desired outcomes (Baer, Wolf, & Risley, 1968, 1987). The later issues, collectively, refer to **social validity.**

Another reason for unfavorable outcomes is that the intervention was not implemented as designed. If information about plan implementation is not assessed, then it is difficult to draw accurate conclusions about intervention outcomes. It is possible that key steps were modified or excluded altogether. Or, maybe the intervention was implemented as planned, but the correct function of the target behavior was not identified (Gresham, Gansle, & Noell, 1993). These issues, collectively, refer to **treatment integrity.**

Yet another possibility for the lack of intervention efficacy may be that the intervention initially produces the desired changes in student behavior, but these changes do not last. For some reason, the effects seem to dissipate or only occur in circumstances that closely parallel the intervention conditions. Perhaps consideration was not given to how to make the intervention outcomes generalize over time, across settings, and in the presence of others (Dunlap, 1993; Ferro & Dunlap, 1993). These issues pertain to **generalization** and **maintenance.**

When designing function-based interventions, it is best to address the three factors that influence intervention outcomes. Social validity data, treatment integrity data, and attention to generalization and maintenance influence the extent to which intervention efforts will produce lasting, meaningful behavioral changes, which is the goal of all intervention work (Baer et al., 1987).

This chapter introduces components that promote or impede intervention outcomes: social validity, treatment integrity, and generalization and maintenance. In addition to defining and justifying the importance of each intervention component, this chapter teaches you to assess and/or program for them in designing function-based interventions.

SOCIAL VALIDITY
Definition and Justification

Social validity addresses three questions: Does (did) the intervention target socially significant goals? Are (were) the intervention procedure socially acceptable in the eyes of the consumers? Will (did) the intervention produce socially important outcomes (Fawcett, 1991; Kazdin, 1977; Lane & Beebe-Frankenberger, 2004; Wolf, 1978)?

You need to address social validity at the onset and conclusion of the intervention. If social validity is high at the onset of the intervention, then the treatments agent (teachers, parents, and/or students) may be more likely to implement the intervention as intended (i.e., with integrity). If the intervention is empirically sound, accurately designed to teach an appropriate replacement behavior, and implemented with fidelity, then the intervention is more likely to produce the desired outcomes. Moreover, the intervention is likely to produce lasting decreases in the target behavior and increases in the replacement behavior that generalize across time, setting, and persons (Lane & Beebe-Frankenberger, 2004; Lane, Beebe-Frankenberger, Lambros, & Pierson, 2001).

Methods of Assessment

There are numerous methods you can use to assess social validity. Specifically, social validity can be assessed using rating scales, interviews, social comparison techniques, and indirectly via future use of intervention procedures (Gresham & Lopez, 1996; Kazdin, 1977; Lane, 1997; Lane & Beebe-Frankenberger, 2004; Lane et al., 2001).

Rating Scales. Rating scales are the most common method of assessing social validity (Lane & Beebe-Frankenberger, 2004). The majority of commercially available rating scales focus on the acceptability of treatment procedures (Finn & Sladeczek, 2001). Two noteworthy instruments are the Treatment Evaluation Inventory (TEI; Kazdin, 1980) and the Intervention Rating Profile-20 (IRP-20; Witt & Martens, 1983). Since the introduction of these two measures, a number of instruments have been developed from these original measures, some of which include the TEI–Short Form (TEI-SF; Kelley, Heffer, Gresham, & Elliott, 1989), the Intervention Rating Profile-15 (IRP-15; Martens & Witt 1982; see Table 12.1), the Children's Intervention Rating Profile (CIRP; Witt & Elliott, 1985; see Table 12.2), and the Behavior Intervention Rating Scales (BIRS; VonBrock & Elliott, 1987; see Lane & Beebe-Frankenberger, 2004, for a list and description of these measures). It is also possible for interventionists (e.g., behavioral specialists and teachers) to develop their own rating scales specific to the function-based intervention at hand (see Tables 12.3 and 12.4).

Interviews. You can also conduct interviews to assess social validity. Gresham and Lopez (1996) designed a semistructured interview for use with classroom teachers. This interview contains three sections to address the three components of social validity: social significance of the goals, social acceptability of procedures, and social importance of effects. Lane (1997) designed a similar interview for children, the Children's Social Validity Interview (CSVI). This 13-item instrument also addresses these three components. In addition, the CSVI contains questions regarding the extent to which the students use the acquired skills in other circumstances. The notion of use was included because use is viewed as a behavioral marker of acceptability. Namely, if students use the skills or techniques acquired during the intervention process, then, by definition, the intervention is acceptable (Gresham & Lopez, 1996).

TABLE 12.1
Intervention Rating Profile-15

The purpose of this questionnaire is to obtain information that will aid in the selection of classroom interventions. These interventions will be used by teachers of children with behavior problems. Please circle the number which best describes your agreement or disagreement with each statement.

	Strongly Disagree	Disagree	Slightly Disagree	Slightly Agree	Agree	Strongly Agree
1. This would be an acceptable intervention for the child's problem behavior.	1	2	3	4	5	6
2. Most teachers would find this intervention appropriate for behavior problems in addition to the one described.	1	2	3	4	5	6
3. This intervention should prove effective in changing the child's problem behavior.	1	2	3	4	5	6
4. I would suggest the use of this intervention to other teachers.	1	2	3	4	5	6
5. The child's behavior problem is severe enough to warrant use of this intervention.	1	2	3	4	5	6
6. Most teachers would find this intervention suitable for the behavior problem described.	1	2	3	4	5	6
7. I would be willing to use this intervention in the classroom setting.	1	2	3	4	5	6
8. This intervention would not result in negative side-effects for the child.	1	2	3	4	5	6
9. This intervention would be appropriate for a variety of children.	1	2	3	4	5	6
10. This intervention is consistent with those I have used in classroom settings.	1	2	3	4	5	6
11. The intervention was a fair way to handle the child's problem behavior.	1	2	3	4	5	6
12. This intervention is reasonable for the behavior problem described.	1	2	3	4	5	6
13. I liked the procedures used in this intervention.	1	2	3	4	5	6
14. This intervention was a good way to handle this child's behavior problem.	1	2	3	4	5	6
15. Overall, this intervention would be beneficial for the child.	1	2	3	4	5	6

Note. From *The Intervention Rating Profile* by B. K. Martens and J. C. Witt, 1982, University of Nebraska–Lincoln. Used with permission of the authors.

TABLE 12.2
Children's Intervention Rating Profile (Witt & Elliott, 1985)

	I agree				I do not agree
1. The method used to deal with the behavior problem was fair.	+ ---- + ---- + ---- + ---- + ---- +				
2. This child's teacher was too harsh on him.	+ ---- + ---- + ---- + ---- + ---- +				
3. The method used to deal with the behavior may cause problems with this child's friends.	+ ---- + ---- + ---- + ---- + ---- +				
4. There are better ways to handle this child's problem than the one described here.	+ ---- + ---- + ---- + ---- + ---- +				
5. The method used by this teacher would be a good one to use with other children.	+ ---- + ---- + ---- + ---- + ---- +				
6. I like the method used for this child's behavior problem.	+ ---- + ---- + ---- + ---- + ---- +				
7. I think that the method used for this problem would help this child do better in school.	+ ---- + ---- + ---- + ---- + ---- +				

Note. From *Advances in School Psychology* (p. 284), by T. R. Kratchowill, Ed., 1985, Mahwah, NJ: Erlbaum. Copyright 1985 by Erlbaum. Reprinted with permission.

TABLE 12.3
Sample Social Validity Form: Preintervention

	Strongly Disagree	Disagree	Slightly Disagree	Slightly Agree	Agree	Strongly Agree
1. This intervention targets an important goal.	1	2	3	4	5	6
2. The child's behavioral concern warrants the use of this intervention.	1	2	3	4	5	6
3. The intervention procedures are reasonable for my classroom.	1	2	3	4	5	6
4. I am likely to implement the procedures as designed.	1	2	3	4	5	6
5. This intervention is likely to improve the concern.	1	2	3	4	5	6
6. This intervention is likely to achieve the targeted goal.	1	2	3	4	5	6

Note. From "Teacher Judgments Concerning the Acceptability of School Based Interventions," by B. K. Martens, J. C. Witt, S. N. Elliott, and D. Darveaux, Eds., 1985, *Professional Psychology: Research and Practice, 16,* p. 107.

TABLE 12.4
Sample Social Validity Form: Postintervention

	Strongly Disagree	Disagree	Slightly Disagree	Slightly Agree	Agree	Strongly Agree
1. This intervention targets an important goal.	1	2	3	4	5	6
2. The child's behavioral concern warranted the use of this intervention.	1	2	3	4	5	6
3. The intervention procedures were reasonable for my classroom.	1	2	3	4	5	6
4. The intervention procedures were put in place as designed.	1	2	3	4	5	6
5. This intervention improved the concern.	1	2	3	4	5	6
6. This intervention achieved the targeted goal.	1	2	3	4	5	6

Note. From "Teacher Judgments Concerning the Acceptability of School Based Interventions," by B. K. Martens, J. C. Witt, S. N. Elliott, and D. Darveaux, Eds., 1985, *Professional Psychology: Research and Practice, 16,* p. 107.

Social Comparison Techniques. You can also assess social validity by making comparisons between the student participating in the function-based intervention and a peer who is competent in the replacement behavior. For example, if the participating student's target behavior is disruptive classroom behavior (e.g., talking out, making rude comments), one could collect data using a given recording system (Chapter 9) on both the participating student and the student with typical classroom behaviors (e.g., raising his or her hand and waiting to be called on). This technique can be used at the onset of the intervention to determine whether the participating student's behavior is substantially different from that of the typical peer. If so, this difference supports intervention efforts. If not, then an individualized intervention may not be warranted. Social comparison techniques can also be used at the conclusion of the intervention to see if the performance levels are more parallel. When employing this technique, Fawcett (1991) recommended establishing ideal, normative, or deficient behavioral levels prior to conducting the observations. These three levels are intended to convey additional information regarding the degree of proficiency.

Future Use. A final mechanism you can use to assess social validity is monitoring the extent to which the teacher (or other treatment agent) actually uses the intervention with subsequent students who present similar concerns. Gresham and Lopez (1996) contended that use serves as a behavioral marker for treatment acceptability. Namely, if teachers independently use the intervention in the future, then, by definition, the intervention is socially valid or acceptable. In addition to ensuring an intervention is socially valid, it is equally important to ensure the proposed intervention procedures are ethical (see Sulzer-Azaroff & Mayer, 1991).

TREATMENT INTEGRITY
Definition and Justification

The next component you must attend to is treatment integrity, which refers to the extent to which a given intervention was implemented as originally designed (Billingsley, White, & Munson, 1980; Gresham, 1989; Yeaton & Sechrest, 1981). In essence, treatment integrity is the reliability of the independent variable—the intervention (Lane & Beebe-Frankenberger, 2004).

Treatment integrity is referred to by many different terms, including treatment fidelity, intervention fidelity, treatment reliability, procedural reliability, and procedural fidelity. Regardless of the terminology, assessing treatment integrity is an essential—and often overlooked—component of function-based interventions (Lane, Umbreit, & Beebe-Frankenberger, 1999) and school-based intervention research in general (Gresham et al., 1993). If the accuracy of implementation is not assessed, then both internal and external validity are threatened. Moreover, it is difficult, if not impossible, for you to draw accurate conclusions about (a) how well the intervention worked in the current situation (internal validity) and (b) how well the intervention might work in other situations (external validity) if treatment integrity is assumed rather than assessed (Gresham et al., 1993).

For example, assume that a function-based intervention (adjusting task difficulty) produced a desired outcome (increased on-task behavior). If you did not collect treatment integrity data, then you cannot be certain that it was the intervention that produced the desired outcomes. It is possible that the behavior change occurred because the intervention was altered in some manner, such as adding additional positive reinforcement from the teacher or allowing the student to work with a peer. Similarly, if the intervention did not produce the desired outcome and treatment integrity data were not collected, we again cannot be sure why the intervention failed. Perhaps the intervention was simply not effective (e.g., the actual function of the target behavior was misidentified), or the intervention was not implemented as designed (e.g., the teacher did not provide the student with the proper assignment).

Furthermore, if accuracy of the independent variable is not assessed, it is difficult for you to generalize from the intervention context to other circumstances (external validity). More specifically, if treatment integrity is not assessed, one cannot be certain that this intervention technique would produce the desired outcomes with other similar individuals who exhibit a similar target behavior and function.

Thus, to ensure internal and external validity, you must assess and report treatment integrity data (Gresham, 1989; Lane, Bocian, MacMillan, & Gresham, 2004). Fortunately, there are several feasible and effective methods you can use to monitor treatment integrity.

Methods of Assessment

There are a variety of direct and indirect methods you can use to assess treatment integrity, including direct observation, rating scales, self-report, and permanent products (Elliott & Busse, 1993; Lane & Beebe-Frankenberger, 2004; Lane et al., 2004). We briefly describe each method and provide sample forms, as appropriate.

Direct Observation. Treatment integrity data can be collected by an outside observer such as a school psychologist, interventionist, or paraprofessional who is trained in the intervention procedures. These observations can take place while the intervention is being implemented in the classroom context or at a later date by reviewing videotapes of the intervention. Prior to collecting treatment integrity data, the outside observer must be familiar with the intervention procedures so the presence or absence of the required components can be evaluated accurately.

Direct observation procedures comprise three steps. First, list and operationally define each component of the intervention. Definitions must include sufficient detail to enable others to determine the extent to which the specific component is implemented. Second, have the outside observer rate either the presence or absence of each component (see Table 12.5). Finally, compute component and session integrity ratings (Gresham, MacMillan, Beebe-Frankenberger, & Bocian, 2000; Lane & Beebe-Frankenberger, 2004). For example, in Table 12.5, component integrity ratings are computed for each component (A to I). For component five, the observer rated a zero for integrity because the teacher did not provide the student with a reminder. Therefore, component five's treatment integrity rating was 80% (E: present 4 out of 5 days). Similarly, session integrity ratings are computed for each session (J to N). Because only nine of the components were implemented on Wednesday, the session integrity (L) was 90%. In Chapter 13 (pages 240–41), you will find a description of another practical and effective method that uses whole intervals to directly measure treatment integrity.

Rating Scales. You can also assess treatment integrity indirectly by using rating scales. In this method, the entire intervention is observed and then evaluated (Gresham, 1989; Gresham et al., 2000). For example, the intervention could be rated using a 4-point Likert-type scale, with values ranging from low integrity to high integrity (see Table 12.6).

Self-Report. Self-report techniques are another indirect approach to assessing treatment integrity. Self-report involves asking the person delivering the intervention (e.g., the teacher or paraprofessional) to evaluate the extent to which each component was implemented (Gresham et al., 2000). Although there are concerns about the accuracy of the data generated from self-report techniques (e.g., intentional or unintentional inaccuracies; Wickstrom, 1995; Witt, Gresham, & Noell, 1996), self-reports are highly practical and may actually remind staff to implement each component

TABLE 12.5
Sample Treatment Integrity Form (Presence or Absence): Shortened Tasks

Teacher: Mr. Fanning Week: 1/5/05   Student: Jillian

Component	Mon.	Tues.	Wed.	Thurs.	Fri.	Component Integrity
1. Introduced the assignment	1	1	1	1	1	A 100%
2. Checked for understanding	1	0	1	1	1	B 80%
3. Distributed the math assignment	1	1	1	1	1	C 100%
4. Indicated a stopping point	1	1	1	1	1	D 100%
5. Reminded the student to raise his hand after completing and checking the required number of problems	1	1	0	1	1	E 80%
6. Responded to the student when he raised his hand by asking if he checked his work	1	1	1	1	1	F 100%
7. Evaluated the first set of problems	1	1	1	1	1	G 100%
8. Provided corrective feedback and verbal praise as appropriate	1	1	1	1	1	H 100%
10. Repeated steps 4 through 10 as necessary	1	1	1	1	1	100%
Session Integrity	J	K	L	M	N	OVERALL MEAN
	100%	90%	90%	100%	100%	

Directions: Write a "1" if the component was completed and a "0" if the component was not completed. Compute session and component integrity at the end of the week.

Note. From *School-Based Interventions: The Tools You Need to Succeed* (p. 135), by K. L. Lane and M. E. Beebe-Frankenberger, 2004, Boston: Allyn & Bacon.

(Lane, Wehby, Menzies, Gregg, Doukas, & Munton, 2002). You can employ self-report methods daily, randomly, at fixed intervals, or at the end of an intervention (Lane & Beebe-Frankenberger, 2004). Furthermore, you can use self-report techniques in isolation or in addition to more direct methods (Lane et al., 2002).

Permanent Products. Another indirect method of assessing treatment integrity is with the use of permanent products. If the intervention yields permanent products, then that information can be used as evidence to support the fidelity of implementation. For example, if the intervention involves reducing task length (Kern, Childs, Dunlap, Clarke, & Falk, 1994) or providing a more challenging assignment (Umbreit, Lane, & Dejud, 2004), then the completed shortened assignment (e.g., worksheet with even or odd problems completed) or alternative assignment could be used to document implementation. Similarly, if the intervention entails having students complete

TABLE 12.6
Sample Treatment Integrity Form (Likert-Type): Shortened Tasks

Teacher: Mr. Fanning   Date: 1/5/05   Student: Jillian

Component	Low Integrity			High Integrity
1. Introduced the assignment	1	2	3	4
2. Checked for understanding	1	2	3	4
3. Distributed the math assignment	1	2	3	4
4. Indicated a stopping point	1	2	3	4
5. Reminded the student to raise his hand after completing and checking the required number of problems	1	2	3	4
6. Responded to the student when he raised his hand by asking if he checked his work	1	2	3	4
7. Evaluated the first set of problems	1	2	3	4
8. Provided corrective feedback and verbal praise as appropriate	1	2	3	4

Directions: Circle the number that corresponds to the level of implementation for each component. Compute session and component integrity at the end of the week.

Note. From *School-Based Interventions: The Tools You Need to Succeed* (p. 138), by K. L. Lane and M. E. Beebe-Frankenberger, 2004, Boston: Allyn & Bacon.

assignments in an alternative manner, such as doing a writing assignment on a computer rather than using the traditional paper–pencil technique (Kern et al., 1994; Kern, Delaney, Clarke, Dunlap, & Childs, 2001), the printed document could serve as data.

Recommendations

When you are determining which assessment method to employ, it is important to achieve a balance between rigor and feasibility. Namely, it is important to select a method that will provide you with accurate information about treatment integrity. However, it is also important to select a method that is practical given your resource constraints (e.g., time, materials, personnel). Wickstrom, Jones, LaFleur, and Witt (1998) illustrated the challenges of assessing treatment integrity by comparing three different methods: direct observation, teacher self-report, and the use of intervention stimulus products across teachers. Results suggested tremendous variability among the three techniques. Treatment integrity ratings were 4%, 54%, and 62%, respectively. Clearly, there was a discrepancy between what teachers said they did and what they were observed doing. This illustrates the need for careful consideration when selecting an assessment technique and supports the use of assessing treatment integrity from more than one perspective (e.g., direct observations and rating scales).

GENERALIZATION AND MAINTENANCE
Definition and Justification

When you are designing function-based interventions, one of the major goals is to teach students a new replacement behavior that will take the place of the undesired target behavior. For example, if a student is acting out to escape an undesirable task (e.g., sustained silent reading), then the goal of a function-based intervention might be to teach the student a more desirable escape method (e.g., raising his or her hand and asking for a break). If the newly acquired replacement behavior is more reliable and more efficient than the target behavior, it is likely that this new behavior will be used outside the intervention conditions with other people, in different environments, and over time (Horner & Billingsley, 1988). In brief, the goal is to teach functionally equivalent behaviors that generalize.

Generalization is defined as the occurrence of the desired behavior in nontraining conditions (i.e., under novel conditions without programming of the same procedures that were structured for the training conditions) (Stokes, 1992; Stokes & Baer, 1977). Maintenance is defined as the occurrence of the desired behavior over time (Stokes & Osnes, 1989). It is important to consider issues of generalization and maintenance at the onset of the intervention process because the overall goal of all school-based interventions is to produce meaningful, lasting behavioral changes (Lane & Beebe-Frankenberger, 2004).

Approaches

There are two main methods of addressing generalization and maintenance: functional generalization and topographic generalization (Gresham, 2002). **Functional generalization** speaks to the reason why the behavior occurs; in contrast, **topographic generalization** focuses on the form of behavior (Gresham, 1994). By definition, functional behavioral assessment involves the functional approach to generalization.

Historically, many interventionists have focused on topographical approaches to generalization. More specifically, topographical generalization refers to the occurrence of the target behavior (e.g., completing assignments in the required time limit) in circumstances other than the training (intervention) conditions (Stokes & Osnes, 1989). For example, if a student has been taught a strategy to complete assignments within the required time limit in language arts and the student then begins to complete math assignments within the allotted time, topographical generalization has occurred. Generalization can occur over time (maintenance), with other people, in different settings, and with variations of the target behavior (Gresham, 1994). However, topographical generalization only addresses the question of whether or not the target behavior has occurred in untrained conditions. It does not answer the question of why the target behavior occurred in those situations.

Stokes and Osnes (1989) designed a topographical system for promoting generalization. Specifically, this system comprises three principles: using functional contingencies, training broadly, and incorporating functional mediators.

Using Functional Contingencies. This category involves techniques for employing naturally occurring contingencies. This is accomplished by (a) contacting and recruiting consequences that take place naturally, (b) adjusting undesirable consequences, and (c) offering reinforcement when the replacement behavior occurs outside the intervention setting.

Contacting and recruiting natural consequences involves capitalizing on consequences that occur over the course of the regular day. For example, if a student is taught a method to self-monitor work completion, natural consequences can be invoked to increase the likelihood that the behavior will occur beyond the intervention setting. Instead of offering students a "point" or a sticker for completing the assigned task, the teacher can provide verbal praise and award a deserving grade. If the task is not completed, the student is likely to receive a less favorable grade and no verbal praise. Similarly, the student can be taught to seek reinforcement. For example, if the teacher does not offer verbal praise, the student can be encouraged to alert the teacher by saying something like "Hey, Mr. Fanning! I finished this whole page!" It is important that students be taught to identify appropriate times to recruit teacher attention (e.g., during down time and not when the teacher is instructing).

Adjusting undesirable consequences involves manipulating consequences that sustain the undesirable behavior. For example, if a student is disrupting the class during sustained silent reading in hopes of being sent out of the room, a teacher can adjust the undesirable consequence by not allowing the student to leave the room during this time. Instead, the student should only be offered a break (escape) contingent on the presence of the replacement behavior (e.g., raising hand to request a break).

Offering reinforcement when the replacement behavior occurs beyond the training setting involves delivering reinforcement when the student uses the replacement behavior outside the training circumstances. For example, if the student who previously demonstrated disruptive behaviors during silent reading now begins to raise his or her hand to request a break during math instruction, the replacement behavior should be reinforced. Ideally, the behavior should be reinforced using behavior-specific praise (e.g., "Yes, you may take a 2-min break to draw a picture about the story you're reading. Thank you for raising your hand to ask for a break."). This provides the students with specific information about which behavior is being reinforced.

These techniques are not only effective, but they are also feasible in terms of your existing resources (time, money, materials, and personnel). When implemented correctly, you can use these techniques—contacting and recruiting consequences that occur naturally, adjusting undesirable consequences, and offering reinforcement when the replacement behaviors occur beyond the training setting—so naturally occurring reinforcers will maintain the replacement behavior (Lane & Beebe-Frankenberger, 2004; Stokes & Osnes, 1989).

Training Broadly. When we teach students new behaviors, there is a delicate balance between discrimination and generalization (Edelstein, 1989; Lane & Beebe-Frankenberger, 2004). Although our initial goal is to ensure a particular behavior will occur precisely under the training conditions (discrimination), the next step is to ensure the behavior will vary in topography (response generalization) and will be used in a range of settings and circumstances (stimulus generalization). To accomplish the latter goal, you must train broadly. In other words, you must systematically vary the training conditions over the course of the intervention program. To do this, consider these variations before beginning the training: using a variety of stimulus and response exemplars, and modifying the antecedents and consequences so they are hard to distinguish from the training conditions.

Using adequate stimulus and response exemplars is similar to training diversely. The key difference is that one involves broadening the antecedent conditions (stimulus exemplars), whereas the other requires broadening the behavioral responses (response exemplars). Varying the training conditions is an example of using stimulus exemplars to enhance generalization. If the goal of a self-regulation intervention is to increase the completion of both classroom and homework assignments, then you will need to provide the intervention in both settings. Response exemplars entail varying the topography of the target response. For example, if you are teaching a child to initiate interactions with his or her peers, then you will want to teach various statements that can be used to begin a conversation (e.g., "Hey, that looks like fun. Can I play?" or "Wow, that's cool! May I play with you guys?").

Modifying antecedents and consequences, so the intervention setting will be similar to other settings, requires that you ask the following questions: Under which additional circumstances (other than the training setting) would you like the new behavior to occur? For example, if you want students to be academically engaged or on-task in other classes (e.g., during science, math, and reading instruction), then it is important to broaden stimulus control. This means you will need to vary the training format so students will not associate the replacement behavior with only one situation (e.g., I only do this in Mr. Fanning's class and not in Mrs. Lane's class). The goal is to ensure more than one antecedent stimulus will prompt the desired behavior.

Similarly, modifying consequences involves broadening the range of acceptable responses. Allowing more time to lapse before delivering reinforcement and allocating reinforcement intermittently can provide ways to vary the consequences that follow the replacement behavior. For example, once a student begins to complete classroom assignments on a regular basis, verbal praise may be offered less frequently by using an intermittent reinforcement schedule.

Collectively, these strategies (using adequate stimulus and response exemplars and modifying antecedents and consequences so they are harder to distinguish from the intervention condition) will help you promote generalization and maintenance by broadening stimulus control and adjusting reinforcement schedules.

Incorporating Functional Mediators. The final category of topographical strategies is to incorporate functional mediators. A mediator is a discriminative stimulus—a stimulus that prompts the occurrence of the desired behavior. This technique involves presenting a mediator that was used in the intervention condition in a novel setting (i.e., the proposed generalization site; Stokes & Osnes, 1989). This can be accomplished by incorporating shared physical stimuli, shared social stimuli, self-mediated physical stimuli, and self-mediated verbal and overt stimuli. Each technique is described as follows.

Incorporating shared physical stimuli involves placing physical objects in both the intervention and generalization environments. For example, if the goal is to generalize a self-monitoring program from a language arts class to a math class, then the self-monitoring sheets initially designed for the language arts class could be used (or be modified for use) in the math class.

Incorporating shared social stimuli involves ensuring similar social aspects are present in both the intervention and generalization settings. For example, if a skill deficit is present and it is necessary to provide explicit instruction in anger management skills, then one method of incorporating shared social stimuli would be to also have the interventionist be present occasionally in the generalization setting. If this is not possible, peer models could participate in the intervention and also serve as discriminative stimuli (prompts) for the student to use proper methods of regulating anger or frustration in the classroom.

Incorporating self-mediated physical stimuli occurs when the target student brings a particular stimulus to both the training and generalization settings. For example, if a student is taught to self-monitor his or her own on-task behavior during social studies by making tally marks on a daily planner, then the daily planner could also be carried to other periods of the day to monitor task engagement. Similarly, if a student is taught to use a "koosh" ball to obtain sensory stimuli during language arts, then the same ball could be used to obtain sensory stimuli during other instructional periods (Lane, Thompson, Reske, Gable, & Barton-Arwood, in press). When using this technique, it is important to inform teachers in the other setting about the self-mediated physical stimulus so they will not remove it or punish its use.

Incorporating self-mediated verbal and overt stimuli involves teaching students to say (overtly) or think about (covertly) the strategies or other content taught in the training settings. For example, if students are taught four steps for improving work accuracy, then the student could recite or think about these steps outside the intervention conditions. It may be necessary to prompt students to use these techniques (Guevremont, Osnes, & Stokes, 1988).

Each strategy (shared physical stimuli, shared social stimuli, self-mediated physical stimuli, and self-mediated verbal and overt stimuli) is an inexpensive technique for incorporating functional mediators. All three categories are topographical approaches to promoting generalization and maintenance of the desired replacement skills (i.e., they focus on the form of the behavior that is to generalize). These techniques have been referred to as "train and hope" techniques and have met with a range of outcomes (Gresham, 2002). Whereas the functional approach to generalization and maintenance is likely to produce the desired changes, building in some topographical approaches to the intervention design may also enhance intervention efforts. Dunlap (1993) recommended the following course of action for enhancing generalization: (a) develop a generalization plan when designing the intervention, (b) evaluate the antecedent and consequent conditions that are present in the environment, (c) implement the interventions (when possible) in the settings to which generalization is desired, (d) build in current generalization technology (e.g., topographical and functional approaches), (e) consider issues of stimulus control (i.e., the conditions that set the occasion for the behavior to occur), (f) evaluate issues of reinforcement (i.e., the consequences that maintain the behavior), and (g) explore generalization of functional alternatives (i.e., replacement behaviors that can be made more efficient than target behaviors).

SUMMARY

To enhance the effectiveness of function-based interventions, it is important to incorporate three components: social validity, treatment integrity, and generalization and maintenance (Lane & Beebe-Frankenberger, 2004). By assessing the social validity of a proposed intervention, you can determine whether the school staff believe the intervention addresses significant goals, includes acceptable procedures, and yields important outcomes (Baer et al., 1987). If social validity is high at the onset, meaning that teachers view the intervention as acceptable, then it is likely that the intervention will be implemented with high treatment integrity (Lane et al., 2001). If the intervention was based on the correct function of the target behavior and was implemented with a high level of fidelity, then it is likely to produce the desired outcomes. Moreover, the intervention is likely to produce behavioral changes that last and generalize to novel circumstances (across environments, in the presence of other people, and with other treatment agents; Dunlap, 1993; Ferro & Dunlap, 1993; Lane et al., 2001). If lasting changes are produced, then it is also likely that postintervention social validity ratings will be high. If this is the case, the teaching staff will conclude that the intervention addressed socially significant goals, incorporated procedures that are reasonable within the classroom, and produced socially important outcomes. In this situation, the teacher may be more likely to use function-based interventions in the future.

Steps for Ensuring Social Validity, Treatment Integrity, and Maintenance and Generalization

Social Validity

Before intervention:

1. Determine which parties (e.g., teachers, parents, students) should assess social validity.

2. Choose a social validity tool (e.g., rating scale, interview).

3. Complete the identified tool(s).

4. Examine the results to determine whether the intervention should be adjusted prior to implementation.

After intervention:

1. Determine which parties (e.g., teachers, parents, students) should assess social validity.

2. Choose a social validity tool (e.g., rating scale, interview).

3. Complete the identified tool(s).

4. Based on the results, make decisions about future interventions.

Treatment Integrity

Before intervention:

1. Select a method of monitoring treatment integrity.

2. Decide who will collect the treatment integrity data.

During intervention:

1. Monitor treatment integrity.

2. Adjust intervention procedures based on the results.

After intervention:

1. Compute final treatment integrity percentages (component and session).

2. Determine if all intervention steps are essential.

Maintenance and Generalization

Before intervention:

1. Identify which approaches you will use to program for maintenance and generalization.

During intervention:

1. Implement maintenance and generalization techniques.

2. Conduct assessments to probe for generalization.

After intervention:

1. Conduct assessments to probe for generalization.

EXERCISES

Directions: Read the following information about a function-based intervention designed to adjust task difficulty to increase on-task behavior (Umbreit et al., 2004). Complete the three activities listed in Table 12.7, which appears after the description.

Student and Background

Jason was a fourth-grade, typically developing general education student attending a public elementary school. Although well liked by his peers, Jason's teacher viewed his behavior to be highly disruptive. Specifically, Mr. Fanning was troubled by Jason's off-task behavior, which occurred frequently during independent work time during math and reading instruction.

FBA Results

Results of the functional assessment interviews, direct observation data, and identification of function indicated that Jason's off-task behavior was maintained by positive reinforcement. More specifically, off-task behavior occurred after he finished his assignments (antecedent condition) when there were no other task demands present. Jason's off-task behavior was maintained by obtaining access to a preferred activity (i.e., the consequence was positive reinforcement—activity).

Intervention

Direct observation data indicated that Jason could perform the tasks (on-task behavior). Thus, there was not a skill deficit. The next question was to determine whether the antecedent conditions in the classroom reflected effective educational practices. Information obtained from Jason and direct observations suggest that the assignments were "too easy" for Jason, who quickly finished his assignments with high levels of accuracy. This left Jason without a task demand for the duration of the independent work period. The interventionists concluded that Jason would be on-task more if he were provided with assignments that more closely matched his ability level and if access to additional preferred activities was available only when he demonstrated high levels of on-task behavior.

Challenging tasks were identified for Jason by allowing him to work ahead in his math and reading workbooks. Once Jason reached an assignment that he could not complete within 10 min with 100% accuracy, this was labeled as a challenging task. The instructional assistant provided the rest of the class with their normal assignment during independent work time, but Jason was given the more challenging assignment to complete.

During each independent activity session, two trained observers recorded Jason's on-task behavior for 15 min using a 30-s whole interval recording procedure. IOA was computed by dividing the total number of intervals in agreement by the total number of intervals with agreements plus disagreements and multiplying by 100% (Kazdin, 1982). IOA was quite high for both math ($M = 96\%$; range: 87%–100%) and reading ($M = 97\%$; range: 90%–100%) sessions.

TABLE 12.7
Exercise Activities

Construct	Activities
Social validity	Explain how you would assess social validity at the onset and at the end of the intervention from both the teacher's and Jason's perspective. Justify your answer.
Treatment integrity	Create your own treatment integrity checklist. Be sure to include all necessary components.
Generalization and maintenance	Assuming the intervention was effective in reducing off-task behavior and increasing on-task behavior, how would you program for generalization? What specific approaches would you employ? Justify your answer.

REFERENCES

Baer, D. M., Wolf, M. M., & Risley, T. R. (1968). Some current dimensions of applied behavior analysis. *Journal of Applied Behavior Analysis, 1,* 91–97.

Baer, D. M., Wolf, M. M., & Risley, T. R. (1987). Some still-current dimensions of applied behavior analysis. *Journal of Applied Behavior Analysis, 20,* 313–327.

Billingsley, F. F., White, O. R., & Munson, R. (1980). Procedural reliability: A rationale and an example. *Behavioral Assessment, 2,* 229–241.

Dunlap, G. (1993). Promoting generalization: Current status and functional considerations. In R. V. Houten, & S. Axelrod (Eds.), *Behavior analysis and treatment* (pp. 269–296). New York: Plenum Press.

Edelstein, B. (1989). Generalization: Terminological, methodological and conceptual issues. *Behavior Therapy, 20,* 311–324.

Elliott, S. N., & Busse, R. (1993). Effective treatments with behavioral consultation. In J. Zins, T. Kratochwill, & S. Elliott (Eds.), *Handbook of consultation service for children* (pp. 179–203). San Francisco: Jossey-Bass.

Fawcett, S. (1991). Social validity: A note on methodology. *Journal of Applied Behavior Analysis, 24,* 235–239.

Ferro, J., & Dunlap, G. (1993). Generalization and maintenance. In M. D. Smith (Ed.), *Behavior modification for exceptional children and youth* (pp. 190–211). Boston: Andover Medical.

Finn, C. A., & Sladeczek, I. E. (2001). Assessing the social validity of behavior interventions: A review of treatment acceptability measures. *School Psychology Quarterly, 16,* 176–206.

Gresham, F. M. (1989). Assessment of treatment integrity in school consultation and prereferral intervention. *School Psychology Review, 18,* 37–50.

Gresham, F. M. (1994). Generalization of social skills: Risks of choosing form over function. *School Psychology Quarterly, 9,* 142–144.

Gresham, F. M. (2002). Social skills assessment and instruction for students with emotional and behavioral disorders. In K. L. Lane, F. M. Gresham, & T. E. O'Shaughnessy (Eds.), *Interventions for children with or at risk for emotional and behavioral disorders* (pp. 242–258). Boston: Allyn & Bacon.

Gresham, F. M., Gansle, K. A., & Noell, G. H. (1993). Treatment integrity in applied behavior analysis with children. *Journal of Applied Behavioral Analysis, 26,* 257–263.

Gresham, F. M., & Lopez, M. F. (1996). Social validation: A unifying construct for school-based consultation research and practice. *School Psychology Quarterly, 11,* 204–227.

Gresham, F. M., MacMillan, D. L., Beebe-Frankenberger, M. E., & Bocian, K. M. (2000). Treatment integrity in learning disabilities intervention research: Do we really know how treatment are implemented? *Learning Disabilities Research & Practice, 15,* 198–205.

Guevremont, D. C., Osnes, P. G., & Stokes, T. F. (1988). The functional role of preschoolers' verbalizations in the generalization of self-instruction training. *Journal of Applied Behavioral Analysis, 21,* 45–55.

Horner, R. H., & Billingsley, F. F. (1988). The effect of competing behavior on the generalization and maintenance of adaptive behavior in applied settings. In R. H. Horner, G. Dunlap, & R. L. Koegel (Eds.), *Generalization and maintenance: Lifestyle changes in applied settings* (pp. 197–220). Baltimore: Paul H. Brookes.

Kazdin, A. E. (1977). Assessing the clinical or applied significance of behavior change through social validation. *Behaviour Modification, 1,* 427–452.

Kazdin, A. E. (1980). Acceptability of alternative treatments for deviant child behavior. *Journal of Applied Behavior Analysis, 13,* 259–273.

Kazdin, A. E. (1982). *Single-case research designs.* New York: Oxford University Press.

Kelley, M. J., Heffer, R. W., Gresham, F. M., & Elliott, S. N. (1989). Development of a modified Treatment Evaluation Inventory. *Journal of Psychopathology & Behavioral Assessment, 11,* 235–247.

Kern, L., Childs, K., Dunlap, G., Clarke, S., & Falk, G. (1994). Using assessment-based curricular intervention to improve the classroom behavior of a student with emotional and behavioral challenges. *Journal of Applied Behavior Analysis, 27,* 7–19.

Kern, L., Delaney, B., Clarke, S., Dunlap, G., & Childs, K. (2001). Improving the classroom behavior of students with emotional and behavioral disorders using individualized curricular modifications. *Journal of Emotional and Behavioral Disorders, 9,* 239–247.

Lane, K. L. (1997). *Students at-risk for antisocial behavior: The utility of academic and social skills interventions.* Doctoral dissertation, University of California, Riverside.

Lane, K. L., & Beebe-Frankenberger, M. E. (2004). *School-based interventions: The tools you need to succeed.* Boston: Allyn & Bacon.

Lane, K. L., Beebe-Frankenberger, M. E., Lambros, K. L., & Pierson, M. E. (2001). Designing effective interventions for children at-risk for antisocial behavior: An integrated model of components necessary for making valid inferences. *Psychology in the Schools, 38,* 365–379.

Lane, K. L., Bocian, K. M., MacMillan, D. L., & Gresham, F. M. (in press). Treatment integrity: An essential—but often forgotten—component of school-based interventions. *Preventing School Failure 48,* 36–43.

Lane, K. L., Thompson, A., Reske, C., Gable, L., & Barton-Arwood, S. (in press). Reducing skin picking behavior via competing activities. *Journal of Applied Behavior Analysis.*

Lane, K. L., Umbreit, J., & Beebe-Frankenberger, M. (1999). A review of functional assessment research with students with or at-risk for emotional and behavioral disorders. *Journal of Positive Behavioral Interventions, 1,* 101–111.

Lane, K. L., Wehby, J. H., Menzies, H. M., Gregg, R. M., Doukas, G. L., & Munton, S. M. (2002). Early literacy instruction for first-grade students at-risk for antisocial behavior. *Education and Treatment of Children, 25,* 438–458.

Mace, F. C. (1994). The significance and future of functional analysis methodologies. *Journal of Applied Behavior Analysis, 27,* 385–392.

Martens, B. K., & Witt, J. C. (1982). *The intervention rating profile.* Copyrighted manuscript, University of Nebraska-Lincoln.

Stokes, T. (1992). Discrimination and generalization. *Journal of Applied Behavior Analysis, 25,* 429–432.

Stokes, T., & Baer, D. M. (1977). An implicit technology of generalization. *Journal of Applied Behavior Analysis, 10,* 349–367.

Stokes, T., & Osnes, P. G. (1989). An operant pursuit of generalization. *Behavior Therapy, 20,* 337–355.

Sulzer-Azaroff, B., & Mayer, G. R. (1991). *Behavior analysis for lasting change.* Ft. Worth, TX: Harcourt Brace College.

Umbreit, J., Lane, K. L., & Dejud, C. (2004). Improving classroom behavior by modifying task difficulty: The effects of increasing the difficulty of too-easy tasks. *Journal of Positive Behavior Interventions, 6,* 13–20.

VonBrock, M., & Elliott, S. N. (1987). The influence of treatment effectiveness information on the acceptability of classroom interventions. *Journal of School Psychology, 25,* 131–144.

Wickstrom, K. (1995). *A study of the relationship among teacher, process and outcome variables with school-based consultation.* Unpublished doctoral dissertation, Louisiana State University, Baton Rouge.

Wickstrom, K., Jones, K., LaFleur, L., & Witt, J. (1998). An analysis of treatment integrity in school-based behavioral consultation. *School Psychology Quarterly, 13,* 141–154.

Witt, J. C., & Elliott, S. N. (1985). Acceptability of classroom intervention strategies. In T. R. Kratochwill (Ed.), *Advances in school psychology* (Vol. 4, pp. 251–288). Mahwah, NJ: Erlbaum.

Witt, J. C., Gresham, F. M., & Noell, G. H. (1996). What's behavioral about behavioral consultation? *Journal of Educational and Psychological Consultation, 7,* 327–344.

Witt, J. C., & Martens, B. (1983). Assessing the acceptability of behavioral interventions used in classrooms. *Psychology in the Schools, 20,* 510–517.

Wolf, M. M. (1978). Social validity: The case for subjective measurement or how applied behavior analysis is finding its heart. *Journal of Applied Behavior Analysis, 11,* 203–214.

Yeaton, W., & Sechrest, L. (1981). Critical dimensions in the choice and maintenance of successful treatments: Strength, integrity, and effectiveness. *Journal of Consulting and Clinical Psychology, 49,* 156–167.

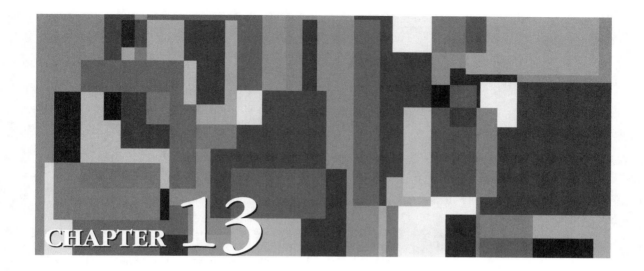

CHAPTER 13

Monitoring the Intervention and Analyzing Outcomes

OUTCOMES

After reading this chapter, you will be able to

- Properly monitor the outcomes of an intervention.
- Properly monitor the implementation of an intervention.
- Organize data into a clear, useful graph.
- Assess social validity at the proper times.
- Use social validity data to improve an intervention or its implementation.
- Assess generalization.
- Identify the appropriate point at which to begin fading an intervention.
- Fade an intervention at the proper speed.

At this point, you have completed the FBA, developed and tested the function-based intervention, and considered a number of key factors that influence whether an intervention is effective. As you now begin to intervene, you must monitor the intervention and analyze student outcomes. During this last step, people often have some specific questions about how to properly monitor an intervention and its implementation. Therefore, this chapter presents a series of commonly asked questions followed by explicit, practical answers. We discuss the mechanics of implementing, monitoring, and evaluating the intervention successfully and practically.

MONITORING STUDENT BEHAVIOR

What does it mean to "monitor" student behavior?

Monitoring the intervention means that you need to collect data to determine how the student's behavior is changing. To do this, you use the same measurement system that you used when collecting baseline data and when you tested the intervention (as described in Chapters 9 and 10).

Is it ever acceptable to use one measurement system for testing the intervention and another measurement system when implementing the intervention? If so, what standard should apply?

In a word—yes. There is some flexibility when moving from testing the intervention to implementing and monitoring the intervention. For example, if a whole interval measurement system was used during the testing phase, it might be possible to use time sampling to monitor the intervention. Similarly, if you used a frequency count during intervention testing, it would be possible to shift to rate data during the intervention implementation. In Chapter 9, we provided some guidelines you can use to determine which types of shifts may be acceptable. When considering making these shifts, it is important to remember that if a change in measurement is going to occur, then the shift must be to another compatible measurement system that provides equivalent data. In other words, you would not shift from a time-based measurement system (e.g., time sampling) to an event-based measurement system (e.g., frequency counts).

Once the intervention is in place, is it possible to switch measurement systems?

No. Once you start the intervention, you should stick with the same measurement system as long as the intervention is being implemented. The purpose of collecting data is to gather accurate information about the effects of the intervention so you can make important decisions about its continuation or modification. If you change from one measurement system to another in midstream, you will have made that task virtually impossible.

How often do I need to collect data on the student's behavior?

There are no explicit guidelines for this question. Data need to be collected often enough to detect change without overburdening the data collector. It may be that data are collected daily, twice a week, or even weekly. The frequency of data collection depends on the frequency of the behavior, the recording system used, and the resources available for data collection.

It is important to recognize that data collection does not occur all day every day. In many cases, data will be collected only during those times in which the target behavior is most likely to occur and only for a specific block of time. For example, if on- and off-task behavior are being measured during reading groups, then time sampling data might be collected using 30-second intervals for a total of 20 min each day.

Is there a point at which I can reduce the number of times I collect data on a student?

Once your data show that the target behavior is declining or has declined, then it is possible to reduce how often you collect data (e.g., from every day

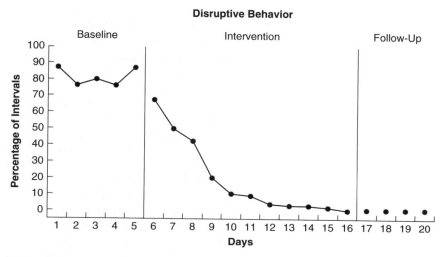

FIGURE 13.1

Illustration of an intervention that decreased disruptive behavior.

to once per week). Before reducing the number of data collection points, verify the behavior has been steadily declining or has leveled off to a desired level for a minimum of three observations. See Figure 13.1 for an example. Figure 13.1 shows the percentage of disruptive behavior a student exhibited during baseline (sessions 1 to 5), intervention (sessions 6 to 16), and follow-up (sessions 17 to 20). Note the vertical lines that separate the graph into three panels, from left to right, marking the three phases. In the baseline and initial intervention phases (sessions 1 to 16), data were collected daily. Because clear and consistent improvement was evident during sessions 10 to 16, data were then collected once each week, rather than once per day, in sessions 17 to 20. Note that these data points are not connected by a line, but rather they stand alone. This change in the graph helps mark these data as being the product of less frequent data collection. Figure 13.1 provides a good example of how and when to reduce the frequency of data collection. The key feature of this example is that data on the student's behavior formed the basis for deciding when to reduce the frequency of data collection.

Do I need to collect IOA data? If so, why? How often?

IOA needs to be collected to ensure the accuracy of your data. If you were conducting research, it would be important to collect IOA data for at least 25% of the sessions in each phase (Horner, Carr, Halle, McGee, Odom, & Wolery, 2005). However, even in the likely event that you are not conducting research, you still need to collect IOA data. The main reason you are collecting data is to be able to draw accurate conclusions about the extent to which an intervention is "working." If your data are not reliable and valid, then you will not be able to determine whether shifts in your data patterns are due to changes in the student's behavior or whether they are due to differences in measurement of the behavior. As mentioned in Chapter 9, IOA is necessary to (a) ensure the data used to evaluate an intervention's effectiveness reflect the student's "true" behavior, (b) reduce the influence of observer bias (the possibility that beliefs or emotional feelings about individual students will influence the data that are recorded), and (c) provide independent evidence about how well a target and replacement behavior have been defined.

Although there are not any "hard and fast" rules about how often to assess IOA for clinical purposes, in general, we recommend that IOA be assessed in every intervention testing session (Chapter 10). When the intervention is initially implemented, IOA should be assessed at least once per week. Once the effectiveness of an intervention has been established, IOA data should be collected approximately once every 2 weeks. Less frequent collection of IOA data introduces potential problems with observer drift (gradual shifts in the criteria for measuring behavior) and creates a risk that important decisions may be based on questionable information.

Should I be measuring both the target and the replacement behaviors?

In general, yes, you should measure both the target and the replacement behaviors. However, there is a situation in which you would measure one or the other—when the behaviors are dichotomous. Behaviors are considered to be **dichotomous** if two behaviors cannot occur at the same time. A good example is on-task/off-task. At any moment, you can be one or the other, but you cannot be both. When the target and replacement behaviors are dichotomous, then the recommendation is to focus on the measurement of the replacement behavior. One of the benefits of function-based intervention is skill building. Rather than simply trying to reduce an undesirable target behavior, the emphasis should be on improving and supporting the level, intensity, or duration of the desirable replacement behavior.

Remember, if the target and replacement behaviors are not dichotomous, then both behaviors should be measured. Each behavior should be measured using an appropriate measurement system. It is possible that they will be measured using different systems. For example, if a young child's target behavior is hitting, the replacement behavior would not be not hitting. Rather, the replacement behavior would identify what the child is supposed to be doing instead (e.g., participating in story-time activities such as sitting, looking at the teacher, or answering questions). In this example, frequency counting might be used to measure hitting. In contrast, time sampling might be used to measure participation (on-task behavior).

Is there some easy way to keep track of all this information? Should I use Excel and create graphs?

We recommend using Microsoft Excel to keep track of your data. You can store and monitor data on both the target and the replacement behaviors in one Excel sheet. Then, the Chart Wizard option can be used to create your graphs. In the exercises at the end of this chapter, you can practice creating a graph in Excel using step-by-step instructions. Carr and Burkholder (1998) also provided instructions for creating graphs using Excel that are suitable for monitoring your data.

Jessica							
		Target Behavior: Disruption		**Replacement Behavior: Academic Engagement**		**IOA Target Behavior**	**IOA Replacement Behavior**	**Treatment Integrity**
Phase A	**Baseline**							
	1	98	1	49		100	100	
	2	92	2	56				
	3	94	3	39				
	4	95	4	54		90	100	
	5	87	5	37				
	6	89	6	37				
	Mean	92.50	**Mean**	45.33				
	SD	4.04	**SD**	8.73				
Phase B	**Treatment**							
	1	30	1	50		100	100	100
	2	22	2	70				100
	3	10	3	80				98
	4	9	4	89		100	90	100
	5	4	5	90				90
	6	3	6	98				97
	Mean	13.00	**Mean**	79.50				
	SD	10.73	**SD**	17.34				
Phase A	**Maintenance**							
	1	0	1	90		90	95	
	2	0	2	96				
	3	0	3	95				
	Mean	0.00	**Mean**	93.67	**Mean**	96	97	97.5
	SD	0.00	**SD**	3.21	**SD**	5.477	4.472	3.886

FIGURE 13.2
Sample Excel spreadsheet.

Figure 13.2 provides an example of an Excel spreadsheet. There are multiple ways to organize your data. Figure 13.2 illustrates one way that allows you to track not only the target and replacement behaviors, but also IOA and treatment integrity data (discussion to follow).

In Figure 13.3, you see a sample graph. The observation or probe numbers are located on the *x*-axis (horizontal line). The percentage of disruptive behavior and academic engagement are presented on the *y*-axis (vertical line). Each observation is presented as a dot (data point) on the graph, and a line is used to connect these observations within each phase. Please note that a solid line is used to connect the target behavior data points (disruptive behavior), and a broken line is used to connect the replacement behavior data points (academic engagement). This is done so the data can be distinguished easily. Another option would be to use color-coded lines. Also, lines should not be connected across phases. This practice is used to separate data from different conditions

FIGURE 13.3
Sample: Jessica's total
disruptive behavior
(TDB) and academic
engaged time (AET).

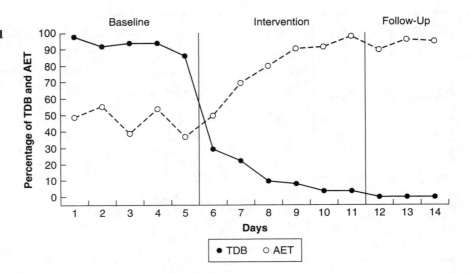

(e.g., baseline, intervention, follow-up). In Figure 13.3, the lines do cross conditions, and the follow-up data points are connected. These are errors that have been presented deliberately so you will avoid them. The correct manner for connecting, and not connecting, data points can be seen in Figure 13.1.

Now, if your target and replacement behaviors are not being measured with the same system, then the graph would need to reflect these differences. Figure 13.4 provides an example of how you can do this. As you can see, the

FIGURE 13.4
Example of a graph
with different
behavior measurement
systems for the target
and replacement
behaviors. AET,
academic engaged
time.

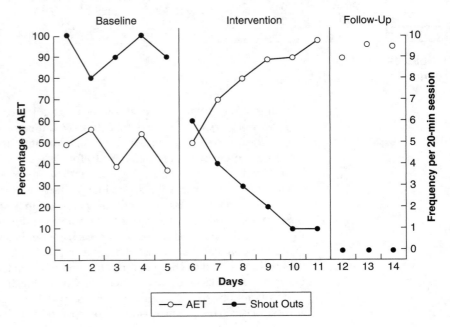

replacement behavior (academic engagement) was measured in a percentage of intervals and is presented on the *y*-axis on the left-hand side; in contrast, the target behavior ("shout outs"—not the kind in a hip hop song, but the kind in a classroom) were measured using event recording, as noted on the *y*-axis on the right-hand side of the graph.

MONITORING THE IMPLEMENTATION OF THE INTERVENTION

Do I need to monitor what the staff and/or teachers are doing (treatment integrity)? Can't I just assume that they will do what they are supposed to do?

We spare you the discussion of what the word "assume" means. Rather than assuming that all staff and/or teachers are doing what is expected of them, you will need to actually assess implementation. In fact, many school staff find that data on implementation often provide the most useful information for improving an intervention's effectiveness.

As you recall from Chapter 12, treatment integrity needs to be assessed so accurate conclusions can be drawn about intervention outcomes. If the plan works, is it because it was a good intervention that was correctly linked to the function of the target behavior? Or, did it work only after the teacher modified the plan in some way? If the plan does not produce the desired outcome, was it because the plan was not correctly linked to the function of the target behavior or because the plan was not properly implemented in some way (e.g., reinforcement was never delivered)? Your goal—to draw accurate conclusions about the effectiveness of the intervention—can be achieved only if you can verify that the intervention was implemented correctly.

Data on treatment integrity can also help you interpret specific performance. For example, take a look at Figure 13.5. You see that the intervention, which involved a self-monitoring plan with teacher reinforcement, appeared to be effective (data points presented as circles), except for data point 13. If you look at the treatment integrity data that are also plotted (the data points presented as triangles), you see that treatment integrity was low on that day. It is likely that, because the plan was not put in place accurately on that day, the student's behavior was influenced negatively. Without the treatment integrity data, you might conclude that the child responded inconsistently to the intervention or that the intervention was only sometimes effective. The treatment integrity data leads you to a very different conclusion.

How often should I monitor implementation (treatment integrity)?

Ideally, treatment integrity should be assessed daily. However, you must also consider other factors, such as the time it takes to assess treatment integrity, how it will be assessed, and the availability of resources to support the assessment. For example, if the teacher is going to be self-evaluating treatment integrity by completing a behavioral checklist, that might be feasible to do on a daily basis. However, if a trained outside observer is going

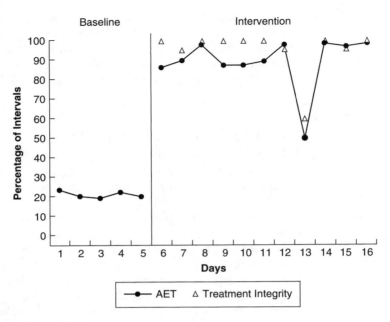

FIGURE 13.5
Using treatment integrity to inform decisions about student behavior. AET, academic engaged time.

to collect treatment integrity, then daily observations may not be reasonable. Instead, the observer might conduct observations once or twice a week.

Is it possible to monitor the student's behavior and the staff's implementation at the same time?

Yes. It is possible to assess the student's behavior while you are also assessing the teacher's or staff's behavior. To assess treatment integrity, you can use any of the methods described in Chapter 12. An additional method would be to use a whole interval measurement system to monitor implementation. This is a very fluid and fairly easy method with many applications. Intervals can be established just as they are when using interval methods to measure the student's behavior. In this case, however, you will be measuring the behavior of the teacher (or other staff members who are implementing the intervention). In many cases, interventions involve multiple components. Different components of the intervention may be called for at different points in time. In scoring each interval, the observer would answer the following question: Were all required intervention components properly implemented throughout the entire interval? Each interval scored "+" indicates that all required components were properly implemented throughout the entire interval. The observer would score a "−" if staff failed to implement any required intervention component at any time during the

Intervals	1	2	3	4	5	6	7	8	9	10	11	12	13	14	15	16	17	18	19	20
On-Task	+	+	+	+	+	+	+	+	+	+	−	+	+	+	−	+	+	+	+	+
Intervention	+	+	+	+	+	+	+	+	+	+	+	+	+	−	+	+	+	+	+	+

Observation Length: 10 min (20 intervals, 30-s each)
On-task behavior: 18/20 intervals = 90%
Implementation: 19/20 intervals = 95%

FIGURE 13.6
Example of a data sheet for simultaneously monitoring behavior and implementation.

interval. Then, a percentage of intervals with proper implementation would be calculated.

Figure 13.6 is an example of such a recording sheet. In this example, an observer simultaneously recorded both the student's behavior and the staff's behavior in implementing the intervention. The child was observed for on- or off-task behavior at the end of every 30 s for a total of 10 min. You should recognize this recording method as time sampling. The observer also used the 30-s intervals to record whether the staff properly implemented all required components of the intervention throughout each 30-s interval. You should recognize this recording method as an example of whole interval measurement. As can be seen in the top row of Figure 13.6, the observer scored that the student was on-task at the end of 18 of the 20 intervals. This equates to a 90% on-task percentage. In the second row, the observer also scored that the staff properly implemented the required intervention components throughout 19 of the 20 intervals. This equates to an implementation percentage (or treatment integrity) of 95%. Using this method, many observers can easily monitor treatment integrity while also measuring the student's behavior.

Regardless of what method is used to assess treatment integrity, how high does the percentage have to be? What if the percentage is not very good? What do I do then?

Ideally, you want to see interventions implemented with 100% integrity. However, interventions can often be effective with less than perfect implementation (e.g., Lane & Menzies, 2003; Stahr, Cushing, Lane, & Fox, in press). In general, you want to have treatment integrity ratings of 85% to 100%. If your percentage is not this strong, then it is time to retrain those involved with implementing the intervention and use the information from your social validity ratings to determine why implementation is low. It may be that there was simply a misunderstanding as to what needed to be done. In some cases, the social validity rating scale may indicate that one or more persons are not comfortable with some aspect of the intervention procedures.

MONITORING OTHER FACTORS THAT ENHANCE AN INTERVENTION'S SUCCESS

You talked about social validity (in Chapter 12). How do I test that? How often? When? What do I do if the social validity is low?

As discussed in Chapter 12, social validity can be assessed in numerous ways, such as interviews and rating scales. Social validity data should be collected at two points: before beginning the intervention, and again at the end.

Social validity data collected at the beginning will give you information about what the parties (e.g., teachers, staff, parents, students) think about the goals, the procedures, and the likelihood of achieving the desired outcomes. If social validity is low, the intervention should be revised further. Staff may think that some of the intervention procedures are too time consuming. If so, then they might not implement the intervention as planned. If the intervention is not implemented with a high degree of fidelity, then the intervention will most likely not produce the desired outcomes. Social validity should also be assessed at the end to help interpret outcomes and to help inform future intervention efforts.

You also talked about generalization. How do I check that? What measurement system should I use? The same measurement system I used to test and monitor the intervention?

Generalization can be checked in a variety of different ways. For example, you could collect additional data using the same measurement system that was used to test and monitor the intervention to see if the same behavior is occurring in different settings or in the presence of different people. This is called **stimulus generalization.** You might also see if different variations of the behavior are occurring in the same settings or with the same people. This is called **response generalization.**

What about fading the intervention? When can I do that? How will I know when I can do it? Is there something in particular I am supposed to be measuring so this part will go correctly?

Once the behavior has been changed, as evidenced by reaching the desired level (e.g., very low levels of disruption or a total absence of disruption, high levels of academic engagement), then it is time to begin fading the intervention. This should be done carefully to avoid causing the undesirable behaviors to rebound.

In brief, you should continue to measure the target and replacement behaviors while you begin to fade. This way, you can make sure the intervention is being faded slowly enough. For example, you might decrease rates of reinforcement by moving from continuous reinforcement to intermittent reinforcement (i.e., reinforcing every second or third occurrence, or an average of every third or fourth occurrence, rather than every occurrence of the behavior). While making these changes, you should continue to collect and chart your data to monitor progress and see how students are responding to this change. You will notice in Figure 13.1 that a vertical line has been added after the second phase (the intervention phase). This is called a **phase**

change line, and it is used, in this case, to show that the intervention is being faded. Data are still being collected and plotted, but the data points are not connected to show that these data are maintenance probes.

Steps and Activities Required in Monitoring Interventions and Outcomes

The following list summarizes the steps and activities involved in monitoring intervention outcomes, monitoring implementation, and making decisions about social validity, generalization, and fading.

Monitoring Intervention Outcomes

1. Identify an appropriate measurement system.
2. Identify an appropriate time to collect data.
3. Collect data on both the target behavior and the replacement behavior, unless you are measuring a dichotomous behavior.
4. When measuring behaviors that are dichotomous, focus on measuring the replacement behavior.
5. Continue with the same measurement system throughout intervention.
6. Collect data frequently when initially implementing the intervention.
7. Reduce the frequency of data collection after the desired changes in behavior have occurred consistently (i.e., for at least three sessions).
8. Collect IOA data at least once per week until the intervention's effects are established, and at least once every 2 weeks after that.
9. Use Excel to organize your data and generate graphs for easy review and analysis of your data.

Monitoring Implementation of the Intervention

1. Identify an appropriate method to collect data on implementation.
2. Collect implementation data frequently until the intervention's effectiveness has been established, and periodically (about once every 2 weeks) after that.
3. If the implementation percentage (treatment integrity) is low, use social validity data to identify the problem(s) and modify the intervention or retrain staff, as needed.

Monitoring Other Factors Related to Intervention Success

1. Assess the intervention's social validity before implementing the intervention and at the end of the intervention.
2. Assess the intervention's generalization across settings and people or through the occurrence of new appropriate behaviors that emerge as the student's behavior improves.

---

3. Begin fading the intervention when your data show that the improvements in the student's behavior are stable.

4. Fade the intervention slowly enough so the intervention's positive effects will continue.

EXERCISES

1. Read the following scenario. Then, follow the instructions in Exercise 2 to create a graph of the data included in the scenario.

   a. Sam, age 7, is physically aggressive with peers, especially during language arts, which lasts for 20 minutes each day. Specifically, he hits, grabs, punches, and/or pinches other children. During baseline sessions, the frequencies of Sam's aggressions were 4, 3, 5, 3, and 4. An FBA was conducted and a function-based intervention was developed and implemented starting on day 6. During intervention, the frequencies of Sam's aggressive behaviors were 2, 1, 2, 0, 0, 1, 0, 1, 0, 0, and 0.

   b. The replacement behavior for Sam was "on-task" behavior (i.e., Sam [a] is seated and engaged in the assigned activity, with his eyes on the teacher or materials, as appropriate, [b] raises his hand when he needs help, and [c] waits quietly for the teacher's assistance). Sam's on-task behavior was measured by using time sampling with a 1-min interval. During baseline, Sam's on-task percentages were 30, 25, 40, 20, and 25. During intervention, Sam's on-task percentages were 70, 90, 90, 85, 100, 95, 90, 100, 95, 100, and 95. Plot these data on the same graph you constructed for exercise 1. Be certain that you correctly label and scale the right-hand y-axis.

2. Following are instructions for creating a graph of Sam's intervention data. You can refer to Figure 13.7 to see the completed graph as you work:

   a. Open Microsoft Excel on your computer. Name and save your file now so you will not lose your work.

   b. On your worksheet, enter the data as shown in Figure 13.8.

   c. Highlight the data that you will graph as shown in Figure 13.9.

   d. In the Standard toolbar, click on the Chart Wizard. If the Standard toolbar is not open, you can select it in the View menu.

   e. A Chart Wizard window labeled, "Step 1 of 4—Chart Type" will open and allow you to pick the type of graph you want to use from a set of thumbnail images of graph types. If you were graphing only one set of data or two sets of data that use the same measurement scale, you would select the Line chart type. However, our target and replacement behavior data use different scales. Click the Custom tab in the Chart Wizard, select the Lines on 2 Axes chart type, and click the Next button.

   f. To ensure that the graph legend will later be properly labeled, we should now name the target and replacement behavior data series. You should now be in the Chart Wizard window labeled "Step 2 of

FIGURE 13.7
Sample graph.

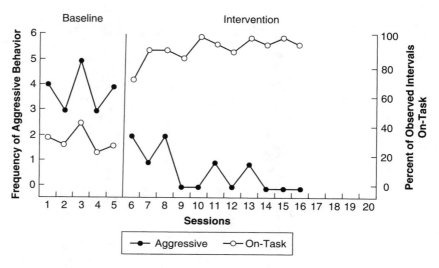

Sam's Intervention Data

FIGURE 13.8
Entering the data.

	A	B	C
1	4	30	
2	3	25	
3	5	40	
4	3	20	
5	4	25	
6	2	70	
7	1	90	
8	2	90	
9	0	85	
10	0	100	
11	1	95	
12	0	90	
13	1	100	
14	0	95	
15	0	100	
16	0	95	
17			
18			
19			
20			
21			
22			

SamData.xls

Sheet1 She

Ready

Sum=0

FIGURE 13.9
Highlighting the data.

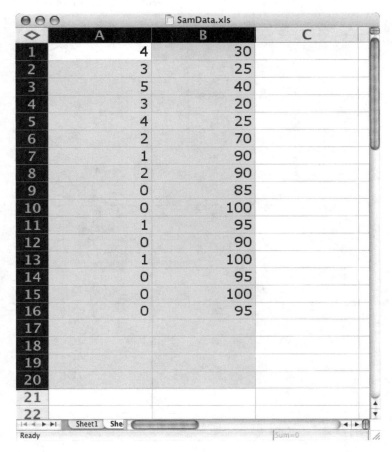

4—Chart Source Data". Click the Series tab. To label your replacement behavior data, click on Series1, and in the Name window, type "On-task". To label your target behavior data, click on Series2 and in the Name window, type "Aggressive". Click the Next button when you are ready to proceed.

g. "Step 3 of 4" in the Chart Wizard presents the Chart Options. The tabs across the top of this window present access to various features.

h. Your window should show options available in the Titles tab. Enter the Title for your chart (Sam's Intervention Data) and label the *x*-axis (Sessions). Then, label the first *y*-axis (Frequency of Aggressive Behavior) and the second *y*-axis (Percent of Observed Intervals On-task).

i. Click the next tab at the top of the Chart Wizard window labeled "Axes." The Category (X) and Value (Y) checkboxes control whether numbers are shown next to each of the axes. You should leave them checked.

j. Click the Gridlines tab. These checkboxes control whether horizontal or vertical lines are included across the graph. Make sure these boxes are unchecked.

k. Click the Legend tab at the top of the Chart Wizard window. This tab allows you to control the presence and location of the legend box. Make sure that the Show Legend checkbox is checked and, for the purposes of this exercise, choose the option that places the legend box at the bottom of the graph. Later, you can change the placement of the legend box by clicking on it and dragging it to a new location.

l. Click the Next button at the bottom of the Chart Wizard. A window appears asking you to choose the location for display of your graph. You can choose to display the graph as a new worksheet or include it on the same worksheet page with your data. Either option will work for the purposes of managing function-based intervention data, but for the purposes of this example, select the As Object In . . . option.

m. You should now be out of the Chart Wizard, and your graph should be on the same page with your intervention data. However, additional features of the graph should be altered to improve the clarity with which it presents your data.

n. Move your graph so it is not positioned over the intervention data. Then, resize the graph so it is approximately twice as long as it is tall. Do this by clicking on the edge of the graph and then clicking and dragging to the right on one of the black squares that appear on the right edge of your graph.

o. Delete the gray background of the graph; your data will show up better on a white background. Right-click on the gray background of the graph to open the Format Plot Area option box. Select None in the Border category and None in the Area category, and then click OK to close this option box.

p. We need to make all data points and lines representing the target behavior the same color and shape. Click once on one of the lines representing the target behavior data to highlight the data series. Then, right-click on the line to open the Format Data Series option window. Select black for the Line color. Select a circle as the Style of data point marker. Then, select black as the Foreground color and black as the Background color. Then, click OK.

q. Repeat the previous steps for the replacement behavior data, but select black as the Foreground color and white as the Background color.

r. The next several steps will adjust the scale of your *y* axes and move your "0" data points above the *x*-axis so "0" frequencies or percentages can be seen clearly. Right-click on the *y*-axis line that represents Frequency of Aggressive Behavior. This will open the Format Axis option window; choose the Scale tab at the top of the window. Set the Minimum value to -1, the Maximum value to 6, the Major unit value to 1, and set the Category (x) axis Crosses at: to $-.5$. Then, click OK.

s. Right-click on the *y*-axis line that represents Percentage of Observed Intervals On-task. Choose the Scale tab in the Format Axis option window. Set the Minimum value to −20, the Maximum value to 100, the Major Unit value to 20, and set the Category (x) axis Crosses at: to −.5. Then, click OK.

t. You now have to remove the −1 and −20 from the bottom of the *y*-axes. We do this by hiding them with a borderless white rectangle. From the View menu, open the Drawing toolbar. Select the Rectangle drawing icon. Draw a small rectangle over the −1 on the bottom of the left-hand *y*-axis. Then, right-click on your rectangle to open the Format AutoShape option window. For the Line color, select No Line from the drop-down menu. Repeat this process to hide the −20 at the bottom of the right-hand *y*-axis.

u. Now, place a phase line on your graph. From the Drawing toolbar, select the Line drawing icon. Draw a line to separate the baseline and intervention data. Holding down the Shift key as you draw and starting the line at the *x*-axis will ensure your line is straight and properly placed.

v. Now label your phases. From the Drawing Toolbar, select the Text Box icon. Click in the area above the baseline data and type "Baseline." Use the same process to label the intervention phase.

w. Data points should not cross phase lines, so next we will remove the lines that connect the data points across sessions 5 and 6 for both the target and replacement behavior data. To remove a line between two data points, click once on the line to highlight all data points. Wait a moment, then click a second time on the exact segment of the line you want to remove; you will notice that now only two data points are highlighted. Finally, right-click on the line segment to open the Format Data Point window. Choose the Patterns tab and select None as the Line option.

3. Review your graph to make sure it looks like Figure 13.7. Then, review the data in your graph and identify the point at which you could begin to fade the intervention.

REFERENCES

Carr, J. E., & Burkholder, E. O. (1998). Creating single-subject design graphs with Microsoft Excel. *Journal of Applied Behavior Analysis, 31,* 245–251.

Horner, R. H., Carr, E. G., Halle, J., McGee, G., Odom, S., & Wolery, M. (2005). The use of single-subject research to identify evidence-based practice in special education. *Exceptional Children, 71,* 165–179.

Lane, K. L., & Menzies, H. M. (2003). A school-wide intervention with primary and secondary levels of support for elementary students: Outcomes and considerations. *Education and Treatment of Children, 26,* 431–451.

Stahr, B., Cushing, D., Lane, K. L., & Fox, J. (in press). Efficacy of a function-based intervention to decrease off-task behavior exhibited by a student with attention deficit hyperactivity disorder. *Journal of Positive Behavior Interventions.*

Part Four

Putting it All Together
From Problem Identification to Effective Intervention

The development and implementation of an effective function-based intervention is a process. This book has presented each step in that process. Development includes defining a target and replacement behavior, collecting interview and observational data, determining the function of the behavior, selecting an appropriate intervention method, selecting a measurement system, testing the intervention, and constructing the BIP. The implementation strategies incorporate methods for effective monitoring, knowledge of the factors that affect the success of an intervention, and the use of effective practices when monitoring the intervention's outcomes and implementation. Your task as an interventionist will be to apply these elements of the function-based intervention process to improve the lives of students who exhibit a wide range of challenging behaviors.

Throughout this book, we have provided examples that illustrate each step in the process. This section provides you with the opportunity to review three new examples that present the entire process. Information is presented in the same order in which you would undertake the tasks that are required to complete the development and implementation of an intervention, beginning with conducting the FBA, then constructing and testing the intervention, then formulating the BIP, and finally implementing and monitoring the function-based intervention. Although these examples present successful interventions, each case will also include a discussion of predictable and preventable errors that would have led to inappropriate or unsuccessful intervention decisions and outcomes.

Each example presents a case study that demonstrates the development and implementation of one of the three function-based intervention methods. Chapter 14 uses the case of a 7-year-old boy who exhibits off-task behavior to describe the implementation of Method 1: Teach the replacement behavior. Chapter 15 follows the case of a 15-year-old girl who exhibits disruptive classroom behavior to show the development of an intervention based on Method 2: Improve the environment. Finally, in Chapter 16, we outline the case of a 13-year-old boy with cerebral palsy who engages in tantruming and benefits from the implementation of Method 3: Adjust the contingencies.

At the end of the book, you will also find a short summary of the text and some suggestions that will help you prepare to practice your newly acquired function-based intervention skills.

CHAPTER 14

The Entire Process When Using Method 1
Teach the Replacement Behavior

OUTCOMES

After reading this chapter, you will be able to

- Explain how the assessment information leads to the selection of the intervention method.
- Summarize the process of implementing the selected intervention method.
- Describe how the intervention is translated into a BIP.
- Identify and prevent common errors in developing and implementing function-based interventions.

This chapter presents a complete example of the function-based intervention process when the student cannot perform the Replacement behavior. This situation calls for the use of Method 1: Teach the replacement behavior, which was presented in Chapter 6. You may want to refer to Chapter 6 for additional information if any part of the process described here is unclear or confusing. This chapter follows the development and implementation of the intervention, step by step, through the use of a case study. Comments that highlight important aspects of the function-based intervention process, as well as common errors, are included throughout the chapter.

CONDUCTING THE FBA
Student and Background

Jamar is a 7-year-old boy in the first grade. The students in Jamar's class are together as a group throughout the entire day. The class, as a whole, changes rooms for art class, music class, and library time. The classroom includes 23 students, with a relatively equal distribution of girls and boys. Jamar has no history of previous problem behavior.

Teacher Interview

Jamar's teacher, Mrs. Lopez, states that Jamar engages in off-task behavior throughout the school day. When asked to give some examples of what he is doing when he is off-task, she states that Jamar is not able to complete his assignments because he is not paying attention when the directions are given. He also frequently draws and colors during class when other students are engaged in the assigned instructional tasks. To deal with these behaviors, Mrs. Lopez has spoken with Jamar individually at breaks, kept Jamar in during recess to do work he has missed, and taken away other materials with which he is playing. She even presents a notebook that was recently confiscated from Jamar. Mrs. Lopez states that she has become so frustrated with Jamar's drawing that she removed the notebook in an attempt to stop him from coloring.

Although Mrs. Lopez initially states that there is no time throughout the day when Jamar is on-task, she does mention that he enjoys when the class reads stories out loud. She notes that Jamar pays attention to the stories and offers frequent comments during story time. When asked if the problem behavior occurs during story time, Mrs. Lopez says that it does not. Mrs. Lopez suggests that the behavior almost always occurs when she is explaining independent work or when others are engaged in independent work.

Mrs. Lopez does not know why these behaviors occur. She has not noticed that Jamar's behavior occurs more frequently in the presence of certain peers and adults or during specific types of instructional tasks. She does wonder whether Jamar simply likes drawing more than schoolwork. Mrs. Lopez identifies other preferred activities for Jamar that include coloring, drawing, computer time, and story time.

Mrs. Lopez suspects Jamar may suffer from an attention deficit disorder, but neither school personnel nor Jamar's parents have explored this possibility. After consulting Jamar's school records and making a quick call to his mother, Mrs. Lopez confirms that Jamar is not on any regular medication, has no known allergies, and does not appear to suffer from any long-term medical condition that might result in his off-task behavior.

Student Interview

When asked how he feels about his class, Jamar states that he does not like school. Although he does like listening to stories and coloring, Jamar reports that he does not like to do the other activities. Jamar mentions that he thinks the other kids do not like him, so he does not want to engage in activities with them. When asked why he sometimes does not do his work, Jamar says it is because the assignments are too hard, so he does not even try to complete them. Jamar does not appear to be able to name any benefits or rewards for doing schoolwork. He also does not think there is a problem with his coloring because it is "more fun" than the other activities that the teacher wants him to do. When asked how he feels when he gets a bad grade, Jamar just shrugs his shoulders and says that he guesses he just does not know that stuff.

Behavioral Definitions

Information collected during interviews with the teacher began with construction of the following behavioral definitions. The target behavior is off-task behavior, which includes engaging in activities such as drawing or playing with materials while the teacher is giving directions and during instructional activities. The replacement behavior is on-task behavior, or more specifically, maintaining eye contact when the teacher is giving instructions and engaging in the assigned instructional task.

> **Comments:** Thus far in the process, the teacher and student interviews have been conducted. The teacher interview began with the identification of the target and replacement behaviors. Note that the target behavior and replacement behavior definitions describe observable behaviors. The target behavior does not describe an outcome of a behavior (e.g., "Jamar will get an 'A' in class") and the replacement behavior does not describe the absence of behavior (e.g., "Jamar will not color or draw during instructional activities"). In addition, the replacement behavior appears to satisfy at least two of the three suggested criteria for an appropriate replacement behavior: (a) It is stated in terms that describe what we want the student to do, and (b) it is something that the student can do or can learn to do. It is unclear at this point whether the replacement behavior fits the third criterion: Reinforcement for the behavior should be available in the natural environment.
>
> The interviews with the teacher and student help prepare the interventionist to collect direct observational data by focusing the observation on a target behavior and suggesting the time of day when the observer is most likely to witness the behavior. In this case, the interventionist will observe during independent classroom activities for the antecedents and consequences of Jamar's off-task behavior, and during reading when the teacher reported that Jamar is on-task.

Observational Data

The A-B-C data collection method is used during two observations in Jamar's classroom. The data are collected during a 40-min period of classroom reading time and a 16-min period of classroom testing time. The focus of the observations is to identify the antecedents and consequences of Jamar's off-task behaviors.

A total of seven instances of off-task behavior occur across the observations. The incidents are of various durations (i.e., some instances are brief and some are lengthy). Although there are brief instances of off-task behavior during story time, longer durations of off-task behavior occur during the observation of independent testing. Jamar's off-task behavior occurs immediately following two different types of antecedents: (a) when the teacher gives oral instructions to the entire class, and (b) when Jamar is supposed to be working independently on a task at his desk. In most instances, the consequence of Jamar's off-task behavior is that he does not participate in the assigned activity for long periods of time. In one situation, the consequence of Jamar's off-task behavior is that Mrs. Lopez comes to his desk and individually repeats a set of instructions.

> **Comments:** Although there were only two observations conducted in this case, in other situations you may need to continue to collect A-B-C data to identify a clear pattern of behavior. There is no magic number of target behavior occurrences that is required during an observation or that will guarantee you will find a clear pattern. Avoid starting with a preset number of occurrences that you will observe; you may fail to identify a clear pattern of A-B-Cs, which is the point of collecting these data in the first place. The data you collect determine when you have enough information.

Determining the Function

The interview and observational data that have been collected are now considered across the six questions posed by the Function Matrix. Do the interview and observational data suggest that the behavior is maintained by

1. Access to attention? No. Jamar's off-task behavior does not often result in peer or adult social interaction. It occurred only once and does not suggest a broader pattern of behavior.

2. Escape from attention? No. The data collected do not show antecedents in which social attention is present.

3. Access to tangibles or activities? Yes. Interviews and observations confirm that Jamar's off-task behavior allows him to engage in preferred activities (e.g., drawing, coloring).

4. Escape from items or activities? Yes. The interviews and observations confirm that Jamar's off-task behavior most often occurs after task demands,

	Positive Reinforcement (Access Something)	Negative Reinforcement (Avoid Something)
Attention		
Tangibles/Activities	X	X
Sensory		

and his engagement in off-task behavior enables him to avoid participating in the assigned activity.

5. Access to sensory stimulation? No. There are no data to suggest Jamar's off-task behavior allows him to access sensory stimulation.

6. Escape from sensory stimulation? No. Jamar does not appear to be engaging in off-task behavior to escape environmental stimulation, and there is no evidence of medical problems that might prompt behavior that would allow escape from pain or discomfort.

Consideration of the data results in a Function Matrix that reveals two functions of Jamar's off-task behavior: positive reinforcement—activity and negative reinforcement—activity (Figure 14.1). The statement of function is developed as follows: When presented with an instructional task or activity, Jamar engages in off-task behavior (e.g., coloring, drawing, playing with materials) to access preferred activities and escape the assigned tasks.

> **Comments:** Note that in this case the interventionist identified two functions of the target behavior. Identifying both functions will be helpful in developing the function-based intervention. If only negative reinforcement had been identified, the interventionist would have missed an important positive reinforcer and used a less effective one. Without the additional information, the interventionist might have used praise to reinforce on-task behavior for lack of a better alternative. Instead, the Function Matrix suggests that access to preferred activities is likely to be the most effective positive reinforcer for on-task behavior.

DEVELOPING AND TESTING THE FUNCTION-BASED INTERVENTION
Selecting an Intervention Method

Following determination of the target and replacement behaviors, collection of interview and observational data, and determination of the function of the behavior, the interventionist asks two questions to select an appropriate intervention method. First, can Jamar perform the replacement behavior? Second, does Jamar's classroom environment reflect effective practice? The interventionist deals with these questions one at a time. In answering Question 1, there are actually two replacement behaviors, which necessitates asking two separate questions: (a) Can Jamar maintain eye contact with the teacher when she gives directions?, and (b) Can he complete the assigned tasks? The teacher interview suggests that Jamar has shown the ability to maintain eye contact during instruction in contexts that he finds reinforcing, such as directions given to facilitate story time.

The question of whether Jamar can complete the assigned tasks has not been adequately answered by the data collected thus far, although the teacher has suggested that Jamar is functioning below grade level. To fully answer this question, Jamar is given a series of curriculum-based measurement tasks. These assessments determine that Jamar is indeed functioning below grade level and is not likely to complete the tasks regularly assigned to the rest of the class. It appears that Jamar can perform the replacement behavior of maintaining eye contact but cannot perform the replacement behavior of completing the assignment.

Now let us consider Question 2: Does Jamar's classroom environment represent effective practice? The interviews and observational data indicate that, in general, the classroom setting does include routines, physical arrangements, rules, and instructional strategies that will support the replacement behavior selected for Jamar. The answer to Question 2 is "Yes."

After asking the two key questions, the interventionist determines that the answer to Question 1 is "No," and the answer to Question 2 is "Yes." Therefore, the interventionist selects Method 1: Teach the replacement behavior as the appropriate model for intervention. Using this method, (a) the antecedent conditions for the task will be adjusted so Jamar can perform the assigned tasks, (b) positive reinforcement will be made available when on-task behavior occurs, and (c) reinforcement will be withheld when Jamar is off-task. In other words, Jamar will be more likely to be on-task if he is given assignments at a lower, more appropriate level of instruction, and if he is reminded that attention to directions and engagement in the task will result in access to preferred activities such as drawing.

Component 1: Adjust Antecedent Conditions. Adjusting the antecedent conditions so Jamar can perform both replacement behaviors is accomplished through three modifications. First, Mrs. Lopez agrees to repeat task directions for Jamar and to ask questions to determine whether he understands the directions. Second, a special education teacher is approached to provide Mrs. Lopez with assistance in adjusting or modifying Jamar's academic work. Third, Mrs. Lopez also agrees to provide Jamar with additional instruction on new material, as necessary, and to monitor his work completion approximately every 3 to 5 min to determine whether he needs additional assistance.

Component 2: Provide Positive Reinforcement for Replacement Behavior. The second element of the selected intervention method requires that consequences be modified to ensure the replacement behavior will be positively reinforced. This element also takes multiple forms. Mrs. Lopez will reinforce Jamar verbally when he correctly restates the directions for the assignment and remind him of the reinforcer for completing the assignment. Mrs. Lopez will also develop a **contingency contract** with Jamar that incorporates an interval schedule of reinforcement. This agreement will state that if Mrs. Lopez sees that Jamar is on-task at the end of any 1-minute interval, he will receive one plastic chip in a clear container that will be located on Mrs. Lopez's desk. These tokens can later be redeemed for time that Jamar can spend on a preferred activity, such as drawing or coloring. Mrs. Lopez will also provide Jamar with verbal praise for on-task behavior as she places a poker chip in the container.

Component 3: Place Target Behavior on Extinction. The third component of the intervention requires the implementation of an extinction procedure to deal with occurrences of the target behavior. This means that Jamar must not be allowed to avoid the class assignment and engage in his preferred activities. Mrs. Lopez should neither reprimand Jamar if he is engaged in off-task behavior nor engage him in conversation or activities that will allow him to avoid completing his assignment. Instead, Mrs. Lopez will remind Jamar of the contingency for on-task behavior and ask him what help he needs to continue the assignment.

> **Comments:** The interventionist used a practice called contingency contracting to organize the elements of the intervention and clarify the elements for both the teacher and the student. For more information on contingency contracting, see the useful descriptions of the practice provided by Kerr and Nelson (2001) and Rhode, Jensen, and Reavis (1993). Also, note that the intervention changes the activities in which Jamar is asked to participate. This allows Jamar to avoid conditions that he finds aversive and addresses the negative reinforcement function of the behavior. Another element of the intervention is the use of an exchangeable reinforcer—poker chips. See Chapter 1 for a review of how reinforcers are categorized.

Identifying a Measurement System

Occurrences of on-task behavior can vary in length, one lasting 5 s, and the next lasting 5 or 10 min. Therefore, on-task behavior is a nonuniform behavior, and its measurement requires the use of a time-based measurement system (Chapter 9). Among the time-based measurement methods, the easiest to implement is time sampling. For these reasons, the interventionist determines that time sampling data will be collected to evaluate the effects of the function-based intervention developed for Jamar.

The intervals will be 30 s in length during all observations. At the end of every 30-s interval, Jamar will be observed to determine whether he is on- or off-task.

If he is on-task, a "+" will be placed in the box that corresponds to that interval. However, if Jamar is off-task, a "−" will be entered. Because on- and off-task behaviors are dichotomous, the interventionist will focus on measuring on-task behavior (i.e., the replacement behavior). The data will be summarized as a percentage of the intervals containing "+" markings. The data collection sheet is depicted in Figure 14.2. The data will also be entered into a computer spreadsheet, and a graph will be developed to allow visual inspection of the results.

To ensure reliability of the data, a second observer will collect data during both baseline sessions and both intervention sessions. Each interval scored the same way by both observers will be considered an agreement. IOA will be calculated by dividing the number of agreements between observers by the number of agreements plus disagreements and expressed as a percentage (multiplied by 100%). The first observer will also monitor whether Mrs. Lopez accurately implements the intervention during the intervention sessions. The whole interval method described in Chapter 13 will be used. At the end of each interval, the observer will record (+ or −) whether Mrs. Lopez correctly implemented all required elements of the intervention.

> **Comments:** A few issues related to selection of a data collection system are brought forth in this example. First, dichotomous behaviors are those that cannot occur at the same time (i.e., off- and on-task). Second, note that the collection of data for each replacement behavior (i.e., eye contact during instruction and engaging in the assigned task) is not necessary if data collection starts when the instructions are being given. In other cases, this might not be true. Third, the interventionist specifically arranges to collect IOA data during both baseline sessions and both intervention sessions to catch any data collection problems prior to going forward with the second round of baseline and intervention sessions. Finally, recall from Chapter 9 that the correct method for calculating IOA of interval data differs from that for calculating IOA for frequency data. Confusing these methods would lead to erroneous conclusions about the accuracy of the data collection across observers.

Testing the Intervention

The intervention is tested by comparing data collected during a baseline session to data collected during an intervention session, followed by a return to baseline, and then reintroduction of the intervention (the A-B-A-B design described in Chapter 10). During baseline sessions, none of the elements of the new intervention were in place. During each intervention session, all elements of the new intervention were in place. The results of the intervention are depicted in Figure 14.3.

Interval Data Recording Form

Observer: _____   Student: _____

Context (Time/Activity/Location): _____

Behavior: _____

Whole/Partial/Momentary Interval Length: _____

Date: _____

Intervals	1	2	3	4	5	6	7	8	9	10	11	12	13	14	15	16	17	18	19	20
On-Task																				
Intervention																				

Summary:

    % of intervals on-task: _____   IOA: _____

    % of intervals with accurate intervention practices: _____

Date: _____

Intervals	1	2	3	4	5	6	7	8	9	10	11	12	13	14	15	16	17	18	19	20
On-Task																				
Intervention																				

Summary:

    % of intervals on-task: _____   IOA: _____

    % of intervals with accurate intervention practices: _____

Date: _____

Intervals	1	2	3	4	5	6	7	8	9	10	11	12	13	14	15	16	17	18	19	20
On-Task																				
Intervention																				

Summary:

    % of intervals on-task: _____   IOA: _____

    % of intervals with accurate intervention practices: _____

Date: _____

Intervals	1	2	3	4	5	6	7	8	9	10	11	12	13	14	15	16	17	18	19	20
On-Task																				
Intervention																				

Summary:

    % of intervals on-task: _____   IOA: _____

    % of intervals with accurate intervention practices: _____

Date: _____

Intervals	1	2	3	4	5	6	7	8	9	10	11	12	13	14	15	16	17	18	19	20
On-Task																				
Intervention																				

Summary:

    % of intervals on-task: _____   IOA: _____

    % of intervals with accurate intervention practices: _____

FIGURE 14.2
Data sheet for Jamar.

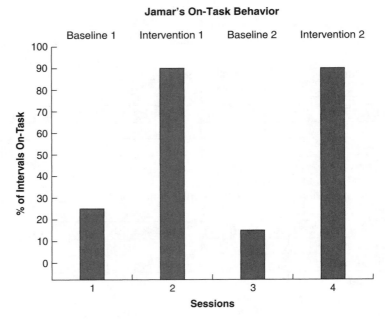

FIGURE 14.3
Example 1: intervention testing graph.

Jamar was observed to be on-task at the end of 27% of the intervals during the first baseline session. IOA for this session was calculated to be 95%. Jamar's on-task behavior rose to 88% of observed intervals during the first intervention session. IOA for the first intervention session was calculated to be 95%. Upon returning to baseline conditions, Jamar's percentage of on-task behavior declined to 16%. During the second intervention session, his on-task behavior rose to a level of 90%. These results demonstrate that the intervention was successful in increasing Jamar's use of the replacement behaviors. The treatment integrity data (100% implementation) also demonstrate that Mrs. Lopez is capable of implementing the intervention.

Comments: The method of testing the intervention that can be used in many situations, as it is used in this one, is called an **A-B-A-B withdrawal design.** That means we present a nonintervention session (A), followed by an intervention session (B), a return to the nonintervention conditions (A), and end with an intervention session (B). If we note a decrease in the frequency of the target behavior and an increase in the replacement behavior only during each intervention session, then we have strong evidence that our intervention is responsible for the changes in behavior.

You should keep in mind that there are situations when a withdrawal design is not appropriate for testing an intervention. The first situation is when we teach a behavior that is not likely to disappear when we return to baseline conditions (e.g., the answers to a set of math facts). The second situation is when it would be unethical to withdraw the intervention, such as when the target behavior is physically harmful to the student or others. In such situations, a simple A-B design is sufficient.

FORMULATING THE BEHAVIOR INTERVENTION PLAN

Based on the data gathered previously, the following BIP was developed for Jamar.

Behavioral Definitions

The target behavior is off-task behavior, which includes engaging in activities such as drawing or playing with materials while the teacher is giving directions and during instructional activities.

The replacement behavior is on-task behavior, or more specifically, maintaining eye contact when the teacher is giving instructions and engaging in the assigned instructional task.

Rationale

Jamar's off-task behavior is causing him to fall further behind his peers in academics.

Baseline Data

Across two observation periods, using a 30-s time sample system, Jamar was on-task at the end of 21% of the intervals.

Function of the Behavior

When presented with an instructional task or activity, Jamar engages in off-task behavior (e.g., coloring, drawing, playing with materials) to access preferred activities (positive reinforcement—activity) and escape the assigned tasks (negative reinforcement—activity).

Behavioral Objective

During individual instructional activities, Jamar will maintain eye contact when the teacher is giving instructions or will be engaged in the assigned instructional task during 75% of observed intervals for 9 of 10 consecutive days.

Intervention Procedures

The intervention will consist of adjusting the task demands, providing Jamar with positive reinforcement for on-task behavior, and ensuring off-task behavior is not reinforced.

The task demands will be modified through the following procedures:

1. Jamar's teacher will repeat task directions for Jamar and ask questions to determine whether he understands the directions.
2. Instructional tasks will be modified to meet Jamar's ability level.
3. Jamar's teacher will provide additional instruction to Jamar on new material.
4. Jamar's teacher will monitor his work completion every 3 to 5 minutes.

Positive reinforcement for on-task behavior will be provided in the following ways:

1. Jamar's teacher will reinforce him verbally when he correctly restates directions and remind him of the reinforcer for completing the assignment.
2. Jamar's teacher will monitor his on-task behavior during individual instructional activities. If Jamar's teacher sees he is on-task at the end of any 1-min interval, he will receive verbal reinforcement and a plastic poker chip in a container that will be located on the teacher's desk. The teacher will provide time each day when the tokens can be redeemed for an activity selected by Jamar from a list of alternatives.
3. Jamar's teacher will develop a simple written agreement with Jamar that describes the goal of the intervention, the method for receiving reinforcement, and the range of possible reinforcers.

Instances of the problem behavior will be handled in the following way: If Jamar does engage in off-task behavior, Mrs. Lopez will remind Jamar of the contingency for on-task behavior and ask him what help he needs to continue the assignment.

A brief test of the function-based intervention revealed that when no intervention was in place, Jamar was on-task only 21% of the time at the end of observed intervals. When the intervention was put into place, Jamar was on-task at the end of 89% of observed intervals. This demonstrates that the function-based intervention was responsible for Jamar's dramatically improved on-task behavior.

Fading and Generalization

A plan to reduce the amount and types of positive reinforcement to levels more natural for the classroom will be developed once Jamar meets the behavioral objective under the initial function-based intervention plan. The district behavior consultant will also collect data weekly to measure the degree to which Jamar engages in on-task behavior during instruction in subject areas other than reading.

Data to Be Collected

Additional data on Jamar's on-/off-task behavior will be collected using the time sampling method with 30-s intervals for at least 20 min during one instructional period every day. In other words, at the end of each interval, the observer will note whether Jamar is on-task and mark a data recording sheet. Data will also be collected to assess IOA (weekly), implementation (weekly), generalization (weekly), and social validity (prior to beginning the intervention, at the end of intervention, and as needed).

Program Review Date

The BIP will be reviewed on 11/15/07.

Personnel and Roles

1. Jamar's teacher will be responsible for discussing the function-based intervention with Jamar, implementing the function-based intervention, and collecting data.
2. The special education teacher will consult twice a week with the teacher to assist with modifications to Jamar's academic work.
3. The district behavior consultant will meet at least once per week with Jamar's teacher. The behavior consultant will assist in developing the simple written reinforcement agreement, preparing a data collection sheet, securing the poker chips and container, collecting IOA and implementation (treatment integrity) data, collecting generalization data, and making summary graphs of progress.

Emergency Procedures

If Jamar becomes disruptive or refuses to do his work, he will be sent to the resource room or to the office to complete his assignment away from his peers. He will not be allowed to earn poker chips and any chips he had earned that day, up to the point that he became disruptive, will be removed from the container. If disruptions or refusals become regular occurrences after the intervention begins, the BIP team will meet to review the intervention.

> **Comments:** As described in Chapter 11, the behavioral objective should include the conditions, the student, the behavior, and the criteria. Setting reasonable criteria can be confusing; how much on-task behavior is enough? Such questions can be answered by asking (a) at what level do other students perform the behavior? and (b) what level of the behavior is necessary for success (reinforcement) in the environment?

IMPLEMENTING AND MONITORING THE INTERVENTION

Mrs. Lopez implemented the intervention because the intervention testing data supported its effectiveness and because the intervention appeared to be manageable. Data for on-task behavior were collected daily, and IOA and implementation data were collected at least once per week (see Figure 14.4). During the intervention, Jamar's on-task behavior maintained at a high level (averaging 86% of intervals) compared with nonintervention sessions during the baseline (intervention testing) phase (21% of intervals). Assessments of IOA (95%) and implementation (90% to 100%) showed that the data on Jamar's on-task behavior were reliable, and the intervention was implemented as planned.

Given that Jamar had met the instructional objective (i.e., maintaining on-task behavior at a level of at least 75% of observed intervals daily for 9 of 10 consecutive days), the interventionist and Mrs. Lopez decided to continue the intervention, but collect data less frequently as a method of monitoring the intervention. They collected data once a week for 3 weeks. This follow-up data demonstrated that Jamar's on-task behavior remained at a

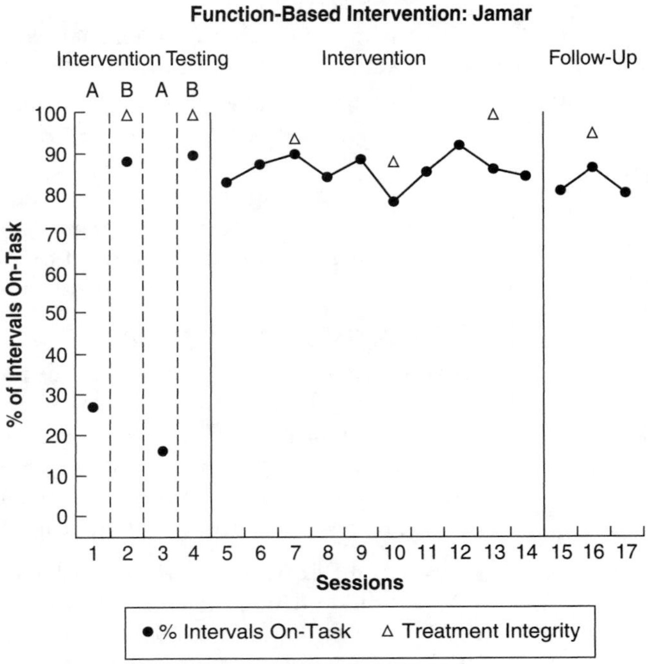

FIGURE 14.4
Example 1: intervention testing, intervention, follow-up graph.

high level and that Mrs. Lopez accurately delivered the components of the intervention when necessary. IOA data collected on these days revealed good reliability.

Understand that the eventual goal is for the reinforcers normally delivered in Mrs. Lopez's classroom to provide sufficient positive reinforcement for Jamar to engage in the replacement behavior. Once Jamar shows a consistent pattern of on-task behavior, the interventionist and teacher will implement a plan to fade the use of the poker chips completely and provide praise and exchangeable reinforcers at a level that is more natural for the classroom.

CHAPTER 15

The Entire Process When Using Method 2
Improve the Environment

OUTCOMES

After reading this chapter, you will be able to

- Explain how the assessment information leads to the selection of the intervention method.
- Summarize the process of implementing the selected intervention method.
- Describe how the intervention is translated into a BIP.
- Identify and prevent common errors in developing and implementing function-based interventions.

This chapter presents a complete example of the function-based intervention process when the environment needs to be improved. This situation calls for the use of Method 2: Improve the environment, which was presented in Chapter 7. You may want to refer to Chapter 7 for additional information if any part of the process described here is unclear or confusing. This chapter follows the development and implementation of the intervention, step by step, through the use of a case study. Comments that highlight important aspects of the function-based intervention process, as well as common errors, are included throughout the chapter.

CONDUCTING THE FBA
Student and Background

June is a 15-year-old female in tenth grade. She failed most of her courses during ninth grade, so she is repeating them this year. June is participating in the traditional curriculum, but attends smaller classes this school year that include team teachers and a learning specialist.

Teacher Interview

Interviews are conducted with two of June's teachers—Mr. Appleton, her math teacher, and Mrs. White, her social studies teacher. Their primary concerns are June's use of profanity and her tendency to leave the classroom without permission when upset. Mr. Appleton states that June is able to joke with other students in class, but that as soon as any comment is directed to her, June swears at the student who made the comment and leaves the room.

Both teachers report that the behaviors only occur at certain times, most often when students are transitioning between activities. They cite instances in which these behaviors occurred when students were asked to move from an independent seat activity into a group activity. June's teachers agree that, if given a choice, she appears to prefer to work alone and that peers seldom select June when activities call for choosing a work partner. Although this pattern is consistent in math and social studies, she has few problems interacting with peers during English and science, even though these classes contain most of the same students. The English and science teachers report that June interacts appropriately with her peers most of the time and asks for "space" when she is upset. Both have occasionally allowed her to leave the room to speak to Miss Brewster. They report that June is most often upset when asked to begin an assignment that she seems to dislike.

Mr. White and Mrs. Appleton concur that June's academic performance is very inconsistent. Some days she completes all assignments and activities with ease. Other days, she resists doing any work. When this happens, June has told Mr. Appleton that she "doesn't care" and would rather go to a private school.

June's teachers know that she failed most her classes during her freshman year of high school and is repeating those classes this year. According to both teachers, June is earning passing grades this time, although they make broad allowances for her behavior. They are concerned that June's behavior will prevent her from being successful in the general classroom environments she will encounter in the future.

Student Interview

June reports that the boys in her classes tend to bother her and that she often feels like hitting them. She also finds working with other students to be frustrating, and she would rather just work independently. She explains further that none of her classes is too difficult, she just does not like some subject areas, especially math and social studies. June indicates that when she feels "angry or frustrated" with the students in her class or with other students, she sometimes yells at them and then leaves the room. June also contends that no one seems to notice when she is doing what is expected and that the only person who says anything nice to her is her learning specialist, Miss Brewster.

Behavioral Definitions

Based on the teacher and student interviews, the interventionist defines the target behavior as **disruptive behavior,** which includes leaving the classroom without permission, punching or destroying objects, and using profanity toward students. The replacement behavior is defined as **cooperative behavior,** which includes asking the teacher permission to leave an assigned area when angry or upset, vocalizing discontent when upset, and ignoring negative comments made by other students.

> **Comments:** Note how the collected data are used to develop accurate behavioral definitions. Also note that "cooperative behavior" is used as a global term to describe the replacement behavior rather than describing the group of behaviors as "nondisruptive behavior." It is better to select a global term that describes what the person is to do, rather than a term that simply describes the absence of the target behavior.

Observational Data

Two formal observations are conducted to collect A-B-C data. The first observation takes place for 75 min during math class. Teacher instruction occurs for the first 10 min, followed by a 15-min independent activity. The remaining 50 min involves a cooperative learning activity in which students work in small groups to construct a tower using straws, marshmallows, and tape. June elects not to work in a small group but instead works with Miss Brewster.

During the 50-min cooperative activity, the interventionist observes June engaging in disruptive behavior three times. The behavior occurs once immediately after the teacher announces the cooperative work task, once while students are busy selecting peers for the task, and once when peers whisper comments and giggle about June's work. The end result of June's behavior is that she is allowed to leave the classroom to talk with Miss Brewster. Furthermore, she is not asked to complete the assignment, nor is she given a failing grade for not completing the activity.

The second observation is 30 min long and takes place in June's social studies class. A substitute teacher is in charge of the class during the observation. June's disruptive behavior occurs once during the observation. Immediately before the instance, the substitute asks June to put her cell phone in her backpack. June initially refuses, then becomes belligerent, curses at the teacher, and eventually walks out of the classroom. A number of consequences result from the behavior: (a) the substitute sends June to the office, (b) an assistant principal sends June to Miss Brewster to discuss the incident, (c) she is suspended for 1 day, and (d) June is not asked to make up the missed assignments.

> **Comments:** The collection of interview data directed the interventionist to observe during specific class periods. However, observation data further clarified particular times and situations in the class (antecedents) when the target behavior was likely to occur.

Determining the Function

The interventionist uses the Function Matrix to reflect on the interview and observational data. Does the interview and observational data suggest that the behavior is maintained by

1. Access to attention? Yes. In her interview, June states that Miss Brewster is her confidant, and June's disruptive behavior results in access to interaction with Miss Brewster during both observations.

2. Escape from attention? Yes. Both the teacher and the student interviews suggest that June seeks situations in which she can be apart from her peers. During the first observation, June succeeded in both working alone and escaping peer comments.

3. Access to tangibles or activities? No. There are no data to suggest that June is accessing an activity or tangible item.

4. Escape from items or activities? Yes. The interviews and observations confirm that June's disruptive behavior most often occurs after group-oriented task demands. In addition, June is not asked to make up missed work.

5. Access to sensory stimulation? No. There are no data to suggest June's target behavior allows her to access sensory stimulation.

6. Escape from sensory stimulation? No. June does not appear to be engaging in disruptive behavior to escape environmental stimulation, and there is no evidence of medical problems that might prompt behavior that would allow escape from pain or discomfort.

Thus, the information from the direct observations of the target behavior and the teacher and student interviews suggests that June was able to gain attention from Miss Brewster, escape the attention of peers, and avoid doing the assigned activities and assignments: positive reinforcement—attention, negative reinforcement—attention, and negative reinforcement—activity (see Figure 15.1). The resulting statement of function is as follows: When presented with a cooperative group task or activity, June engages in disruptive behavior (e.g., leaving the classroom without permission, punching

**FIGURE 15.1
Example 2: Function
Matrix for June.**

	Positive Reinforcement (Access Something)	Negative Reinforcement (Avoid Something)
Attention	X	X
Tangibles/Activities		X
Sensory		

or destroying objects, or using profanity) to access adult attention, escape peer attention, and avoid the task or activity. That is, June is able to interact with Miss Brewster, avoids contact with peers and escapes their comments, and does not have to complete the instructional task or activity.

DEVELOPING AND TESTING THE FUNCTION-BASED INTERVENTION

Selecting an Intervention Method

Two questions guide the interventionist's selection of an intervention method. First, can the student perform the replacement behavior? The answer to this question appears to be "Yes." June has demonstrated that she can perform the replacement behavior in other classes, as evidenced by ignoring negative comments from peers, using appropriate words when interacting with others, and asking for permission to leave when upset. We have also determined that June can complete the assignments. Although it is not part of the replacement behavior, one concern is that June does not like to work in groups because she does not know how to do the work. However, both June and her teachers indicated that she understands and can complete assignments. Second, do the antecedent conditions represent effective practice? The answer is "No." June's disruptive behavior often occur during lengthy, unstructured transitions in which the teacher is giving instructions and groups are forming, as well as during cooperative work activities that involve little supervision. Therefore, the interventionist selects Method 2: Improve the environment. This method involves the following three components: (a) adjusting the antecedent conditions so the conditions that set the occasion for the target behavior are eliminated and the replacement behavior is more likely to occur, (b) providing appropriate positive reinforcement for the replacement behavior, and (c) withholding consequences that previously reinforced the target behavior when it occurs (extinction).

Component 1: Adjust Antecedent Conditions. This component involves several steps. First, June's teachers will be asked to establish an independent entry activity that is within all students' instructional abilities and is to be completed within the first 5 min of the period. Second, the teachers will transition into instruction immediately following the entry activity to eliminate down/wait time. Both the first and the second steps are intended to limit the amount of time that students have for engaging in counterproductive conversations. Third, the teachers will move around the classroom to be in close proximity to students during guided and independent activities to prompt appropriate social interaction and praise students for desired performance. Fourth, the teachers will be encouraged to increase the amount of instructional time devoted to independent practice activities. Fifth, June will be required to work with a student partner during cooperative activities. However, the work partner will be selected ahead of time by June and the teacher (with cooperation from the intended student). Sixth, June will be offered an opportunity to spend some time working independently provided that she asks politely.

Component 2: Provide Positive Reinforcement for Replacement Behavior. This component will involve praising June when she demonstrates the replacement behavior. In addition, June will be allowed to visit Miss Brewster when she has demonstrated cooperative behavior during class. Finally, June will be given positive notes at least twice a week regarding her success in class that she can show to Miss Brewster and her parents.

Component 3: Place Target Behavior on Extinction. June will not be allowed to make contact with Miss Brewster if she leaves class without permission. June will also be required to complete missed assignments and activities when she returns to class. If June is belligerent or swears at other students, she will be allowed a short period to cool off, and then she will be required to complete assignments and activities.

When Mr. Appleton is approached with this plan, he is skeptical at first. However, after discussion with the interventionist, Mr. Appleton concurs with the need for each component of the intervention and suggests that he is willing and able to take part in implementation within his classroom.

> **Comments:** Note how the intervention addresses each function served by June's disruptive behavior. June's desire to access attention from Miss Brewster (positive reinforcement—attention) is dealt with by providing access when the replacement behavior is used and by not allowing access when the target behavior occurs. June's use of the target behavior to avoid inappropriate peer comments (negative reinforcement—attention) is managed by preselecting an appropriate peer, providing more supervision during practice activities, and decreasing the amount of unstructured time. Finally, June's ability to get out of assignments (negative reinforcement—activities) is put on extinction; she is required to complete assignments. Finally, note that the teacher's social validity assessment found he was skeptical. This information enabled the interventionist to discuss and further explain all components so the teacher was able to readily agree to the intervention.

Identifying a Measurement System

Cooperative behavior is nonuniform, so only the time-based measurement methods would be appropriate. Among these methods, time sampling is easier to implement than either duration or interval recording. However, the interventionist and teaching staff want June to be cooperative continuously, not occasionally. To measure continuous engagement, you would have to use either duration recording or the whole interval method. Between these two methods, the whole interval method is easier to implement, so it is selected as the measurement system for June. Furthermore, cooperation and disruption are dichotomous, so attention is placed on measuring the replacement behavior.

Observations will take place daily in math class. Each observation session will last for 20 min with 1-min intervals. If June engages in cooperative behavior across the entire 1-min interval, a "+" will be placed in the box that corresponds to that interval. If June engages in disruptive behavior at any point during an interval, a "−" will be placed in the box corresponding to the interval. The data will be summarized as a percentage of intervals containing "+" markings. The data will be entered into a computer spreadsheet, and graphs from the data will be generated at least once a week. The data collection sheet is shown in Figure 15.2. Once a week, data will also be collected in the same manner in social studies to assess generalization.

IOA data will be collected during both baseline sessions, and during both intervention sessions. IOA will be computed by dividing the number of agreements by the sum of agreements and disagreements, and multiplying the quantity by 100%.

A second observer will monitor the degree to which the intervention is properly implemented. These observations will occur during the two intervention testing sessions. Using a whole interval method, the observer will record at the end of each 1-min interval whether the intervention procedures were properly implemented (+) or not properly implemented (−) throughout the interval.

> **Comments:** You probably noticed that although June exhibits problems in two environments, only one was selected for initial implementation of the function-based intervention. Given the resources necessary to implement a function-based intervention and the fact that replacement behaviors can indeed generalize to other environments in which the intervention is not in place, it is often more efficient to begin with implementation on a small scale and monitor generalization to other environments in which it is deemed that the replacement behavior should occur.
>
> You probably also noticed that the measurement system focuses on the replacement behavior. With dichotomous behaviors, the recommended practice is to concentrate on replacement behaviors rather than the target behavior. In other words, when dealing with dichotomous behaviors, our effort is best spent in promoting and measuring appropriate rather than inappropriate behaviors.

Interval Data Recording Form

Observer: _____   Student: _____

Context (Time/Activity/Location): _____

Behavior: _____

Whole/Partial/Momentary   Interval Length: _____

Date: _____

Intervals	1	2	3	4	5	6	7	8	9	10	11	12	13	14	15	16	17	18	19	20
Behavior																				
Intervention																				

Summary:
     % of "+" intervals: _____   IOA: _____
     % of intervals with accurate intervention practices: _____

Date: _____

Intervals	1	2	3	4	5	6	7	8	9	10	11	12	13	14	15	16	17	18	19	20
Behavior																				
Intervention																				

Summary:
     % of "+" intervals: _____   IOA: _____
     % of intervals with accurate intervention practices: _____

Date: _____

Intervals	1	2	3	4	5	6	7	8	9	10	11	12	13	14	15	16	17	18	19	20
Behavior																				
Intervention																				

Summary:
     % of "+" intervals: _____   IOA: _____
     % of intervals with accurate intervention practices: _____

Date: _____

Intervals	1	2	3	4	5	6	7	8	9	10	11	12	13	14	15	16	17	18	19	20
Behavior																				
Intervention																				

Summary:
     % of "+" intervals: _____   IOA: _____
     % of intervals with accurate intervention practices: _____

Date: _____

Intervals	1	2	3	4	5	6	7	8	9	10	11	12	13	14	15	16	17	18	19	20
Behavior																				
Intervention																				

Summary:
     % of "+" intervals: _____   IOA: _____
     % of intervals with accurate intervention practices: _____

FIGURE 15.2
Data sheet to monitor function-based intervention for June.

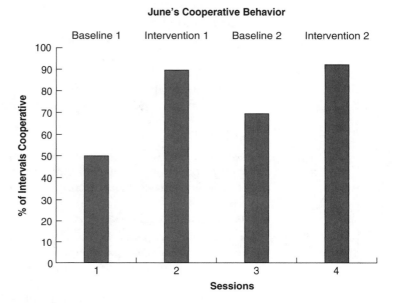

FIGURE 15.3
Example 2: intervention testing graph.

Testing the Intervention

The function-based intervention is evaluated using an A-B-A-B design to determine the effects of the intervention on June's disruptive behavior. The results are presented in Figure 15.3. During the first and third (baseline) sessions, June engaged in cooperative behavior during 50% and 70% of intervals, respectively. During the second and fourth (intervention) sessions, June's cooperative behavior occurred throughout 90% and 95% of intervals, respectively. IOA across intervention testing sessions was 95%. Implementation (treatment integrity) across intervention sessions was 95% and 100%, respectively. The data suggest that the intervention was successful in increasing June's engagement in cooperative behavior and that the teacher is capable of implementing the intervention.

FORMULATING THE BEHAVIOR INTERVENTION PLAN

The interventionist uses the information collected thus far to create the following BIP for June.

Behavioral Definitions

The target behavior is disruptive behavior, which includes leaving the classroom without permission, punching or destroying objects, and using profanity toward students. The replacement behavior is cooperative behavior, which includes asking the teacher permission to leave the assigned area when angry or upset, vocalizing discontent when upset, and ignoring negative comments made by other students.

Rationale

June's disruptive behavior is preventing her from (a) engaging in peer social interactions in class and (b) completing her classwork.

Baseline Data

Across two 20-min whole interval observations, June displayed cooperative behavior throughout 60% of the 1-min intervals. During the remaining intervals, disruptive behaviors occurred.

Function of the Behavior

When presented with a cooperative group task or activity, June engages in disruptive behavior (e.g., leaving the classroom without permission, punching or destroying objects, using profanity) to access adult attention, escape peer attention, and avoid the task or activity. That is, June is able to interact with Miss Brewster (positive reinforcement—attention), avoids contact with peers and escapes their comments (negative reinforcement—attention), and does not have to complete the instructional task or activity (negative reinforcement—activity).

Behavioral Objective

During group instructional activities, June will demonstrate cooperative behaviors that will include asking permission to leave the assigned area when angry or upset, vocalizing discontent when upset, and ignoring negative comments made by other students. June will demonstrate cooperative behaviors throughout an average of 95% of observed intervals over 10 consecutive days.

Intervention Procedures

The intervention will consist of adjusting the antecedent conditions, providing June with positive reinforcement for cooperative behavior, and ensuring disruptive behavior is not reinforced.

The task demands will be modified through the following procedures:

1. June's math teacher will establish independent entry activities during the first few minutes of class.
2. June's math teacher will transition quickly between activities.
3. June's math teacher will closely monitor independent and group activities.
4. June's math teacher will increase the amount of time spent in independent activities.
5. When activities call for group work, June's work partner will be selected ahead of time.

6. June will be offered the opportunity to work independently when she asks politely.

Positive reinforcement for cooperative behavior will be provided in the following ways:

1. June's math teacher will reinforce her verbally when she is engaged in cooperative behavior and remind her of the consequences of her cooperative behavior.

2. June will be allowed to visit Miss Brewster if she has demonstrated cooperative behavior throughout class and if she asks politely.

3. June will be given positive notes at least twice a week when she demonstrates cooperative behavior in multiple class sessions.

Instances of disruptive behavior will be handled in the following ways:

1. June's math teacher will remind her of the contingency for cooperative behavior.

2. June will not be allowed to contact Miss Brewster if she leaves the room without permission.

3. June will be required to complete any missed assignments.

A brief test of the function-based intervention showed that when no intervention was in place, June was engaged in cooperative behavior across only 60% of the observed intervals. When the intervention was implemented, June displayed cooperative behavior across 92.5% of the observed intervals. This demonstrates that the function-based intervention was responsible for June's cooperative behavior.

Fading and Generalization

As soon as June meets the behavioral objective under the function-based intervention plan, the intervention team will meet to develop a plan to reduce the amount and types of positive reinforcement to levels that are appropriate for the classroom. Review of data generated in the social studies classroom will provide information as to whether the replacement behavior has generalized or the intervention must be implemented in that class as well.

Data to Be Collected

Data on June's cooperative behavior will be collected using the whole interval method with 1-min intervals for at least 20 min during one instructional period every day in math and once a week in social studies. In other words, at the end of each interval, the observer will note whether June displayed cooperative behavior across the entire interval and mark a data recording sheet. Data will also be collected to assess IOA (weekly), implementation (weekly) using the whole interval method, generalization (weekly), and social validity using the IRP-15 and the CIRP (prior to beginning the intervention, at the end of intervention, and as needed).

Program Review Date

The BIP will be reviewed on 11/20/07.

Personnel and Roles

1. June's math teacher will be responsible for discussing the function-based intervention with June, implementing the function-based intervention, and collecting daily data on cooperative behavior.

2. The district behavior consultant will meet at least once per week with June's math teacher. The behavior consultant will assist the teacher in altering the structure of classroom activities, preparing a data collection sheet, collecting IOA and implementation (treatment integrity) data, collecting generalization data, and making summary graphs of progress. The district behavior consultant will also collect data to assess social validity of the function-based intervention plan.

3. Miss Brewster will agree to meet with June only when she has demonstrated appropriate cooperative behavior in class or when it is deemed appropriate for her to work with June on educational tasks in the classroom.

Emergency Procedures

If June becomes physically aggressive, the school plan for dealing with physically aggressive students will be put into action. She will be allowed to return to the classroom when she states to office personnel that she is ready. If removal for physical aggression occurs twice, the BIP team will meet to review the intervention.

> **Comments:** The failure of the interventionist to carefully detail the emergency procedures for this plan is not simply a "cop-out"; a well-thought out plan is necessary. In this case, the interventionist simply refers to a plan that is already in place. Most schools have an established plan for dealing with acts of physical aggression. In fact, a school is not fully prepared to implement function-based interventions if such a plan is not in place (Walker, Ramsey, & Gresham, 2004). In some situations the school's general emergency plan will suffice, whereas in other cases it may be necessary to make additional arrangements.

IMPLEMENTING AND MONITORING THE INTERVENTION

The function-based intervention was implemented and observational data were collected daily, with IOA and implementation data collected at least once a week (see Figure 15.4). June's cooperative behavior was maintained at a high level across the intervention (averaging 96% of observed intervals).

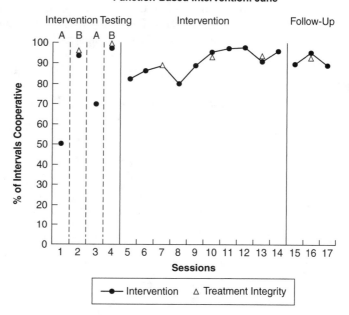

FIGURE 15.4
Intervention testing, intervention, follow-up graph.

The teacher's data collection was deemed accurate due to acceptable IOA data (90%). Weekly treatment integrity data averaged 97.5% (range: 95%–100%) and showed that the teacher consistently followed the function-based intervention plan. When Mr. Appleton was asked whether he considered the intervention to be effective, he said that it was and that he was pleased with the changes in June's behavior.

When June met the behavioral objective of demonstrating cooperative behavior at an average level of 95% of observed intervals across 10 consecutive days, the interventionist, Mr. Appleton, Mrs. White, and Ms. Brewster met to determine the next step to take. Because a review of the weekly generalization data showed that June's cooperative behavior had not carried over to social studies class, it was decided that the function-based intervention should be continued in Mr. Appleton's math class and that it should also be implemented in Mrs. White's social studies class. Data were collected once a week for 3 weeks after intervention was established in both classes. The follow-up data showed that June used the replacement behavior at high levels in both classes.

At the end of the 3-week period, the group met once again to plan fading of the function-based intervention. They agreed that much of the plan could simply remain in place and that the only element requiring adjustment would be the "preselection" of the peer that June would work with on group-based activities. They decided to fade this element of the plan by simply reminding June to make these arrangements herself with a peer at the beginning of class. The team would meet again if any member of the team determined that further adjustments to the plan were necessary.

REFERENCE

Walker, H. M., Ramsey, E., & Gresham, F. M. (2004). *Antisocial Behavior in School: Evidence-Based Practices.* Belmont, CA: Thomson/Wadsworth.

CHAPTER 16

The Entire Process When Using Method 3
Adjust the Contingencies

OUTCOMES

After reading this chapter, you will be able to

- Explain how the assessment information leads to the selection of the intervention method.
- Summarize the process of implementing the selected intervention method.
- Describe how the intervention is translated into a BIP.
- Identify and prevent common errors in developing and implementing function-based interventions.

This chapter presents a complete example of the function-based intervention process when the contingencies of reinforcement are misaligned. This situation calls for the use of Method 3: Adjust the contingencies, which was presented in Chapter 8. You may want to refer to Chapter 8 for additional information if any part of the process described here is unclear or confusing. This chapter follows the development and implementation of the intervention, step by step, through the use of a case study. Comments that highlight important aspects of the function-based intervention process, as well as common errors, are included throughout the chapter.

CONDUCTING THE FBA
Student and Background

Steven is a 13-year-old seventh grader who has been diagnosed with cerebral palsy and receives special education services. Steven spends half of every day in a life skills classroom and the rest of each day either in inclusive classroom settings or in internships with same-age peers. He has numerous motor issues; thus, he uses a wheelchair and walker for mobility. Steven uses his walker for moving short distances, such as around the classroom, but his teachers prefer that he use his wheelchair when he needs to travel longer distances. In these situations, Steven often begins to tantrum as soon as he realizes he is supposed to use his wheelchair. Tantrums always begin with cursing and mumbling but continue to escalate until staff can no longer ignore the behaviors.

Teacher Interview

Interviews are conducted with Steven's life skills teacher (Mrs. Longette), the paraprofessional who assists him throughout the day (Mrs. Babbage), and one of the inclusive classroom teachers (Mr. Martinez). All three staff report that Steven often refuses to use his wheelchair to move between classes or to distant locations around the school. When asked what the refusal behavior looks like, they describe the refusals as tantrums consisting of behaviors such as swearing; throwing objects; and hitting, pinching, and scratching staff members. Steven's teachers encourage him to use his wheelchair when moving longer distances so he will not become fatigued and will arrive in time for the beginning of his next class or activity. They report that these tantrums have been occurring for approximately 3 months and are most likely to occur when he is expected to transition from his fourth-period class to lunch in the cafeteria.

Steven's paraprofessional notes that, during the transition to lunch, several students in the class who use wheelchairs for mobility receive assistance from staff in transferring to their wheelchairs. However, staff generally leave Steven to perform this transfer himself because he has the skills and mobility to perform the task on his own. None of the staff members believe Steven tantrums to avoid the cafeteria; they state that he has many friends he interacts with at lunch. When asked what usually happens immediately after a tantrum, the staff report they have tried to ignore the behavior, but often end up taking the rest of the students to the cafeteria and leaving one staff member behind to try to calm Steven. Eventually, that staff member takes Steven to lunch, and the incident is not discussed further for fear of igniting another tantrum.

Student Interview

Steven avoids answering direct questions about his behavior during transitions. Instead, he directs the conversation to other topics. He indicates that lunch is his favorite time of day because he has time to see friends and because he likes to eat. He also states that he likes his classes and is able to do the work that is given to him. Steven suggests that other students in his life skills class get more help than he does; he feels he is sometimes ignored. When asked if he likes using his walker more than his wheelchair, Steven declares no preference; he likes using both.

Behavioral Definitions

The interviews with the teachers and Steven lead the interventionist to define the target behavior as tantruming, which includes swearing; throwing objects; and hitting, pinching, and scratching staff members. The replacement behavior selected is requesting assistance, or more specifically, getting a staff member's attention by saying his or her name, and then expressing his desire to make a choice of mobility devices or to receive assistance in transferring to his wheelchair.

> **Comments:** The paraprofessional provided a critical piece of information; that Steven's tantrums occur when peers are receiving assistance with transfers and Steven is left to fend for himself. It will often be the case that interviews will uncover patterns of staff behavior that may appear obvious to the observer but that are simply overlooked by staff members.

Observational Data

The interventionist collects A-B-C data twice. Both observations begin 10 min prior to the end of Steven's fourth-period class and continue 5 min into the lunch period. Steven's tantruming behavior is observed during both sessions. In each case, Steven's behavior occurs after he is asked to transfer to his wheelchair and the staff member moves on to assist another student.

The consequences that follow each incident vary slightly across the observations. During the first observation, Steven's paraprofessional ignores his swearing for 3 min. However, when Steven throws a plastic cup at the wall, Mrs. Babbage comes over and tries to calm him down. A few minutes later, Steven lets Mrs. Babbage help him transfer to his wheelchair, and Mrs. Babbage accompanies him to lunch. During the second observation, Steven swears and goes to his walker rather than his wheelchair. His classroom teacher, who is assisting another student and preparing lunch materials, asks Steven to use his wheelchair instead of the walker. Steven curses more and sits down in a regular desk chair, folds his arms, and mutters under his breath. The rest of the class leaves, and Steven's teacher stays behind to talk with him. Steven eventually uses the walker with the teacher's assistance. In both cases, Steven is at least 10 min late for lunch. However, Steven's friends are still present so he sits with them.

> **Comments:** Note the timing of the observations. The interview data suggested that to catch the antecedents to the problem, the

observations should begin several minutes prior to the daily transition. To ensure all immediate consequences were captured, the observations were continued until shortly after Steven and the teacher arrived at lunch. In addition, multiple observations provided a better overall picture of variations in antecedents and consequences.

Determining the Function

The Function Matrix guides the interventionist in asking six questions key to determining the function of Steven's behavior. Do the interview and observational data suggest that the behavior is maintained by

1. Access to attention? Yes. Both interview and observational data contain information showing that prior to incidents, staff is engaged with other students. The common consequence across the incidents is that Steven gains the attention of staff members.

2. Escape from attention? No. There are no data to suggest that Steven's behavior functions to allow escape from either staff or peer attention.

3. Access to tangibles or activities? No. Steven does not seem to prefer the walker to the wheelchair; arguing over the walker is more likely an additional method for gaining attention.

4. Escape from items or activities? No. The data suggest Steven is not trying to avoid the next class period (lunch) and is not trying to avoid use of the wheelchair.

5. Access to sensory stimulation? No. There are no data to suggest Steven's target behavior allows him to access sensory stimulation.

6. Escape from sensory stimulation? No. Steven does not appear to be engaging in disruptive behavior to escape environmental stimulation, and there is no evidence of medical problems that might prompt behavior that would enable escape from pain or discomfort.

The resulting Function Matrix is marked as shown in Figure 16.1 (positive reinforcement—attention). The resulting statement of function is as follows: When asked to transfer to his wheelchair, Steven engages in tantruming

FIGURE 16.1
Example 3: Function Matrix for Steven.

	Positive Reinforcement (Access Something)	Negative Reinforcement (Avoid Something)
Attention	X	
Tangibles/Activities		
Sensory		

behavior (which includes cursing; throwing objects; and hitting, pinching, and scratching staff) to access adult attention. That is, Steven is able to gain access to adult attention for assistance with transfer to his wheelchair and social interaction on the way to the cafeteria (positive reinforcement—attention).

DEVELOPING AND TESTING THE FUNCTION-BASED INTERVENTION

Selecting an Intervention Method

Two questions guide the selection of the intervention method. First, can the student perform the replacement behavior? The answer to this question is "Yes." Although Steven has not asked for assistance with transferring to his wheelchair, he has often asked for assistance with other tasks. Second, do the antecedent conditions represent effective educational practice? Again, the answer is "Yes." Although some antecedents specific to the target behavior will require adjustment, the overall classroom environment accurately implements instructionally sound rules, routines, and physical arrangements. Therefore, the interventionist selects Method 3: Adjust the contingencies. This method involves development and implementation of the following three components: (a) providing the consequence that previously reinforced the target behavior only when the replacement behavior occurs, (b) withholding the consequence that previously maintained the target behavior when the target behavior occurs, and (c) adjusting the antecedent conditions to make it more likely that Steven's replacement behavior will occur.

Component 1: Reinforce the Replacement Behavior. In applying this component to Steven's case, staff will provide attention only when Steven calls them by name and asks politely.

Component 2: Place Target Behavior on Extinction. Component 2 will involve withholding attention from Steven when he is engaged in tantruming. The staff will briefly remind Steven of the replacement behavior, ensure he and others are safe, and refrain from further attention for the target behavior.

Component 3: Adjust Antecedent Conditions. Steven's teachers and paraprofessional will remind him of the replacement behaviors 2 min prior to transition times. They will also ensure a staff member is within hearing distance of Steven's expected requests.

> **Comments:** In this intervention plan, notice that changing the reinforcement contingencies basically changes which of Steven's behaviors is more effective. Prior to the intervention, the more effective way for Steven to get attention was to use the target

behavior. With the intervention, the more effective way for him to gain attention is to use the replacement behavior.

This intervention plan also requires that if Steven selects the walker, the staff have to go along with it. This may require some changes on the part of staff, as well as some accommodations (e.g., leaving a few minutes earlier so he can walk rather than ride). Dealing properly with such issues increases the social validity of the plan, which should be discussed with the staff prior to finalizing the intervention procedures so that "follow-through" with the intervention (treatment integrity) does not suffer.

Identifying a Measurement System

Data will be collected to measure use of the replacement behavior and occurrences of the target behavior. Data will be collected daily beginning 5 min prior to the transition from fourth period to lunch and continuing until Steven leaves the room for lunch. Event recording will be used to measure Steven's use of the replacement behavior, which is discrete or uniform (see Figure 16.2). More specifically, if Steven calls a staff member by name, a tally mark will be recorded on the data recording sheet. The event data will be summarized by tallying the marks made during each observation.

FIGURE 16.2
Data sheet for Steven: replacement behavior.

Frequency Data Recording Form						
Observer: _____ Student: _____						
Context (Time/Activity/Location): _____						
Behavior: _____						
Date	Start	Frequency	Stop	Total Time	Rate

The target behavior is not uniform, so measurement will require a time-based method. Among the options, the whole interval method would underestimate the behavior because it would be counted only if it lasted an entire interval. Duration recording could be used, but it is more demanding than time sampling, which will give a good overall estimate of the behavior. Therefore, time sampling will be used (see Figure 16.3). The intervals will be 1 min in length. If Steven is engaged in tantruming behavior (i.e., swearing; throwing objects; or hitting, pinching, or scratching staff members) at the end of any interval, that interval will be marked with a "+" in the row labeled "Behavior." If Steven is not tantruming, the interval will be marked with a "−". The data on the strength of the target behavior will be summarized as a percentage of intervals containing "+" marks.

IOA data will be collected during both nonintervention sessions, both intervention sessions, and once a week during the course of the intervention. IOA for event data will be calculated by dividing the larger number of events by the smaller number of events and expressed as a percentage (multiplied by 100%). IOA for time sampling data will be computed by dividing the number of agreements by the sum of agreements and disagreements, and it will be expressed as a percentage (multiplied by 100%).

Implementation of the function-based intervention will be measured during both intervention testing sessions and once a week during the course of the intervention. A whole interval measurement will be used to assess treatment integrity. Again, a 1-min interval will be used that corresponds to the intervals used for measuring the target behavior. If the intervention was accurately applied throughout the entire interval, a "+" will be entered in the row labeled "Intervention" (see Figure 16.3). Otherwise, the interval will be marked with a "−". These data will be summarized in the same manner as the target behavior data.

The data will be entered into a computer database and summarized in graphic format at least once a week.

> **Comments:** As described in Chapter 14, it is appropriate to collect data on only the replacement behavior if the target and replacement behaviors cannot occur at the same time (i.e., if they are dichotomous behaviors). In this case, the target behavior and replacement behavior could actually occur at the same time, so it is necessary to collect data on both. In other words, our goal is to not only see an increase in the use of the replacement behavior, but also a reduction in the use of the target behavior.
>
> Another wrinkle in the measurement of the target and replacement behaviors and treatment integrity in this situation is that accurately measuring them requires the use of different data collection methods. The replacement behavior is discrete (uniform) and can be measured with event recording, whereas the target behavior of tantruming is continuous (nonuniform)

Interval Data Recording Form

Observer: _____   Student: _____

Context (Time/Activity/Location): _____

Behavior: _____

Whole/Partial/Momentary   Interval Length: _____

Date: _____

Intervals	1	2	3	4	5	6	7	8	9	10	11	12	13	14	15	16	17	18	19	20
Behavior																				
Intervention																				

Summary:
    % of "+" intervals: _____   IOA: _____
    % of intervals with accurate intervention practices: _____

Date: _____

Intervals	1	2	3	4	5	6	7	8	9	10	11	12	13	14	15	16	17	18	19	20
Behavior																				
Intervention																				

Summary:
    % of "+" intervals: _____   IOA: _____
    % of intervals with accurate intervention practices: _____

Date: _____

Intervals	1	2	3	4	5	6	7	8	9	10	11	12	13	14	15	16	17	18	19	20
Behavior																				
Intervention																				

Summary:
    % of "+" intervals: _____   IOA: _____
    % of intervals with accurate intervention practices: _____

Date: _____

Intervals	1	2	3	4	5	6	7	8	9	10	11	12	13	14	15	16	17	18	19	20
Behavior																				
Intervention																				

Summary:
    % of "+" intervals: _____   IOA: _____
    % of intervals with accurate intervention practices: _____

Date: _____

Intervals	1	2	3	4	5	6	7	8	9	10	11	12	13	14	15	16	17	18	19	20
Behavior																				
Intervention																				

Summary:
    % of "+" intervals: _____   IOA: _____
    % of intervals with accurate intervention practices: _____

FIGURE 16.3
Data sheet for Steven: target behavior and treatment integrity.

and requires the use of a time-based method. Finally, the measurement of treatment integrity requires a different time-based system than the measurement of tantrums.

Testing the Intervention

An A-A-B-B design was used to test the effectiveness of the function-based intervention. The testing results are presented in Figures 16.4 and 16.5. During the first and second baseline sessions, Steven engaged in tantruming behavior during 25% and 35% of intervals, respectively. He did not use the replacement behavior at all. During the two intervention sessions that followed, Steven's tantruming behavior did not occur. In addition, he used the replacement behavior once during the first intervention session and twice during the second session but not at all during the two baseline sessions. IOA across intervention testing sessions was 100%. Treatment integrity across intervention sessions was 95% and 100%, respectively. These data suggest the intervention is likely responsible for the reduction in tantruming and the increase in use of the replacement behavior. In addition, the teacher appeared to be able to accurately implement the intervention.

> **Comments:** You may have noticed the use of an A-A-B-B evaluation design for intervention testing rather than the A-B-A-B design used for the examples in previous chapters. The interventionist selected the A-A-B-B design because Steven's tantruming includes behaviors that might be dangerous to himself or others. Unfortunately, because there was no alternation between the baseline (A) and intervention (B) conditions, we

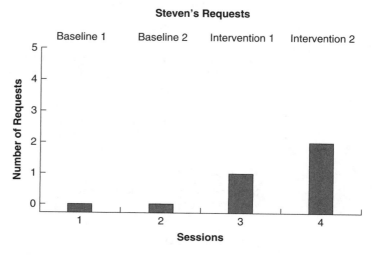

FIGURE 16.4
Example 3: intervention testing graph/replacement behavior.

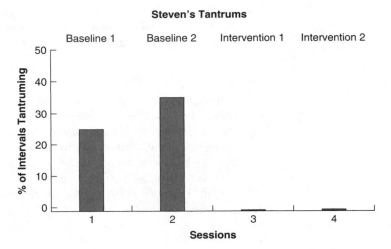

FIGURE 16.5
Example 3: intervention testing graph/target behavior.

cannot be as confident that our intervention is responsible for the effects on the target and replacement behaviors. However, because it would be unethical to withdraw the intervention, the interventionist and teachers will simply begin implementation and monitor the outcomes.

FORMULATING THE BEHAVIOR INTERVENTION PLAN
The following BIP is developed to carefully outline the intervention.

Behavioral Definitions
The target behavior is tantruming, which includes swearing; throwing objects; and hitting, pinching, and scratching staff members. The replacement behavior is requesting assistance, or more specifically, getting a staff member's attention by saying his or her name, and expressing his desire to make a choice of mobility devices or to receive assistance in transferring to his wheelchair.

Rationale
Steven's tantruming causes dangerous situations in the classroom for Steven, peers, and staff.

Baseline Data
Across two observations, Steven displayed tantruming behavior at the end of 30% of the 1-min intervals. The replacement behavior did not occur at all.

Function of the Behavior

When asked to transfer to his wheelchair, Steven engages in tantruming behavior (which includes cursing; throwing objects; and hitting, pinching, and scratching staff) to gain adult attention. That is, Steven is able to gain access to adult attention for assistance with transfer to his wheelchair and social interaction on the way to the cafeteria (positive reinforcement—attention).

Behavioral Objective

During the transition to lunch, Steven will exhibit the behavior of requesting assistance at least once each day for 7 consecutive days.

During the transition to lunch, Steven will exhibit the behavior of tantruming for 0% of intervals observed for 7 consecutive days.

Intervention Procedures

This intervention will include three main steps: (a) adjusting the antecedent conditions to promote use of the replacement behavior, (b) providing Steven with positive reinforcement when he requests assistance, and (c) ensuring that Steven's tantrums are not reinforced.

The antecedent conditions will be modified in the following ways:

1. Steven's teacher and paraprofessional will provide reminders to use the replacement behavior and of the consequences for appropriate behavior approximately 2 min prior to transitions.
2. The teacher and paraprofessional will ensure they are within hearing distance of Steven's expected requests.

During transitions, Steven will receive positive reinforcement in the form of teacher assistance and staff attention only when he appropriately requests assistance.

Instances of disruptive behavior will be handled in the following ways:

1. Staff will withhold attention or assistance from Steven when he is engaged in tantruming.
2. During or immediately after an occurrence of tantruming, staff will remind Steven of the replacement behavior, ensure he and others are safe, and refrain from giving further attention to the target behavior.

A brief test of the function-based intervention showed that when no intervention was in place during the two baseline observation sessions, Steven did not use the behavior of requesting assistance during either session and engaged in tantruming behavior an average of 30% of the observed intervals. When the intervention was put into place, Steven requested assistance once during the first session and twice during the second session, and did not engage in tantruming across either observation. This outcome suggests that the function-based intervention was responsible for Steven's use of requests for assistance.

Fading and Generalization

As soon as Steven meets the previous behavioral objectives, the intervention team will meet to develop a plan to reduce the amount and types of positive reinforcement to levels that are appropriate for the environment.

Data to Be Collected

Data will be collected on both requests for assistance and tantruming. Instances of requests for assistance will be measured using an event recording method and summarized as a frequency count. Steven's tantruming behavior will be measured using the time sampling method with 1-min intervals. Data collection will occur daily, beginning when the transition to lunch is announced and ending when Steven reaches the lunchroom. Data will also be collected to assess IOA (weekly), implementation (weekly), and social validity (prior to beginning the intervention and at the end of intervention).

Program Review Date

The BIP will be reviewed on 10/15/07.

Personnel and Roles

1. Both the teacher and the paraprofessional will discuss the function-based intervention with Steven, and both will be responsible for implementing it.

2. The paraprofessional will collect data daily on Steven's requests for assistance and tantruming behaviors.

3. The district behavior consultant will meet weekly with Steven's teacher and paraprofessional. The behavior consultant will assist the teacher and paraprofessional in preparing data collection sheets, collecting IOA and implementation (treatment integrity) data, and making summary graphs of progress.

Emergency Procedures

This intervention plan requires responding to minor instances of aggression by ensuring individuals in the classroom are safe, withholding attention, and reminding Steven of the replacement behavior and consequences for appropriate behavior. The principal and assistant principal should be notified that these procedures are in place. If Steven becomes physically aggressive to the point that persons in the classroom are at risk, the school plan for dealing with physically aggressive students will be put into action.

> **Comments:** Unlike the previous examples in this chapter, you will note that this plan includes two separate behavioral objectives. As you will recall, the replacement and target

behaviors are not dichotomous behaviors, so both are being measured. In such situations, determining the degree to which the intervention is successful requires the development of a behavioral objective for both the target and the replacement behavior.

Also note that the Emergency Procedures section of the plan is structured to make allowances for dealing with the risky nature of Steven's tantruming behavior within the structure of the intervention. The section also suggests that the building administrators be made aware of what may be a deviation from school policy with regard to minor incidents of this type.

IMPLEMENTING AND MONITORING THE INTERVENTION

The function-based intervention was implemented and data were collected daily on the replacement and target behaviors. IOA and implementation data were collected at least once a week (see Figure 16.6). During the first two intervention sessions, Steven requested assistance both days and did not

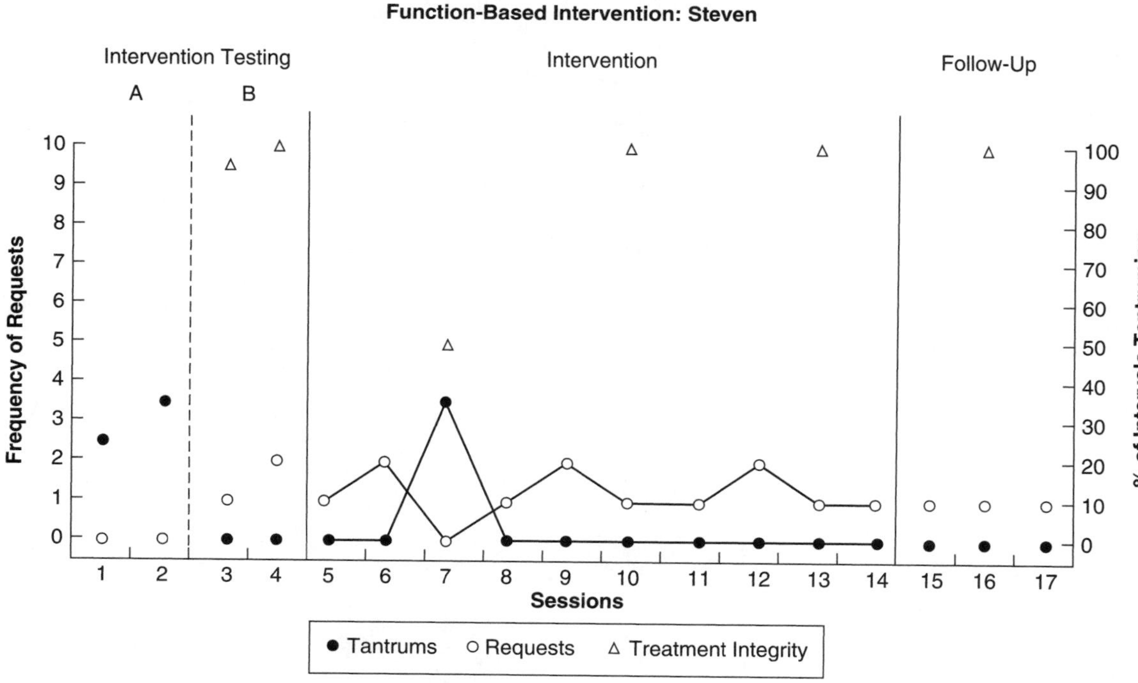

FIGURE 16.6
Intervention testing, intervention, and follow-up graph.

exhibit tantrums. However, during the third day of intervention (Session 7), Steven did not request assistance and tantrumed during 35% of observed intervals. Data collected showed a low level of treatment integrity; neither the teacher nor the paraprofessional provided Steven with prompts prior to transition, and they responded to two instances of tantruming with reprimands (i.e., attention). The interventionist discussed this problem with both staff members prior to the next intervention session, drawing attention to the success of the intervention during the two previous sessions. Treatment integrity then remained at a high level across the remainder of the intervention. Across the next seven sessions, Steven used requests for assistance at least once during each intervention session and tantruming occurred during 0% of observed intervals.

After Steven met the behavioral objectives established in the intervention plan, the staff responsible for the intervention reconvened to consider the next steps to take. Because the end of the school year was only a few weeks away, they decided to keep the plan in place without any major changes. However, they did decide to reduce the frequency of data collection to one session per week. These follow-up data showed that the teacher and paraprofessional faithfully implemented the intervention and that Steven maintained his use of the behavior of requesting assistance without engaging in tantruming.

Conclusion . . . and Some Suggestions

This book could not possibly address every situation you might come across, but if you have read the preceding chapters and engaged in the exercises at the end of Chapters 2 to 13, you should be prepared to start practicing your new skills. As you begin to implement what you have learned here, it may be helpful to find an individual who can serve as a mentor as you develop and refine your skills. Perhaps you read this book as part of a course dealing with behavioral problems. If so, consider asking your course instructor if you can contact him or her when you have problems or questions about specific cases. Perhaps your job requires you to deal with behavioral problems and you read this book to improve your skills in this area. If so, consider consulting with knowledgeable professionals (e.g., school psychologists or behavioral consultants) in your area.

If your job includes providing behavioral assessment and intervention services across a school, a district, or some other type of organization, consider taking a few steps to build your organization's capacity to effectively and efficiently implement the function-based intervention planning process. Many of your coworkers will not be familiar with the ideas underlying function-based intervention planning. One useful action would be to introduce these staff members to some of the key concepts of this approach. Raising awareness about the issue of behavioral function across an entire staff can aid the assessment and planning process in a few ways. Teaching staff who understand the basics of function-based intervention planning can provide more focused responses during interviews. They can also contribute more effectively to the development of the intervention. To help your staff develop this understanding, consider offering a short (e.g., 15- to 20-min) presentation about behavioral function and how understanding it can result in more effective interventions. Brief descriptions and examples of each step in the assessment and intervention process will improve your staff's capacity to participate effectively.

In addition to providing all staff with a basic understanding of key concepts, it can be helpful if a core of people in an organization receive in-depth instruction and develop proficiency in applying function-based intervention methods. In most organizations, there are staff who regularly assist with intervention planning, such as counselors, school psychologists, administrators, or select general and special education teachers. Encourage these individuals to take a course in function-based intervention planning or to seek professional development experiences that are consistent with the skills and tools you learned in this book.

A function-based approach to assessment and intervention is best practiced when dealing with significant behavioral challenges. Most behavioral problems develop and persist for one simple reason—they work (i.e., they provide an individual with the most efficient and effective way to gain desirable outcomes or avoid undesirable ones). Understanding this fact begins the process of function-based intervention planning. Completing the process requires knowledge and skill in accomplishing three broad tasks. First, you must systematically assess the individual's behavior so you can identify the function(s) it serves in the natural contexts in which it is causing concern. Second, you must develop an intervention that adequately addresses the behavior's function(s). Finally, you must accurately implement the intervention in ways that are lasting, generalizable, and socially valid. Accomplishing these tasks requires knowledge and proficiency in applying specific methods that will enable you to successfully complete each step in the process. We wrote this book to provide you with all the tools you will need to complete these tasks in ways that benefit both the students and the staff you serve.

Name Index

Subject Index

301